STRUCTURE, SYSTEM AND ECONOMIC POLICY

STRUCTURE, SYSTEM AND ECONOMIC POLICY

Proceedings of Section F of the British
Association for the Advancement of Science, *Section F (Economics)*
held at the University of Lancaster
1-8 September 1976

EDITED BY
WASSILY LEONTIEF
Professor of Economics, New York University

CAMBRIDGE UNIVERSITY PRESS

CAMBRIDGE

LONDON · NEW YORK · MELBOURNE

Published by the Syndics of the Cambridge University Press
The Pitt Building, Trumpington Street, Cambridge CB2 1RP
Bentley House, 200 Euston Road, London NW1 2DB
32 East 57th Street, New York, NY 10022, USA
296 Beaconsfield Parade, Middle Park, Melbourne 3206, Australia

© Cambridge University Press 1977
The paper by Nankivell is Crown Copyright and is reproduced by permission of the
Controller of Her Majesty's Stationery Office

First published 1977

Typeset by The Alden Press (London and Northampton) Ltd.
Printed in Great Britain at the University Press, Cambridge

Library of Congress Cataloguing in Publication Data
British Association for the Advancement of Science.
Section F (Economics)
Structure, system, and economic policy.
1. Economics – Congresses. 2. Economic policy –
Congresses. 3. Interindustry economics – Congresses.
4. Great Britain – Economic conditions – 1945–
Congresses. I. Leontief, Wassily W., 1906–
HB21.B7 1977   338.9   77–8581
ISBN 0 521 21724 5

CONTENTS

Contributors   vii

Preface   ix

1   Projecting the future of the world economy   1
Wassily Leontief

2   Input—output, technological change and inflation: the end of the Keynesian era?   19
W. F. Gossling

3   A study of sectoral prices and their movements in the British economy in an input—output framework   29
P. N. Mathur

4   Linkages, key sectors and development strategy   49
J. McGilvray

5   Government policy and the structure of the economy   57
V. H. Woodward

6   Use of an input—output framework for monitoring current developments in the economy   75
O. Nankivell

7   Controlling urban change: models of the urban economy   85
W. I. Morrison and T. A. Broadbent

8   Regional interdependence in the United Kingdom economy   111
I. R. Gordon

9   The Scottish balance of payments — 1973   123
V. G. Bulmer-Thomas

10   Materials, resources and production: an engineer's view   143
H. J. Pick

11 Unemployment in Britain: an interpretation of the last
    twenty-five years   165
    J. Taylor

12 Industry and technical progress   189
    C. F. Carter

13 Energy policy formulation   201
    P. Lesley Cook

14 Adam Smith and market capitalism   211
    D. A. Reisman

CONTRIBUTORS

Wassily Leontief	Department of Economics, New York University
W. F. Gossling	Economic and Social Studies, University of East Anglia
P. N. Mathur	Department of Economics, University College of Wales, Aberystwyth
J. McGilvray	Fraser of Allander Institute, Strathclyde University
V. H. Woodward	Department of Applied Economics, Cambridge University
O. Nankivell	Central Statistical Office
W. I. Morrison	Centre for Environmental Studies
T. A. Broadbent	Centre for Environmental Studies
I. R. Gordon	Urban and Regional Studies Unit, University of Kent
V. G. Bulmer-Thomas	Fraser of Allander Institute, Strathclyde University
H. J. Pick	Department of Mechanical Engineering, University of Aston
J. Taylor	Department of Economics, University of Lancaster
C. F. Carter	Vice-Chancellor, University of Lancaster
P. L. Cook	Department of Economics, University of Sussex
D. A. Reisman	Department of Economics, University of Surrey

PREFACE

The title of this volume describes succinctly the common theme of papers collected in this volume. They were presented at the annual meeting of Section F (The Economic Section) of the British Association for the Advancement of Science held in Lancaster in the fall of 1976.

While the mainstream of British economic thought seems to be still dominated by the aggregative theorizing with emphasis on monetary phenomena that came into vogue with the advent of the Keynesian approach, a small but steadily increasing number of economists seem to doubt that an appropriate combination of Phillips Curves, Full Employment Gaps and, say, summary indices of the Average Productivity of Labor could possibly provide a basis for realistic description of, not to say effective explanation of, the operating characteristics of a modern national economy. While the authors of these papers address themselves to a great variety of subjects, in each instance they probe below the surface of the aggregates in search of concrete, preferably directly observable — rather than statistically 'fitted' — structural relationships. These, in their turn, are used as building blocks for the construction first of small and simple, then of larger and more and more complex analytical systems or models. It is such combination of detailed factual information with a concise but flexible theoretical design that makes an effective analytical tool.

On an occasion, such as that of the annual British Association meeting, at which economists have an opportunity to share their interests with pure and applied scientists, the shift from abstract generalities to concrete specificity seems to be particularly appropriate. It is on this level — the level on which an economist can meaningfully discuss, say, direct reduction of ore to steel with a metallurgist, or questions of fertilizer production with an agronomist and a chemist — that not only can a common language be found, but a foundation can be laid for designing analytical systems capable of crossing the boundaries of different disciplines.

One of the procedures capable of mobilizing a large volume of detailed structural information without suppressing its fine grain is the so-called input—output analysis. In Britain, in contrast to the United States, the application of this approach has up to now been very limited. This volume contains several good examples of its effective use.

To prove a theorem or to formulate a general theory, one needs only paper and pencil. To demonstrate how a theoretical scheme can be implemented empirically (not all of them can pass that test), one needs data. For didactic purposes any set of figures will do. But when it comes to practical application, the data have to be sufficiently complete, detailed and accurate. Many of the contributors to this volume wrote their papers with specific policy applications in mind, and all of them deplore the paucity of adequate statistics. Hence, Mr Nankivell's brief but informative contribution deserves to be read with particular attention — for he is Assistant Director of the Central Statistical Office.

The book opens with the Presidential address, in which I describe in some detail a recent attempt to quantify economic interdependencies at a global level. Dr Gossling seeks to find common ground between at least four factions of economists in his paper on 'Input—Output, Technological Change, and Inflation: The End of the Keynesian Era?' He concludes that improved data on input—output flows and the application of a disaggregated medium-term 'dynamic-inverse' type of model would more usefully illuminate the relationship between technological change and inflation than would the extended short-term Keynesian approach (even if highly disaggregative in presentation). Professor Mathur, too, is concerned with the marriage of technology and the price system within the framework of input—output analysis. In his paper on sectoral prices and their movements in the British Economy in an Input—Output Framework', he seeks to quantify disaggregated price and commodity movements in the United Kingdom over the last two decades, and by means of that approach to examine crucial strengths and weaknesses in the economy. And Professor McGilvray, writing on 'Linkages, key sectors and development strategy', demonstrates the use of input—output tables to identify key sectors (with special reference to the case of a small economy highly dependent on foreign trade).

The book then moves from the primarily theoretical to the fundamentally practical. Mr Woodward makes two points in 'Government Policy and the Structure of the Economy'. He argues, firstly, that excessive preoccupation with macroeconomic aggregates conceals the reasons for the poor performance of the British economy in recent years and himself presents disaggregated estimates of employment levels and the overseas trade balance for four groups of industries within the key manufacturing sector. Then, secondly, he proposes government subsidies, both selective (available for all investment by technologically-backward industries, particularly those facing a strong trend growth in demand) and general (available in all industries, but based on past success in expanding capital per worker), because he thinks that adequate stimulus to investment in manufacturing industry will not be forthcoming via the unaided market mechanism with or without aggregate demand policies (which are insufficient to deal with a problem increasingly structural in nature). It is naturally interesting, in the light of Mr Woodward's strictures concerning British economic statistics, to read Mr

Nankivell's paper on the 'Use of an Input—Output Framework for Monitoring Current Developments in the Economy'. In it he describes some of the difficulties now facing the input—output practitioner in the United Kingdom, notably the lack of data, of spectacular forecasting successes, of theoretical interest within the academic community, of dialogues with businessmen and other policy makers. He is, however, more hopeful about the future in view of improvements in data collection and computer techniques, and also because of the increasing awareness that the Keynesian framework inadequately pictures inter-industry activity. He notes, too, that an input—output matrix is useful for short-run policy purposes (as where it is used, say, to predict the effects on a wide range of industries of a sudden rise in oil prices) as well as for identifying long-term structural changes, a fact which is likely, in the future, to increase substantially the influence of the approach.

Next come three papers concerned with inter-regional flows. Dr Morrison and Dr Broadbent, in 'Controlling Urban Change: Models of the Urban Economy', examine some of the social and economic problems of urban development in the United Kingdom, using new research on activity analysis and input—output techniques. Mr Gordon's paper on 'Regional Interdependence in the United Kingdom Economy' considers flows of labor migrants as well as inter-regional input—output relationships and argues that economists must examine these linkages more explicitly if they are to make a real contribution to regional policy making. Mr Bulmer-Thomas has, in his paper on 'The Scottish Balance of Payments — 1973', constructed the first ever regional balance of payments account for Scotland; the estimate is based on the difference between capital formation and domestic savings. The latter is broken down into the savings of the three domestic sectors: households, Government and business. There is also an estimate of the balance of payments in 1980 based on various assumptions about North Sea oil.

Turning now to more specialized areas of enquiry, the next four papers belong together. Professor Pick's essay on 'Materials, Resources and Production' attempts to bridge the gap between economists and engineers by demonstrating how the use of input—output analysis can help to illuminate inter-industry flows of intermediate products. Inputs and their destination (and, in the view of Professor Pick, inputs of materials in particular) are, after all, as interesting to the student of economic structures as final value added. Dr Taylor's paper on 'Unemployment in Britain' considers the causes of the upward trend in Britain's unemployment rate in the period from 1951 to 1975. He draws attention to the significance of the fall in search costs for unemployed workers engendered by higher unemployment benefits (flat-rate and earnings related); and notes that differential unemployment rates between males and females in the labor force may be explained by this hypothesis. The fall in search costs, it is argued, has permitted the unemployed to study the labor market more carefully and to extend the duration of the spell between jobs. Mr Carter, in his paper on 'Industry and Technical Progress', returns to the work he has done previously on the industrial applications of scientific and technical knowledge, and notes the urgent economic necessity to remove existing hindrances to such applications. He argues that a spectrum of types and degrees of specialization ought to be provided so as to ensure that the supply of skilled manpower corresponds to the demands of the economy. His recommendations for streaming and for elitist education aimed at maximizing the productive potential of the gifted are likely to prove particularly controversial. And Dr Cook's paper on 'Energy Policy Formulation' examines the problems of a sector characterized by the need to make vital decisions in conditions of considerable uncertainty. She argues that the market mechanism is inadequate and public policy indispensable if the energy industry sector is to plan ahead; and recommends that a system of decentralized decision making be supplemented by government guidelines for various periods into the future designed in accordance with social valuations of the trade-off between the present and the probable future.

Finally, there is Dr Reisman's paper on 'Adam Smith and Market Capitalism', in which he places Smith firmly in the general rather than the partial equilibrium tradition, and also argues that social, political and psychological as well as purely economic variables are mutually determinant within the context of Smith's large-scale multidisciplinary matrix.

As President of Section F residing on the other side of the Atlantic, I could not have organized the Program of which this volume is a record without the invaluable counsel of Mr E. J. Cleary, the Recorder of the Section; and without the help and generosity of the British Academy and Shell International Limited. Dr Reisman took charge of the preparation of the manuscript for publication.

On behalf of the members of Section F who attended the annual meeting, I express appreciation to Dr Magnus Pike, Secretary of the Association and the University, for the excellent arrangements and friendly hospitality that made our stay in Lancaster so pleasant.

Wassily Leontief

New York University
January 1977

PROJECTING THE FUTURE OF
THE WORLD ECONOMY

WASSILY LEONTIEF

1. The general equilibrium approach gained a dominant position in the study of the structure and function of national economies a long time ago. More recently, the traditional analysis conducted in terms of a few broad aggregates, such as the Gross National Income, Total Consumption, or Total Employment, began to be supplemented and, occasionally, supplanted by a much more detailed and, because of that, a much more concrete description and analysis of intersectoral relationships within the framework of a disaggregated input—output formulation.

While the general equilibrium — I would prefer to call it the general inter-dependence — approach dominates the past record of international trade even more than theoretical analysis of an individual national economy, concrete factual explanation of international economic transactions is still being conducted. External economic transactions of an individual country are usually explained from the point of view of its internal economic structure or, occasionally, the economic structures of one or two of its principal trading partners.

When it comes to consideration of the world economy as a whole, most studies were based on a grossly aggregative approach in which the identities of different areas were drowned out completely in global figures or took the form of comparative studies in which the difference between the economic status of different countries was being commented upon without any systematic con-sideration of their mutual interrelationships.

The study of the developmental prospects of the various countries over the period of thirty years from 1970 to 1980, 1990 and the year 2000, some of whose results are presented in this paper, is based on disaggregated descriptions of the input—output structure of the world economy.

All projections have been derived on the basis of a fully integrated theoretical model in which the internal intersectoral flows of goods and services within each of the different areas are tied together through the network of interregional transactions into a single multisectoral, multiregional, global system.

2. The 2625 equations contained in the model consist of 15 interconnected regional sets, one for each of the fifteen regional blocks. Each regional set consists of 175 equations that describe — in terms of 269 variables — the inter-relationships between the production and consumption of various goods and

Figure 1.   Classification of regions[1]

Name	Population 1970		GDP		
	millions	% of world	billions of '1970' dollars	% of world	GDP/capita ('1970' dollars)
Developed:	979	0.27	2631	0.82	2687
North America	229	0.060	1060	0.329	4625
Western Europe, high income	282	0.080	729	0.226	2574
USSR	243	0.070	435	0.145	1791
Eastern Europe	105	0.030	164	0.051	1564
Japan	104	0.030	200	0.062	1916
Oceania	15	0.004	43	0.013	2799
Developing Class I (Developing with major mineral resource endowment):	358	0.10	100	0.03	278
Latin America, low income	90	0.027	40	0.012	443
Middle East – Africa, oil producers	127	0.034	36	0.011	286
Africa, tropical	141	0.039	24	0.007	168
Developing Class II (other Developing):	2284	0.63	490	0.15	214
Latin America, medium income	191	0.053	114	0.035	594
Asia, low-medium income	1023	0.283	123	0.038	120
Africa, arid	131	0.036	27	0.008	205
Asia, centrally-planned	808	0.223	135	0.042	167
Africa, medium income	22	0.006	17	0.005	786
Western Europe, medium income	108	0.029	76	0.023	698

[1]The classification is influenced by the level of development the regions are likely to reach by the year 2000.

services — and in particular of specific natural resources — within a particular region; 229 of these variables are region specific, while 40 represent the export—import pools of internationally traded goods and the balance or imbalance, as the case may be, of that region's international financial transactions.

The fifteen regions and their groupings as used in tables and graphs below, as well as the corresponding population and average per capita GDP figures for the year 1970, are listed in Figure 1.

Basically, the geographic groupings aim at a reasonable degree of homogeneity in the economic variables that characterize the political entities combined in a single regional unit. The primary criterion employed in this classification scheme was the level of economic development as measured by per capita income levels and the share of manufacturing activity in total GDP. Further aggregation was based on the identification of certain variables that are of particular importance to the Study. Thus, the major oil exporting countries were grouped together and, for African nations, a distinction was made between those receiving less than ten inches of rainfull annually, and those receiving more. As might be expected, the criteria outlined were not applied without exceptions. In general, the regional groupings respect continental boundaries so as to facilitate the comparison of the projected results with the economic data produced by various international agencies. An exception to this rule was made for the oil producing countries of the Middle East and Africa which were grouped into one region. In a few other instances, geo-political considerations overrode the economic basis for aggregation.

3. The input–output method used in this Study provides the means of describing the complex and highly differentiated structure of the world economy in great detail. Each of the fifteen regions into which all the developed and less developed countries are grouped for the purposes of this analysis is visualized as a set of forty-eight producing and consuming sectors connected with each other and with the goods. Extractive industries absorb, in addition to inputs received from other sectors, renewable or non-renewable primary, i.e. natural, resources. Households absorb consumers' goods and supply labor; the public sector is represented by government activities of several different kinds. Pollutants are treated as by-products of regular production or consumption processes, and their elimination (abatement) as a special type of 'productive' activity. Besides the flows of current inputs, each sector also employs 'stocks' of buildings, machinery, inventories of raw and semi-fabricated materials (usually referred to, respectively, as fixed and working capital) and – in the case of the household sector – residential housing, sewage systems, etc.

The 'cooking recipe' (technological input mix) used in a particular industry at any given place and time determines the amounts of all the inputs, including labor, required to produce a given amount of its output. In the case of households, it is the 'consumption recipe' (which depends on the income level and the combination of biological needs, social conditions and cultural standards) that determines the contents of a typical household shopping basket.

4. The economies of individual regions are linked with each other through flows of internationally, or rather interregionally, traded goods.

While the inputs and outputs of services and goods classified as 'domestic' must be balanced within each region, the consumption of internationally traded goods has to be balanced only for the world as a whole. Export surpluses and import surpluses of each commodity or commodity group must add up to zero on the international scale. The worldwide input–output system must contain a set of equations stating this in algebraic terms.

In principle the composition of each region's exports and imports should be examinable and, consequently, also predictable in terms of comparative production costs and the structures of demand. However, the lack of sufficiently detailed factual information precludes, at this stage of analysis, the possibility of explaining interregional commodity flows in such fundamental terms.

The quantity of a particular type of good, say, steel, exported from a given region, say, North America, is treated as a fixed share of aggregate world exports (which, of course, are equal to aggregate world imports) of that good. The quantity of steel imported into the North American region is, on the other hand, determined as representing a given share of the total amount of steel consumed in that region. Thus, the domestic outputs and the global input — or rather its separate regional components — are the variables that enter into the determination of the internal input—output balances of the trading regions.

With sets of appropriate 'trade coefficients' incorporated in our system of equations, any projected change in regional inputs and outputs of internationally traded goods will thus be accompanied by corresponding shifts in each region's pattern of exports and imports.

Moreover, the quantities of internationally traded goods flowing into and out of every region are related to — and determined simultaneously with — their flows between the different sectors of each region.

In terms of this approach, all the exports of a particular good can be viewed as if they were delivered to a single international trading pool and all the imports as if they were drawn from that pool. The worldwide balance of trade (to be distinguished from the balance of payments, considered below) requires that the sum total of all regional exports of each good delivered to its pool equal the sum total of all regional imports drawn from that pool.

The same sets of technical coefficients that govern the physical relationships between the inputs and the outputs within the structural framework of a particular economy determine also the relationship between prices of various goods and services, on the one hand, and the 'value added', i.e. the wages, rents, and profits earned and taxes paid by the industries that produce them, on the other.

The fact that this formulation does not involve any analysis of bilateral (i.e. region to region) trade flows should be viewed, at this stage, as its strength rather than its weakness. Detailed analysis and explanation of the network of interregional shipments — involving the consideration of such factors as differential transportation costs — can and should be separated from the analysis of long-run patterns of what might be called the interregional division of labor.

5. The introduction of prices and income variables leads, as explained below, to the important question of the total value of the exported and imported goods and the problem of capital flows and of other types of international transfers.

Interregional capital movements and the flows of direct development grants are described in similar terms. All capital exports are combined into a single international pool from which the funds are being distributed to the individual regions. The amount exported by a particular region is controlled by a capital export coefficient that relates it to that region's Gross Domestic Product and varies – as do domestic saving coefficients – with the level of per capita income. The amount of capital imported is determined by a given share (that changes, however, as time goes on) in the worldwide export–import pool.

In addition to payments for traded goods and services, the annual financial benefits and outlays of each region include payments and receipts on accumulated foreign assets (i.e. on accumulated amounts of foreign borrowing and lending).

In case regular capital flows and developmental grants do not cover the surplus or deficit, as the case may be, of a particular region, the difference must, obviously, be covered by 'extraordinary' loans, grants or other special financial measures. The annual amount of payments received or made by a particular region on this account is referred to in our model as its positive or negative Balance of Payments.

6. The model presented above served first of all as a basis for an internally consistent, fully integrated description of the actual state of the world economy in the year 1970. Next it provides a framework for systematic projection of changes in the structural – mainly technical – and consumption coefficients that will determine the operating properties of the fifteen regions and their mutual interrelation shifts from 1970 through 1980 and 1990 to the year 2000. This major piece of empirical research absorbed the major part of efforts that went into preparation of the UN Report. The method – or rather the great variety of different methods – used is described in the official UN publication.

Finally, the empirically implemented mathematical formulation of the model was translated into a computer program capable of generating multiregional and multisectoral projections of developmental paths that this world economy might follow from 1970 on; specifically, through 1980 and 1990 to the year 2000. Eight alternative scenarios were selected to trace out, on the one hand, the implication of alternative assumptions concerning the future rates of population growth and available reserves of primary natural resources and, on the other, of alternative policies in respect to capital transfer and other types of developmental assistance made available by the developed to the less developed countries.

The complete printout of each projection reads like a combination of the economic sections of Statistical Abstracts of the fifteen regions for the years 1970, 1980, 1990 and 2000 with separate tabulations of levels of sectoral output and investment, sectoral deliveries to private and public consumption, export and imports, current and cumulative use of inputs of principal natural resources, generation and abatement of some of the most important pollutants and so on.

The rest of this paper is devoted to the presentation of some of the answers to the latter question derived from a comparison of these contrasting projections. One is based on scenario 'X' that incorporates some of the principal objectives of the New Economic Order. The other, based on scenario 'A', can be

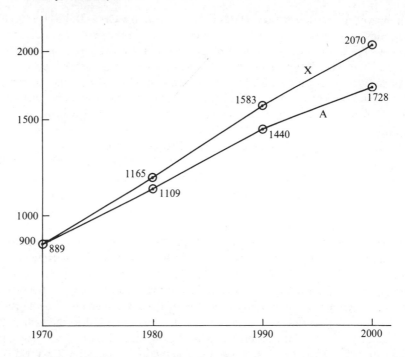

Figure 2.   GDP per capita — World (constant '1970' dollars on log scale)

said to carry the imprint of the Old Economic Order since it specifies that the constellation of behaviour patterns that govern how the level of saving and investment in all the regions and, in particular, the level and direction of international capital flows as well as of the flows of developmental aid will continue to operate up to the year 2000 in the same form as they do now.

Both projections are, however, based on the same sets of structural coefficients describing the state of technology and of consumption patterns as different regions pass from one stage of economic development to the next. The same estimated rates of future regional population growth were used in both of these projections. They correspond to the 'medium' UN estimates and average 0.7 per cent per annum for the Developed and 2.3 per cent for the Less Developed regions. So far as the estimated total regional reserves of various natural resources are concerned, both of these projections are based on what, in a complete tabulation of all the eight scenarios, is referred to as 'conservative', i.e. relatively low estimates.

7. For purposes of graphic presentation, the figures pertaining to the fifteen separate regions are aggregated in their sets. As shown on Figure 1 above, one is identified as Developed Countries, the second as Developing Countries Class I, the third Developing Countries Class II. Countries assigned to Class I possess relatively large reserves of natural resources, while those included in Class II do

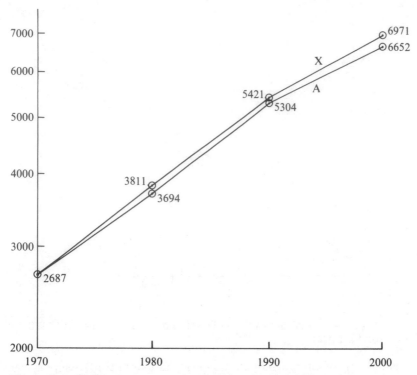

Figure 3.   GDP per capita — Developed countries (constant '1970' dollars on log scale)

not. Developed countries held, in 1970, 27 per cent of the total world population but produced 82 per cent of the total world Gross Domestic Product; Developing Countries Class I contained 10 per cent of the world population and generated 3 per cent of the global Gross Domestic Product, while those belonging to Class II held 63 per cent of the world population and produced 15 per cent of the total world's output.

Curves A and X in Figures 3, 4, and 5 trace out the prospective growth of per capita Gross Domestic Product from 1970 to 2000 in the Developed Countries and the two groups of Developing Countries under the Old and the New Economic Order. Curves A trace out the end results of computation A based on the assumption that saving, investment and international transfer of capital and developmental aid will operate in the future under the same conditions under which they are operating now. Curves X describe, on the other hand, the fixed 'income targets', the combination of which constituted — so to say — the starting point for computation X.

The fact that — as can be seen on Figure 2 — the per capita (and consequently also the total) World Income is expected to grow under the forced draft of a New Economic Order faster than it would in the presently prevailing

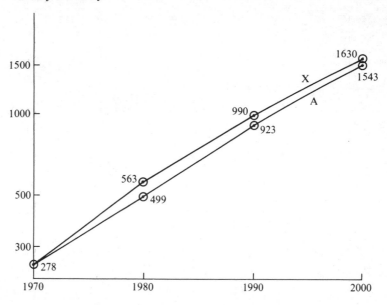

Figure 4.   GDP per capita — Developing Class I (constant '1970' dollars on log scale)

condition, is not surprising. It reflects the aspirations of the Developing countries and the readiness of the UN economic experts to explore systematically the possibility of their actual realization.

Figure 3 shows that even in the Developed countries the per capita GNP is intended to be higher under the New regime than it can be expected to be under the Old. The flatter slopes in the last decade reflect the commonly observed tendency to slow down when consumption reaches a very high level: By the year 2000 even under the Old regime the per capita income has been computed to reach $6652 as compared to $2687 in 1970 (both measured in base year, i.e. 1970, purchasing power).

An examination of Figure 4 shows that the target rates of future income growth provided for the Developing Countries Class I, i.e. resource rich developing countries, do not differ very much from the rates projected on the basis of the A scenario. Curve A rises above curve X in the first decade, but falls below by the year 2000.

The contrast between the developed and less developed regions comes to the fore, however, in Figure 5, which describes the two alternative paths of income in Developing Countries Class II. The bold ascent of curve X, which brings the average per capita income in these regions by the year 2000 to a level nearly twice as high as that projected on the basis of the A scenario, is, obviously, intended to make a major contribution toward narrowing the income gap between the developed and the less developed countries.

8. As explained above — for purposes of projection based on scenario

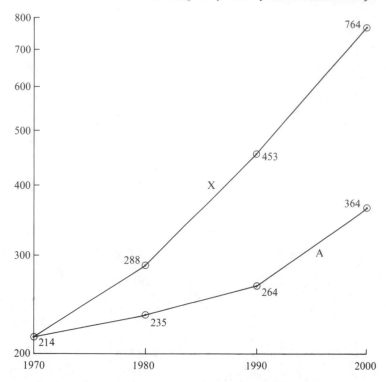

Figure 5. GDP per capita – Developing Class II (constant '1970' dollars on log scale).

X – having inserted in our system of input–output equations a set of externally fixed income targets, we computed the levels of sectoral investments and the levels of special foreign credits or of other types of extraordinary financial transfers that would have to be received or granted, as the case may be, to balance the regional surpluses or deficits in the Balance of Payments not covered by ordinary financial transactions.

Scenario A, describing the long-run implications of the Old Economic Order, on the contrary, does not permit the appearance of extraordinary shortfalls or surpluses on either the domestic savings or the external financial accounts of Developing Countries Class II.

The Middle Eastern countries are, however, assumed to attain, even under this Old Economic Order scenario A, the UN per capita income targets prescribed in scenario X. That implies that their Balance of Payments is also treated in this case as an unknown, the magnitude of which has to be determined as those of all the other unknowns through the solution of the given system of equations. While all other countries included in Class II of the Developing countries are not permitted under scenario A to have a Balance of Payments different from zero (and while the levels of their future per capita incomes are treated as dependent rather than exogenously fixed variables) the group as a whole can and, as can be

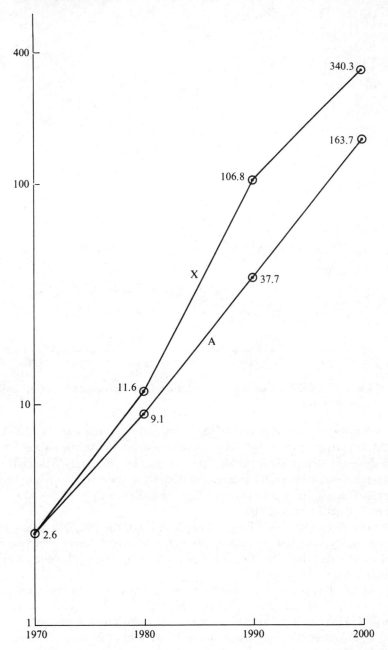

Figure 6.   Balance of trade — Developed countries (billions of current dollars on log scale).

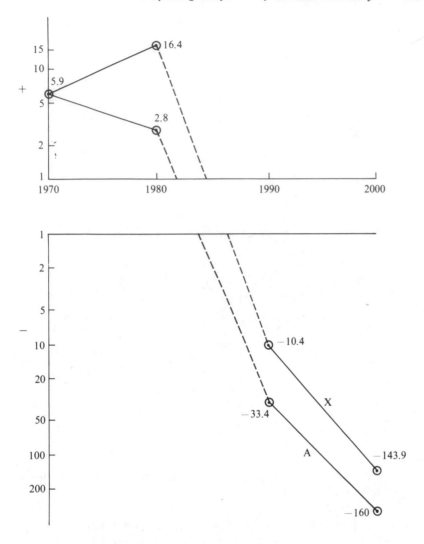

Figure 7.   Balance of trade — Developing Class I (billions of current dollars on log scale)

seen on one of the graphs, actually does show a plus on its aggregate Balance of Payments account.

The International aspects of the differences between the Old and the New Economic Order are traced out on six graphs reproduced in this paper.

Figures 6, 7, and 8 show changes in the Balance of Trade of each of the three groups of countries projected alternatively on the basis of scenarios X and A. Defined as a surplus of the aggregate value of goods and services exported over the aggregate value of goods and services imported — both expressed in current

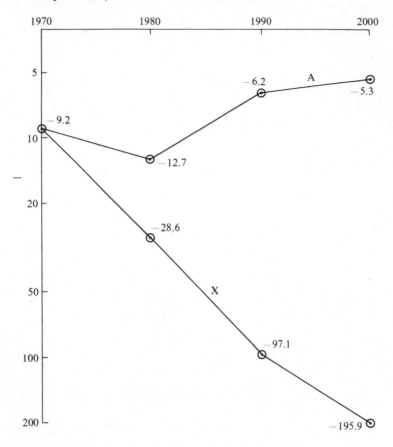

Figure 8.   Balance of trade — Developing Class II (billions of current dollars on log scale)

prices — such a balance can be positive or negative. Not willing to forgo the advantage of a logarithmic scale, I measured the logs of positive figures upward and the logs of the absolute magnitudes of the negative figures downward from their respective horizontal (time) axes. When a curve passes from the positive into the negative domain or vice versa, its path across the blank strip separating the positive from the negative domain is traced by a broken line.

Figure 6 indicates that the annual export surplus of the Developed areas can be expected to grow under both scenarios. By the year 2000 it becomes, under the New Economic Order, twice as large as under the Old. Developing countries Class I, after maintaining export surpluses in 1970 and 1980, show large import surpluses in 1990 and still larger ones by the year 2000. Curve A runs below curve X throughout the entire length. Figure 8 displays the leveling effect of the external credit limitations imposed on the Developing countries Class II under the

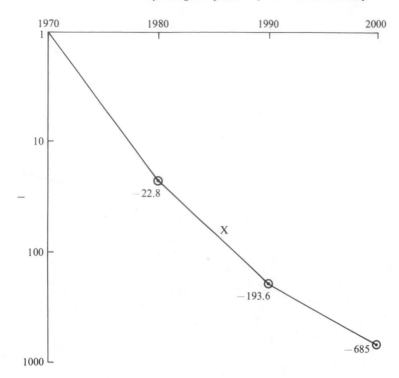

Figure 9.   Balance of payments — Developing Class II (billions of current dollars on log scale).

Old Economic Order: The even, nearly horizontal course of curve A tracing out a very small, and gradually shrinking, import surplus should please a most conservative international banker. The downward plunge of curve X indicates that a sharply rising import surplus seems to represent a necessary condition for rapid economic growth required to attain the ambitious UN income target.

9. Figures 9, 10, 11 and 12 display essentially the same inexorable economic logic, only they do so even more glaringly. The Balance of Payments represents, as has been explained before, the gap between the annual outflow and inflow of purchasing power that remains after all trading transactions as well as all regular capital movements, external interest payments and official developmental aid have been accounted for.

To understand the meaning and the implications of these figures, it is best to examine first the Balance of Payments of Developing countries belonging to Class II. Scenario A imposes on them the iron discipline of perfect balance between 'regular' external receipts and payments. Hence, curve A is not even shown on Figure 9: On a natural scale it would coincide with the horizontal zero-line. The plunging X curve, however, shows the rising volume of 'extra-ordinary' indebtedness that these countries would have to incur each year in order to attain the ambitious UN income targets.

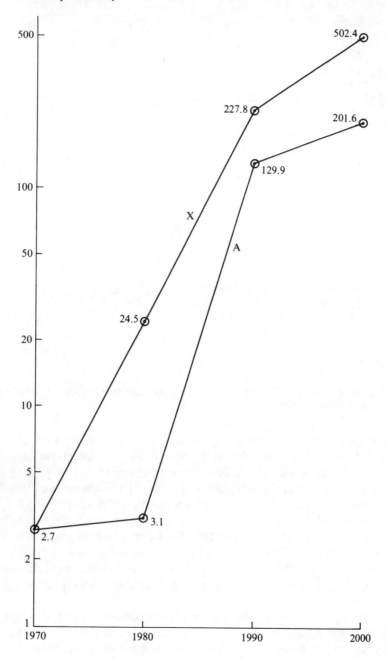

Figure 10.   Balance of payments — Developing Class I (billions of current dollars on log scale).

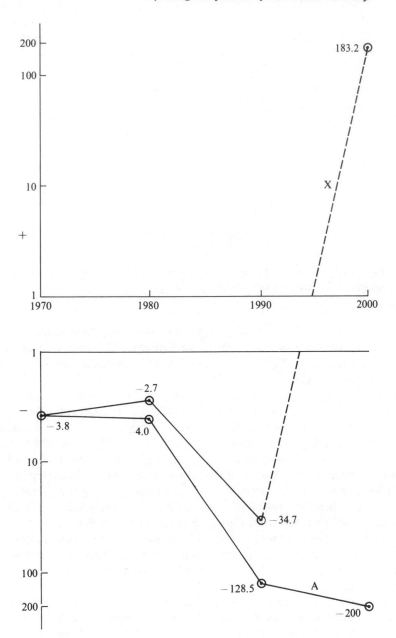

Figure 11.   Balance of payments — Developed countries (billions of current dollars on log scale).

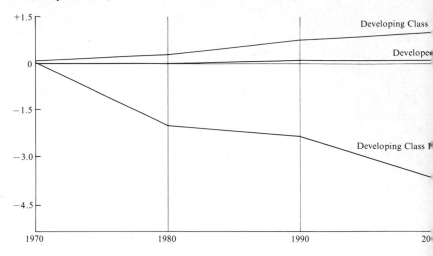

Figure 12.   Ratio of balance of payments to exports (both valued in billions of current dollars) (scenario X).

Figure 10, on the other hand, shows that the resource rich Developing countries Class I would have to maintain a rising positive Balance of Payments under the Old as well as under the New Economic Order, although under the new it would have to be much larger.

Turning, finally, to the Developed countries, we see on Figure 11 that, continuing to operate under the rules of the Old Economic Order (curve A), they would have to incur at first a small and later on a sharply rising deficit in their regular Balance of Payments. Since Developing countries Class II would show, under these conditions, a Balance of Payments deficit as well, both, obviously, would be covered by the Balance of Payments surplus of Class I Developing countries (Figure 10). An examination of the disaggregated regional figures (not presented here) indicates that, as should have been expected, all of these surpluses come from the Middle Eastern oil-exporting countries.

Returning to Figure 11 we see that under scenario X the negative Balance of Payments of the Developed countries would, in the years 1980 and 1990, be smaller than under scenario A, but that it would have to turn into a large positive balance by the year 2000.

The Balance of Payments problems that each of the three groups of countries would face along the development path designed to attain the objectives of the New Economic Order are brought out in full relief in Figure 12. The points along each of the three curves represent the Balance of Payments divided by the value of the total exports of the respective region. For the Developed countries these ratios stay very small throughout the entire period covered by this projection. In the case of resource rich Developing countries Class I, the relative magnitude of their Balance of Payments surplus grows much faster than the total value of their exports, and by the year 2000 it becomes nearly as large as the value of the exports themselves. The corresponding curve for the resource poor Developing countries Class II reflects a more explosive trend but in a negative domain.

Let me conclude by pointing out again that the broad aggregates shown on these graphs represent only a minute part of a detailed but at the same time fully integrated, i.e. internally consistent, picture based on the multiregional, multi-sectoral model of the world economy described in the first part of this paper.

2

INPUT–OUTPUT, TECHNOLOGICAL CHANGE, AND INFLATION: THE END OF THE KEYNESIAN ERA?[1]

W. F. GOSSLING

At least four factions of economists are involved in the title of this paper. That title is enough to make all readers very cross, since the experts from each faction are both involved, and, at the same time, slightly out of their depth. It is my wish to confound their disagreeabilities, and to produce at the core of this paper a model, different views of which are clear to the respective factions. Combining such views may allow us to see the economic reality in better relief.

Before we get to the core, we have to spend a little time on the outside. The Keynesian standard hang-up about the non-measurability of current input–output flows comes from Keynes' *General Theory* [8] (hereafter *GT*) Chapter 3, p. 24n2. National income was not very well measured in February 1936; in August 1936 Professor Leontief's *Review of Economics and Statistics* paper appeared with measurements of input–output flows [10]. Since then, for a few decades, a state of duopoly (comparable to that illustrated in *Let's All Hate Toronto* [22]) has reigned with {national income / input–output} statisticians in governments' statistical services. Recently, in 1973–4, the order of the entries in those brackets has been permanently reversed, but this no longer matters, since harmony, outside academic circles, has been reached for some time. More- over, in a 'group therapy' session with certain mostly-British economists in the autumn of 1974, I noted a sequence of conceptual difficulties: firstly, with an accounting system larger than 'GNP'; secondly, acceptance of inter-industry but not intra-industry flows, the latter still thought to be 'unmeasurable'; thirdly, the same problem with intra-firm flows; fourthly, that these 'intra' nettings-out in the input–output equations would lead to different results; and, lastly, that price changes would 'upset' the (commodity) input–output equations. My respective pieces of advice were: stare at the system for a few weeks; go and get some more technology data; ditto, ditto; read my *Productivity Trends* [4] ; and ditto, ditto, Appendix B. We do have some social survivals. Those economists' objections were mental excuses to reject input–output flows, netted out in the *GT* in order to separate the income and expenditure variables (conveniently forgetting servants and housewives); in their view, all models were sub-models of the Keynesian model.

It is now the other way round. We shall soon see why. Meanwhile, one has to ask why economists, American and British included, not forgetting 'input– outputters', have seemingly failed to appreciate the quasi-Schliemannesque endeavour of exploring changes and contrasts in production technology in the context of an unchanging set of consumption goods, as found in [17] Professor Joan Robinson's book *The Accumulation of Capital.* The short answer is that that work contains a net-national-product accounting framework: necessary for incorporating Wicksell's ideas. The model, in that difficult but rewarding work, can be extended to an input—output framework (at the cost of relaxing some special assumptions), and has so been, in *Productivity Trends* [4] and in *Capital Coefficients* [5] by me at Illinois and by myself and others at Manchester; we have examined the technical progress(?) of a sector, relative prices and wages-bills of an economy's industries, and a 'traverse' or 'process of transition' from slow to fast growth and vice versa, using empirical data from American, not British, sources. (Only half the needed data for the UK was available; BA [Section F] please note).

Up to now, I have mentioned models mostly set in a single time-period, even though, paradoxically, they can handle several time-periods; but with the arrival of the Leontief 'Dynamic Inverse' model in 1968, we could build multi-time-period input—output models with technological[2] change included [11]. Originally, the 'Dynamic Inverse' arrived in an 'operational' form absorbing all the available American empirical information in coefficient form. Petri [15, 16] and myself [6, 5] and others have modified it to include respectively gestation and replacement of capital, etc., and the model can be joined to Paolo Leon's account of the demand side of a Western economy where new commodities enter and old ones fade away and there is a spectrum of rates of profit as theoretically implied by Engel's Law [9, 7]. As with all the 'capital-coefficient' models, the capital stock is not (as in the von Neumann [14] model) directly involved, and there is the implicit assumption that capital is fully employed unless worn out; such models, including the 'Dynamic Inverse', should embrace the in-use, usable-but-shut-down, and unusable, fractions of the capital stock: and thus knotty problems such as 'to extend or to reopen' industrial plant.

Of course, against the increasing capabilities of disaggregated models, it is a major tragedy that British microeconomic studies of technology and its change over time remain unexpressed in physical, both input—output and capital, coefficient-tableau form. The UK has £/£ *input—output* coefficients for years at intervals in the postwar period, and from these tables one can catch a few glimpses, but not the whole picture, and other data has to be imported from abroad.

(Merely as a footnote to the foregoing, in case someone asks, let me add that I doubt that the monetarists can tell us anything more, in micro terms, than the Keynesians, and will not make a useful contribution until they have studied the micro-accounting of firms and its inter-relations with finance and credit).

All factions of economists should now be properly inter-confounded (but holding the view that larger, flexible, disaggregated, trans-temporal models are useful and computable), while leaving me with some degrees of freedom. Let me now turn the question in the title round, and ask 'Input-output, technological change, and deflation: the start of the Keynesian era?'

This question can be answered briefly by quoting from a not-so-recent review in *Capital Coefficients,* Chapter 7 [5]:

'At the time he wrote his *General Theory* (1936) Keynes could never have known – from statistics – the longer-run changes in technology which had produced the slack – the lack of his 'Effective Demand'. Leontief had found out part of the answer by 1941 when he published his [12] *Structure of American Economy:* input–output ratios fell over the '20's[3] – the economy could produce the same output with (overall) less inputs of current materials and services. Kuznets' (*et al.*) research on the inter-war years (published over the 1950's) pointed to a similar effect for capital goods: ratios of capital(s) to capacity outputs fell in the inter-war period. D.H. Robertson, much earlier, had noticed the fall in both physical and financial working capital requirements (or inventory-to-sales ratios). Producing the same amounts for consumption required less inter-industry flows, capital investment, and stocks, than before; result: a lack of "Effective Demand". Under Keynes' leadership the slack was taken up by concentrating on methods to boost public consumption and investment and income.'

Under those economic conditions* the Keynesian techniques of thinking were relevant. In contradistinction we can consider the extreme opposite:† 'Producing the same amounts for consumption will require more interindustry flows, capital investment, and stocks, than before; result: a lack of "Effective Supply" ' which is embraced by the 'Doom Men' (Forrester *et al.*) and can be used for maximal support of the position posed in the title of this paper.

But there are intermediates between these extremes, where technology allows economies on input–output flows at the expense of diseconomies in capital investment,‡ or the other way round. §

Before we can think more about all these cases, we have to look at the proportions that demands bear to supplies. Let us define:

A = Grand total of input–output flows;
B = Gross investment, entire;
C = Consumption, private and public;

and their sum:

$T = A + B + C$ = Total demands (= Total supplies, in equilibrium).

We can then remind ourselves, from the empirical evidence of the past three decades, that for a Western economy closed to trade and growing at about five percent a year the usual ratios are, approximately:

$$\frac{A}{T} = 0.50; \qquad \frac{B}{T} = 0.10; \qquad \frac{C}{T} = 0.40;$$

and for the United Kingdom, as a trading economy, the domestically produced part of A divided by the domestically produced part of T works out at about 0.43, for the 1960s.

Technology directly influences A/T, the largest ratio; *cet. par.* it influences B/T (via changes in the physical bits and pieces of capital needed per unit of capacity output for industries' plant and equipment – if there are economies, then B/T is less), the smallest ratio.

*Case 4. †Case 3. ‡Case 2. §Case 1.

As a close parallel to Case 1, the ratio of total input—output flows (domestic plus imported) to total domestic supplies must have risen, in the United Kingdom's case, from about 0.54 to about 0.60 as a result of the September 1973 crude oil price rise. Moreover, if crude oil had become *technologically* more difficult to produce, and in real economic terms more costly, then the trend of technological change is no longer the one that ushered in the start of the Keynesian era.

Embroiled in the problems — incipient or otherwise — of Effective Supply, we are forced to take note of technology, as described by input—output coefficients, capital coefficients, gestation (or lead-)times and lengths of life of capitals, and its change over the years, including new goods and services both of the producer and consumer variety and new processes of production, with old goods, services, and processes fading out. Inevitably, we have to disaggregate, and consider models covering a considerable number of time-periods; however, some old habits die hard, and if it seems to help the economist to summarise 'where the economy is/was/will be' in terms of aggregate figures and ratios like A, B, T, and A/T above, well then, 'a little of what you "macro" does you good'.

In Table 1 sequences of ratios of A/T are presented for the USA, the UK, and even one (1972) figure for the USSR. There are also three computed values of λ for the UK; λ being the proportion of each industry's output used up in the economy's production when the economy's industries grow at the same maximal rate R assuming zero fixed capital requirements for each industry $(\lambda = 1/(1 + R))$. An improvement on λ is r_{max}: the maximal rate of growth of a closed economy with fixed-capital requirements included, the two values of which are given for the USA. Values of r_{max} for the UK have been computed, but need recomputing; an estimate is entered for the time being.

Some capital—output ratios for the USA are entered in Table 2; the figures go only to 1958, but we can glean some indications from the column sums of the Battelle-Scientific American capital matrix, which were higher in 1975 (projected) than in 1958 in 30 industries, about the same in 22 industries, and *lower* in the remaining 49 industries. Recently (1975—76), statisticians in America have indicated slight concern about *rising* values of industries' capital—output ratios.

Capital figures for the UK are lacking, notably matrices of capital coefficients, but economic statisticians at the NEDO tell me that UK industries' capital—output ratios are apparently steady, even if, as some of the figures in Table 1 indicate, input—output coefficients are *in*creasing, particularly in recent years (cf. also the recent work by H.J. Pick, P. Becker, *et al.*, at the University of Aston).

From the statistics in Tables 1 and 2, the following conclusions might be drawn:

(i) in the USA over 1919—67, input—output coefficients were falling, indicating a preference for processes and products with better materials conversion and lighter dependence on industrial services; similar trends are apparent for the capital—output ratios;

Table 1   *Various ratios of A/T, eigenvalues λ, and maximal growth rates: USA, UK, and USSR*

Year	A/T	λ	r_{max} in percent per year	Country	Source
1919	0.536			USA	*Productivity Trends* [4]
1929	0.504			USA	(Appendix C), after Leontief [12] Tables 5 and 6 (in purchasers' prices).
1939	0.488			USA	Anne P. Carter, *Structural*
1947	0.493			USA	*Change in the American*
1958	0.488			USA	*Economy* [3]: in constant
1961	0.488			USA	(1947) dollars.
1947	0.491			USA	United States Department of
1958	0.483			USA	Commerce: in current dollars,
1963	0.472			USA	subject to further revision.
1967	0.466			USA	
1968	0.4996			USA	United States Department of
1969	0.4988			USA	Commerce [21]: projected
1970	0.4987			USA	tables.
1939			46	USA	*Capital Coefficients* [5],
1958			55	USA	Chapter 5; used eighteen industry-groups for both years.
1972*			42	UK	Estimate: after Barker [2]; see also Gossling [6].
1954		0.455		UK	Drs S.P. Gupta and I.W.
1963		0.495		UK	Steedman, Manchester University (mimeo) *c.* 1970.
1970†		0.504		UK	versity (mimeo) *c.* 1970.
1963	0.502			UK	Published CSO Tables [18,
1968	0.509			UK	19, 20]; domestic *plus* imported input–output flows.
1970‡	0.539			UK	ported input–output flows.
1972	0.559			USSR	Vladimir Treml (mimeo), *c.* 1974 (in purchasers' prices); quoted with the author's permission.

*1972 projected. †1970 projected from 1954 and 1963.
‡1970 projected from 1968.

Table 2   *Net capital–output ratios, USA census years, 1919–58*

Year	US domestic economy: net capital to net national product ratio*
1919	1.97
1929	1.46
1939	1.43
1954†	1.22
1958	1.33

*Numerator and denominator in current dollars   † Intercensal year.
Source: *Productivity Trends* [4], Table 15, p. 105.

(ii) in the UK over the postwar decades, input—output coefficients might be rising, at least from time to time; I ask whether the Selwyn Lloyd emergency budget in July 1961, and the inflation-rate increase in the fourth quarter of 1969, were 'hiccoughs' caused by increased pressure in the economy's tummy.

Additionally one might advance the following hypotheses, for the past decade, about 'hybrid' technological advances:

(*a*) in the USA, were the input—output coefficients falling while capital coefficients rose? ‡

(*b*) in the UK, were input—output coefficients rising while capital coefficients were steady or possibly falling? §

I ask would-be researchers to use the mid-sixties as a starting point and to endeavour to remove the distorting effects of the crude oil price rise in the mid seventies. Moreover, I raise these questions, because, in Western economies we might talk ourselves into accepting Diminishing Returns in the form of higher materials and services input both into processes per unit of output *and* capital outfits per unit of capacity output; or either. Or we might find such a state of affairs creeping in because economists failed to observe technological variables adequately and systematically.

A concluding endeavour is made to crystallise technological variables' comparison on to one diagram, Figure 1, below, which is an extension of Figure 24 in *Productivity Trends* [4] which in turn was an extension of the Robinson—Wicksell diagram ([17] p. 420). Quite a number of variables go on to this two-dimensional diagram in its fully extended form.

If we wish to chain up most of the 'index-number birds', the total gross output (per person if one wishes) of the closed economy, CZ, consists of standard commodity, as do its components, a restrictive assumption forcing us to change the technology if the growth rate is changed — the changes are minimal if the fixed capitals share the same lifetime (ten years, in Figure 1), and gestation time (one year). The components of CZ, also total gross outlay, comprise CA, consumption, equal to the wages bill; AB, net new investment, equal to net profits; BX, replacement investment, equal to amortisation; and XZ, the current input—output flows. The area $OCAE$ equals the gross physical capital stock (of constant efficiency), undepreciated and undiscounted. Thus OC is that capital stock (per person) deflated by the wages bill (per person), both in units of standard commodity; OC is what I call the gross real capital ratio (undiscounted). Thanks to Euclid, similar triangles give the reciprocal of ON as the growth rate of the capital stock and of total gross output. This diagram can be redrawn, following Joan Robinson, to show the (discounted) real capital ratio and the inverse of the rate of profit — for the benefit of stockbrokers *et al.*

Making the further assumption that CA $(= OE)$, consumption (and/or the wages bill), stays constant, or else redrawing the diagram making appropriate changes in OC so that $OCAE$ stays constant in area, one can then consider sets of alternative technologies. As the diagram is drawn, the vertical distance between EAQ and TBQ, for example AB, gives the net new investment, and on changing

‡Case 2. §Case 1.

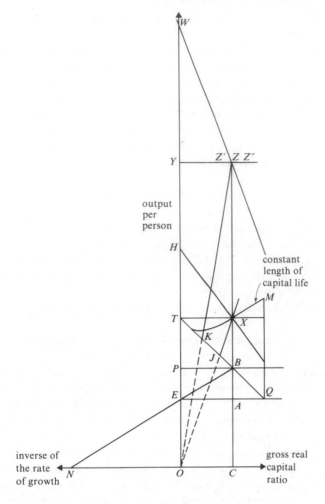

Figure 1.

to a technology more *saving* on physical capital the economy goes over to *higher* growth rate, and vice versa; by so drawing *EAQ* and *TBQ* we incorporate a behavioural investment assumption. [Other versions of this diagram, respectively derivable from Figures 22 and 23 in *Productivity Trends* [4], allow a constant level of net new investment (whatever the physical capital is under the new technology), or a level given by the upright distance between *EA* and *EB* which means a constant growth rate whatever the technology. Each diagram, like Figure 1, explores but a restricted field of hypothetical technologies.] Returning to Figure 1, one can see that the constancy of *OE* allows the drawing of rays from *O* through *K* and *J* on *TB* to *Z* and *X* respectively, locating technologies with constant capital/total gross output and capital/GNP ratios. Also *OE*'s constancy and the behavioural investment assumption allows *computation* of the constant-length-of-capital-life *curve TXM*— looking like an uphill Lancashire clothes line. There are two other straight lines: *HX* picks up technologies with capital replacements a constant proportion of GNP (capital life shorter, except at *X*), and *WZ* threads through technologies with a constant input—output coefficient, given capital replacements are a constant proportion of GNP.

We can now embark on two exercises, drawing a level line through *Z* which reaches the upright axis at *Y*; of course, *YZ* (produced) picks up technologies with constant labour productivities. Consumption per person *OE* stays constant, and the wage; *Z'* on *YZ*, near *Z*, allows a number of possibilities, with a lowered capital—output coefficient and gross real capital ratio, and sharply increased growth rate:

I(*a*)   the input—output coefficient would be increased, with capital life constant;

I(*b*)   the input—output coefficient would be constant, with capital life reduced and capital replacements greater than under I(*a*).

With similar provisos, consider *Z"*, on *YZ* produced, near *Z*. This too allows several possibilities, with a raised capital—output coefficient and gross real capital ratio, and sharply reduced growth rate:

II(*a*)   the input—output coefficient would be reduced, with capital life constant;

II(*b*)   the input—output coefficient would be constant, with capital life increased and capital replacements less than under II(*a*).

These two exercises merely illustrate hybrid technological changes,‡ using long-run comparative statics. One can rework them with a constant growth rate — *TXM* becomes *EX* produced and *HX* becomes *GX* with *G* just above *P*, etc. — but the above results still hold, with the important condition that the growth rate, among other things, stays constant.

Returning to Figure 1, again consider *Z'* in relation to *Z*: the growth rate has sharply increased, faster than constant labour productivity, under the stimulus of capital-saving technology—the post-war labour-shortage inflation. If *Z'* drops so as to reduce the increase in the input—output coefficient, labour productivity drops, but if it stays constant then employment decreases (temporarily). We can extend this line of thought to show more generally that technological change, by making savings on materials for capital requirements, can engender 'a continuous conflict between the pressure for higher wages and final consumption per person on the one hand, and on the other hand industries desiring to grow faster than before' and faster than the increase in labour productivity; insofar as technology suddenly (and in addition to the foregoing) starts to allow labour productivity to increase sharply, unemployment can be generated with inflation still continuing (stretch the diagram upwards and shrink it sideways, leaving the capital stock unchanged).

Resort to geometry inevitably restricts the possibilities; if, however, I encounter protests to the effect that the computable dynamic-inverse model in conjunction with Paolo Leon's demand, growth and *rates* of profit analysis

‡Cases 1 and 2.

(including superior techniques) covers a much greater range of possible worlds, and that furthermore we live in a continuously changing world so that its 'traverses' or 'processes of transition' are somewhat more important, then I shall have achieved my objective — because the various factions that I mentioned at the beginning will have found the common ground floor of an expanding subject.

Notes

1   An abstracted preliminary version of this paper was given by the author as the Chairman's Address to the 1975 London Conference of the Input–Output Research Association.

2   Not necessarily reflected in numerical changes in input–output and capital coefficients as Almon [1] reminds us.

3   And over the thirties, but slightly less markedly: see *Studies in the Structure of the American Economy* [13] pp. 28–29.

References

[1]   Almon, Clopper, Jr, *et al.*, *1985: Interindustry Forecasts of the American Economy*, D.C. Heath and Co., Lexington Books, Lexington, Mass., USA, 1974.

[2]   Barker, T.S., Paper in the *Review of Economic Studies*, vol. XXXVIII, July 1971, pp. 369–75.

[3]   Carter, Anne P., *Structural Change in the American Economy*, Harvard University Press, Cambridge, Mass., USA, 1970.

[4]   Gossling, W.F., *Productivity Trends in a Sectoral Macro-Economic Model*, Input–Output Publishing Company, London, 1972.

[5]   Gossling, W.F., *Capital Coefficients and Dynamic Input–Output Models*, Input–Output Publishing Company, London, 1975.

[6]   Gossling, W.F., 'Correct Fixed-Capital Replacement in Input–Output Growth Models', *Review of Economic Studies*, vol. XLI, October, 1974.

[7]   Gossling, W.F., 'Some Productive Consequences of Engel's Law', Occasional Paper No. 2 of the Input–Output Research Association, Input–Output Publishing Company, London, 1974.

[8]   Keynes, J.M., *The General Theory of Employment Interest and Money*, Macmillan and Co. Ltd, London, 1936.

[9]   Leon, Paolo, *Structural Change and Growth in Capitalism*, Johns Hopkins, USA, 1967 (*Ipotesi sullo sviluppo dell'economia capitalistica*, Editori Boringhieri, Torino, 1965).

[10]   Leontief, W.W., 'Quantitative Input and Output Relations in the Economic System of the United States', *The Review of Economics and Statistics*, XVIII, 1936.

[11]   Leontief, W.W., 'The Dynamic Inverse' in *Contributions to Input–Output Analysis*, A.P. Carter and A. Brody (eds.), North-Holland Publishing Company, Amsterdam, 1969.

[12]   Leontief, W.W., *The Structure of American Economy, 1919–1929*, Oxford University Press, 1941, and *ibid. 1919–1939*, Oxford University Press, New York, 1951.

[13]   Leontief, W.W., *et al.*, *Studies in the Structure of the American Economy*, Oxford University Press, New York, 1953.

[14]   von Neumann, J., 'A Model of General Economic Equilibrium', *Review of Economic Studies*, XIII, 1945–46.

[15] Petri, Peter A., 'Convergence and Temporal Structure in the Leontief Dynamic [-Inverse] Model', in Carter, A.P., and Brody, A., *Input–Output Techniques,* North-Holland Publishing Co., Amsterdam and London, 1972.

[16] Petri, Peter A., 'Research on the Dynamic Inverse', *Research Papers* (Progress Report) vol. II, no. 2, Harvard Economic Research Project, 1970.

[17] Robinson, Joan, *The Accumulation of Capital,* 3rd edn, Macmillan and Co. Ltd, London, 1968.

[18] United Kingdom, Central Statistical Office, *Input–Output Tables for the U.K., 1963,* Studies in Official Statistics No. 16.

[19] United Kingdom, Central Statistical Office, *Input–Output Tables for the U.K., 1968,* Studies in Official Statistics No. 22.

[20] United Kingdom, Central Statistical Office, *Input–Output Tables for the U.K., 1970,* Business Monitor PA 1004.

[21] United States Department of Commerce, *Summary Input–Output Tables of the U.S. Economy: 1968, 1969, 1970,* Bureau of Economic Analysis Staff Paper No. 27, September 1975.

[22] *Let's All Hate Toronto* (a humorous study *inter alia* of duopoly), author unknown, c. 1960.

3

A STUDY OF SECTORAL PRICES AND THEIR MOVEMENTS IN THE BRITISH ECONOMY IN AN INPUT–OUTPUT FRAMEWORK

P.N. MATHUR

'When profit diminishes, merchants are very apt to complain that trade decays; though the diminution of profit is a natural effect of its prosperity.' Adam Smith, *The Wealth of Nations*, p. 196, Pelican edition, 1976.

Introduction

The economic tribulations of the United Kingdom in the post-war decades can be mainly traced to a largely successful drive towards the progressive achievement of a higher standard of living for the average wage/salary earner. It is for this reason that the economy is continuously transformed from that of one vintage to that of a later vintage; consequently, the price structure is moving from that relating to the technology of the former to that of the latter. In the process, it is not only confronted with recurring resource 'bottle-necks', but also with the particularly difficult socioeconomic problems of a society trying to achieve these changes through democratic means. The observed price movements and structural changes in the British economy are the direct result of this process.

Determination of price structure

Adam Smith's theory of prices may be mathematically written as

$$p_j = \sum_{i=1}^{n} a_{ij}p_i + wl_j + \pi_j \tag{1}$$

where p_j is the price of jth commodity, a_{ij} is the input of ith commodity for producing one unit of jth commodity l_j is the labour units required for it and π_j is per unit profit rate for jth commodity, while w is per unit wage rate. According to Adam Smith, in the long run, with the creation of sufficient capacity to meet the demand, π_j tends to zero and thus p_j tends to become equal to

$$\sum_{i=1}^{n} a_{ij}p_i + wl_j$$

Using Matrix terminology, we may write (1) for time t as:

$$P^t = P^t A + w^t L + \pi^t \tag{1'}$$

where superscript t denotes the time period P, L and π are respective vectors having n elements and where A is the input—output matrix. Then

$$P^t = (w^t L + \pi^t)(I - A)^{-1}. \tag{2}$$

Then Smith maintains that π^t tends to 0 as t tends to infinity. Or long run price (value) is

$$P = wL(I - A)^{-1}. \tag{3}$$

Marx[1] changed (3) into

$$P = w(1 + s)L(I - A)^{-1} \tag{4}$$

where s is the rate of surplus value. This does not effectively change the value structure given by (3) as $(1 + s)$ is only a constant and multiplication of each value with a constant keeps relative prices the same.

In Volume III of *Capital*, he developed (2) on the hypothesis that profit rate π_j is proportional to the investment of capital for a unit of output of the jth commodity per unit of time, say, K_j. Then $\pi_j = rK_j$, and (2) becomes

$$P = (wl + rK)(I - A)^{-1}. \tag{5}$$

Schumpeter, on the other hand, distinguished between interest and profit. While interest is a permanent stream of income related to the value of capital, profits are the surplus value in development, which after a longer or shorter period of progressive diminution are wiped out by competition.

Further, 'profit is not a return to capital, however one may define capital. So that there is no reason of speaking about a tendency towards equalisation of profits which does not exist at all in reality: for only the jumbling together of interest and profit explains why many authors contend for such a tendency although we can observe such extraordinarily different profits in one and the same place, at the same time and in the same industry.'[2]

Leontief's theory of price structure

It has been complained (Solow, 1959)[3] that Leontief in his *locus classicus* has not spelled out any price system. In spelling out a price system, several assumptions like uniformity of wage rates, interest rates, etc., become inevitable. And that gives us only the supply price, or the long-run price. To assume that it will be observable in an economy leads to an assumption that demand does not play any part in determining profit rate, etc., or either that the economy is at a stationary state or follows what Hicks[4] has termed as 'Fix Price System', in which the adjustment of demand and supply is not done through price flexibility but through output and stock management. If these assumptions are not made, the utmost one can go in specifying the price system is to find out from technological relationships the dependence of the price vector of commodities with the value-added vector of various industries. And this is what Leontief has done in his first book.[5] If value added in the industry i is represented by v_i, from the static input–output system, we get:

$$v_i = p_i - \sum_{j=1}^{n} a_{ji} p_j$$

or (6)

$$V = P(I - A) \quad \text{and} \quad P = V(I - A)^{-1}$$

where V is the value added vector and P is the price vector.

When the uniformity of the wage rate and the interest rate is assumed, the specifications required for the static input–output system are not enough. We require extra knowledge of labour units employed in each industry, as well as a disaggregative specification of capital requirements, viz. the matrix of capital coefficients. Then, with the assumption that the income generated in each process is completely exhausted in wages and interest payments, viz. there is no profit in the residual sense, we see that:

$$v_i = p_0 a_{0i} + \Pi_k \sum_{k=1}^{n} b_{ki} p_k \qquad i = 1, \ldots, n.$$

Substituting in (1), we get:

$$p_0 a_{0i} = p_i - \sum_{j=1}^{n} a_{ji} p_j - \pi \sum_{k=1}^{n} b_{ki} p_k$$

or

$$P = p_0 A_0 (I - A - \pi B)^{-1}$$

or

$$\frac{1}{p_0} \{P\} = A_0 (I - A - \pi B)^{-1} \qquad (7)$$

where A_0 is the labour requirement row-vector (a_{0i}) and π is the rate of interest; and p_0 is the wage rate. It will be seen from (7) that as far as the structure of prices (including wage rate) is concerned, the whole system is technologically determined (viz. by A_0, A, and B), except for the interest rate. Or, given the interest rate and the input–output technology, the price structure is uniquely determined. We can say that the price structure has one degree of freedom. Of course, there is an upper limit to the interest rate.[6] When we put the interest rate equal to zero, we get a price structure corresponding to the system where the whole of the national product is distributed to the wage earners. This we may call the 'price structure corresponding to the labour theory of value'.

The above formulation may be alright for a stationary state, but in the observed world we find that returns to working capital are different from those on fixed capital. Returns on working capital are governed by the prevailing interest rate, as primarily it is financed from bank loans. Even in the case where it is financed from internal funds, there is an alternative use of those internal funds — as a loan to the banking system at the prevailing interest rate. While the fixed capital is more in the nature of a long-term investment done on the expectation of future markets. However, once bought, it can either be used for production, or kept idle (of course, in the end it can be sold for scrap). Thus, its opportunity cost is almost zero. Therefore, once fixed capital is invested in, an entrepreneur has only the option on whether to keep the firm working or not, and if he keeps it working he has to take as profit whatever market prices will give him, which may be not only different from the prevailing interest rate but also different for different industries.[7] On these considerations the price equation will become:

$$p_i = p_0 a_{0i} + \sum_{j=1}^{n} a_{ji} p_j + r \sum_{j=1}^{n} {}^w b_{ji} p_j + \pi^i \sum_{j=1}^{n} {}^f b_{ji} p_j \qquad (8)$$

where ${}^w b_{ji}$ is the working-capital coefficient and ${}^f b_{ji}$ is the fixed-capital coefficient, r is the rate of interest and π^i is the profit rate in ith industry. Or

$$P = p_0 A_0 \{I - A - {}^w Br - {}^f B\hat{\pi}\}^{-1} \qquad (8')$$

where $\hat{\pi}$ is the matrix with π^i along the diagonal.

Determination of price structure in a state of flux, viz. when capacity of various vintages is simultaneously utilised

The above description of the input—output theory of price structure refers to a single set of techniques producing the commodities at any time. However, a growing economy has in *situ* various amounts of fixed capital equipment belonging to different vintages. The equipment or the fixed capital embodies the technology at the time when it was newly installed. This technology remains almost the same up to the time it is scrapped. The technological progress or growth in the economy comes about by the installation of new equipment — embodying more profitable techniques at the current price structure. At a particular moment of time equipment installed at different past dates will be simultaneously working, having, of course, different productivities and profit rates. In understanding the working of an economy, we can neglect this embodiment of technological change in the equipment only at the cost of relevance. Thus in a state of flux there will be a spectrum of technologies of different productivities working simultaneously.

For the commodity j, we may represent the available processes as follows:

$$
\begin{bmatrix}
a_{1j}^1 & a_{1j}^2 & \cdots & a_{1j}^k & \cdot & a_{1j}^{mj} \\
a_{2j}^1 & a_{2j}^2 & \cdot & a_{2j}^k & \cdot & a_{2j}^{mj} \\
\cdot & \cdot & \cdot & \cdot & \cdot & \cdot \\
\cdot & \cdot & \cdot & \cdot & \cdot & \cdot \\
a_{nj}^1 & a_{nj}^2 & \cdot & a_{nj}^k & \cdot & a_{nj}^{mj} \\
a_{0j}^1 & a_{0j}^2 & \cdot & a_{0j}^k & \cdot & a_{0j}^{mj} \\
C_j^1 & C_j^2 & \cdot & C_j^k & \cdot & C_j^{mj}
\end{bmatrix}
\quad ; \quad
\begin{bmatrix}
{}^wb_{1j}^1 & {}^wb_{1j}^2 & \cdots & {}^wb_{1j}^k & \cdot & {}^wb_{1j}^{mj} \\
{}^wb_{2j}^1 & {}^wb_{2j}^2 & & {}^wb_{2j}^k & \cdot & {}^wb_{2j}^{mj} \\
\cdot & \cdot & \cdot & \cdot & \cdot & \cdot \\
\cdot & \cdot & \cdot & \cdot & \cdot & \cdot \\
{}^wb_{nj}^1 & {}^wb_{nj}^2 & & {}^wb_{nj}^k & \cdot & {}^wb_{nj}^{mj}
\end{bmatrix}
$$

and

$$
\begin{bmatrix}
{}^fb_{1j}^1 & {}^fb_{1j}^2 & \cdots & {}^fb_{1j}^k & \cdot & {}^fb_{1j}^{mj} \\
{}^fb_{2j}^1 & {}^fb_{2j}^2 & \cdot & {}^fb_{2j}^k & \cdot & {}^fb_{2j}^{mj} \\
\cdot & \cdot & \cdot & \cdot & \cdot & \cdot \\
\cdot & \cdot & \cdot & \cdot & \cdot & \cdot \\
{}^fb_{nj}^1 & {}^fb_{nj}^2 & \cdot & {}^fb_{nj}^k & \cdot & {}^fb_{nj}^{mj}
\end{bmatrix}
$$

where a_{ij}^k represents the input coefficient of the ith commodity in the jth industry for the kth technique for producing jth commodity which is available to the economy. ${}^wb_{ij}^k$ and ${}^fb_{ij}^k$ are similarly the working-capital and fixed-capital coefficients respectively; a_{0j}^k represents the labour coefficient for the kth technique for producing the jth commodity, and C_j^k the capacity of the equipment in *situ* of the kth technique.

If, at a particular time, equipment relating to the techniques $1, \ldots, m_j$ is being worked at each one's full capacity respectively, then the average input–output coefficient as found in the table constructed for that time will be

$$
a_{ij} = \left[\sum_{k=1}^{mj} C_j^k \, a_{ij}^k \right] \left[\sum_{k=1}^{mj} C_j^k \right]^{-1}. \tag{9}
$$

Similarly, working stock coefficients will be given by:

$$
{}^wb_{ij} = \left[\sum_{k=1}^{mj} C_j^k \, {}^wb_{ij}^k \right] \left[\sum_{k=1}^{mj} C_j^k \right] \tag{10}
$$

and the total output of the jth commodity will be given by $X_j = \sum_{k=1}^{mj} C_j^k$

The price strcuture at that time should be such that:

$$
p_j = p_0 a_{0j}^k + \sum_{i=1}^n p_i a_{ij}^k + r \sum_{i=1}^n p_i {}^wb_{ij}^k + \pi_k^j \sum_{i=1}^n p_i {}^fb_{ij}^k \qquad (k = 1, 2, \ldots, m_j). \tag{11}
$$

It may be noticed that while prices, the wage rate and the interest rate is the same for all the technologies, the profit rate on fixed capital will be different for each. For the kth technique to be in use, the price of jth commodity should at least cover the wage cost, input cost and the interest cost on the working capital. Otherwise it may be better for the firm not to produce at all. However, return on fixed capital is not essential. For once it is installed, a firm can get only scrap value, if it is not profitable to work with. So its opportunity cost is almost zero (this does not imply that sufficient returns need not be expected before it is installed at all). Thus we can say that for all the techniques working

$$p_j \geqslant p_0 a_{0j} + \sum_{i=1}^{n} p_i{}^w b_{ij}^k. \tag{12}$$

Now if we look at a technique which is not in use, and assume a non-monopolistic market, the reason for closing down at the micro level may be only the fact that at the current price structure the technique is not able to earn even its current cost. That is

$$p_j < p_0 a_{0j}^k + \sum_{i=1}^{n} p_i a_{ij}^k + r \sum_{i=1}^{n} p_i{}^w b_{ij}^k \tag{13}$$

for all ks corresponding to techniques which are not in use.

If there are a sufficient number of techniques in the industry, we can say that there will be a technique on the margin which though working will hardly be producing any profit on the fixed capital. That is, for such a technique at the margin the prices will be such that:

$$p_j \simeq p_0 a_{0j}^v + \sum_{i=1}^{n} p_i a_{ij}^v + r \sum_{i=1}^{n} p_i{}^w b_{ij}^v \tag{14}$$

where r is the technique which, though working, is on the verge of becoming obsolete.

Equations of the above type will be true for one technique of each of the industries, viz. the marginal technique which is on the verge of obsolescence.

Collecting them, we have a marginal technology for the whole economy which is such that no industry in it makes any profit. Let A^v denote the input–output coefficient matrix for such a set of techniques and $^wB^v$ the corresponding working-capital-coefficient matrix, then:

$$P \simeq p_0 A_0^v + PA^v + rP^w B^v$$
or
$$p_0^{-1} \{P\} \simeq A_0^v \{I - A^v - r^w B^v\}^{-1}. \tag{15}$$

Thus we see that the current price structure is related to the current interest rate and the marginal technology which is on the verge of obsolescence, and not with the average technology or the best technology working in the economy.

We may standardise the price–wage unit in such a way that

$$p_0 + \sum_{i=1}^{n} w_i p_i \equiv 1 \tag{16}$$

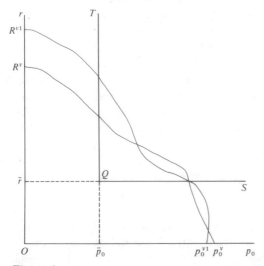

Figure 1.

where w_i may be any weights, but it may be interesting to put them proportional to those used in constructing the cost-of-living index.

Then the maximum value of p_0 will be given by equation (15), when r is zero and it will be $\ll 1$.[8] Given r, the value of p_0 as well as the vector P will be uniquely determined for each technology. We have seen above that given a technology, a technologically determined maximum value of $r \equiv R$ can be calculated. Substituting the values of p_i ($i = 1, \ldots, n$) from equation system (11) in equation (12) we can get a functional relationship between r and p_0 for each technology.[9] They will delineate curves like $R^v p_0^v$, $R^{v1} p_0^{v1}$, etc. for each technology on the rp_0 graph. For any value of $\bar{r} \bar{p}_0$, all the technologies whose curves pass through its north-east would be feasible.

Thus, in Figure 1, point Q represents the wage rate $\bar{p}_0$ and interest rate $\bar{r}$. Then, each and every technology whose feasibility curve has any point in common with the space east of the line QT extended and north of QS extended will be a feasible technology, and the price structure will be determined by the one which passes through Q, or the nearest to Q. (It is not maintained that there will be only one technology which will pass through it, and hence the price structure will be unique.) Once the price structure is determined, equation system (12) will determine the total number of techniques for each industry that is working; and then equation system (10) will determine the total amount of each commodity that will be produced. From that, given input–output and labour coefficients, final availability of each commodity, as well as the total labour force employed, is easily calculated.

Demand induced modification in price structure – Fix–Flex price structure

In the whole of the above formulation we have not tackled the problem of the effect of demand on prices. In the neoclassical theory it is the flexibility of the

price structure that ensures the equality of supply and demand of each commodity. There, in the shortrun, the supply of commodities is given, and then the
price is determined in the market so as to clear it. Only in long period, that is
in a stationary state, may the price structure be determined by the cost of
production. On the other hand, Keynesian macro-economics, which is shortrun,
is based on the fixed-price assumption. In this the adjustment of supply and
demand is achieved by changes in output rather than by changes in relative
prices. In the fixed-price system the prices change only in response to changes in
wages, in the rate of foreign exchange, etc., which affect the real cost. Professor
Hicks[10] has recently come to the conclusion that in the real world certain commodities, when faced with changes in demand, behave as if they follow the flex-
price rule, while the others follow the fixed-price system. In the flex-price
market there are usually intermediate traders, by whose manipulation of stocks
prices are really determined. They may serve to moderate the price rise if
shortages are expected to be very temporary. However, if shortages were not
expected to be temporary they would tend to hold on to their stocks rather
longer, and we may be faced with a short-term backward-sloping supply curve
for flex-price commodities. However, for fixed-price commodities, the additional
or reduced demand shows up as extra or reduced production, and when 'bottle-
necks' occur it will be exhibited as a lengthened order book rather than as an
increased price. In a closed economy, shortages cause 'bottle-necks' leading to
delays; and if shortages are widespread, the demand-generated expansion will
not get started. In an open economy, this problem becomes the problem of the
balance-of-payments.

In the literature, the fixed-price phenomenon is juxtaposed with the situation
in which monopoly or monopolistic competition prevails. In our framework we
may look at it as follows: an increase in price, given equation (12), will imply
either a decrease in the wage rate or in the prices of other commodities. This
would lead to various other techniques of producing the commodity becoming
feasible; while if it means a decrease in the price of other commodities, it may
make some techniques of producing these non-feasible. This will change the
supply position of different commodities in the economy, and if the market
really demands that set of commodities, it would mean that supply will be at the
cost of production of certain other vintages. If the change in demand is considered temporary the current producers will be reluctant to see an obsolete
technique reactivated, causing the threat of a glut in the particular market. This
potential threat should keep them to the artifice of lengthening the order book
rather than increasing the price to meet such temporary increase in demand. The
same should be true with decreasing demand, as closing down a firm of a
particular vintage will not be undertaken on temporary considerations. However,
it is not possible to have an increase in prices without bringing other vintages
into the production line. This would be possible only where such vintages do not
exist, or where to get them activated is a time-consuming process, such as
agriculture; especially for perishable goods like vegetables, fish, etc., and there-

fore in agriculture, the flex-price system is likely to prevail, while in all other it is the fixed-price system that prevails.

However, the cost of production is not an unequivocal description. Though the cost of all other inputs can be accounted, the appropriate rate of profit remains an open question. It is well-known that no economic study in the UK has been able to track the problem of determination of the rate of profit for goods, which are here called 'fixed-price commodities'. The system described above skirts around this problem by making the rate of profit simply a residual for non-marginal techniques, while it is zero for the marginal techniques. Once that specification is given, the price structure of fixed-price commodities becomes determinate and the input—output model, as described above, becomes the right tool for analysis of the price structure.

Thus for short-term adjustment of the price structure the commodities can be divided into two groups — flex and fix. Flex are those whose demand/supply adjustments are done through price-flexibility, while for fix they are done through output changes. The model developed above will be useful only for the fix-price commodities. Let commodities $(1, \ldots, n_1)$ follow the fix-price rule and $(n_1 + 1, \ldots, n)$ follow the flex-price rule. Let matrices A, ^wB, and ^fB be partitioned accordingly, to form

$$\begin{bmatrix} A_{11} & A_{12} \\ A_{21} & A_{22} \end{bmatrix} \qquad \begin{bmatrix} ^wB_{11} & ^wB_{12} \\ ^wB_{21} & ^wB_{22} \end{bmatrix} \quad \text{and} \quad \begin{bmatrix} ^fB_{11} & ^fB_{12} \\ ^fB_{21} & ^fB_{22} \end{bmatrix} \quad \text{respectively}$$

and vectors P, C, V, A_0 as $[P_1 P_2]$, $[C_1 C_2]$, $[V_1 V_2]$ and $[A_{01} A_{02}]$. Then the price of fix-price commodities will be given by:

$$P_1 = p_0 A_{01}^v + P_1 A_{11}^v + P_2 A_{21}^v + rP_1{}^wB_{11}^v + rP_2{}^wB_{21}^v$$

or
$$P_1 = \{p_0 A_{01}^v + P_2 A_{21}^v + rP_2{}^wB_{21}^v\} \{I - A_{11}^v - rB_{11}^v\}^{-1} \qquad (17)$$

where superscript v, as before, denotes the marginal technique. We thus see that not only r is exogenously given, but also the prices of all the flex-price commodities P_2 are given outside this system.

In developed countries agricultural prices are often state-determined support prices and most of the service industries are also organised on fixed-price basis. In such an economy, too, prices of imported goods behave as those of flex commodities, and so are to be included in P_2 in the above system. Thus, while the short-term changes in prices will be governed by the system (17), medium-term changes will be determined by changes in the marginal techniques themselves, viz. changes in v for the individual industries.

The feasibility of vintage techniques with changing prices in Britain[11]

With the above framework in view, we have looked at the UK data of industrial cost. The data about industrial cost vintage-wise is just not available. The information that is collected in the Census of Manufactures relates only to the average cost of each industry, and from that it is not possible to find out the cost structure of production done with the help of equipment of different vintages.

In Tables A and B^{12} we have examined the feasibility of the average technologies of 1963 and 1968, with the changing wage–price structure up to the year 1973. The wage rates of individual industries have been adjusted according to the movement of wages in each industry. A detailed commodity-wise adjustment of the prices of imported goods has also been done. An indirect tax, commodity-wise, has been roughly estimated. After taking these costs out, the residual, as a proportion of total value of production, is tabulated. That is, this residual ($\equiv R$) is given by

$$R_i^t = \frac{1}{p_i^t} \left\{ p_i^t - \sum_{j=1}^{n} p_j^t a_{ji} - \sum_{j=1}^{n} p_k^{mt} a_{ji}^m - w_i^t a_{n+1\ i} (1 - g_i) \right\} \tag{18}$$

where R_i^t is the residual of industry i in tth period, p_i^t is its price, p_j^{mt} is the import price of the kth commodity in the tth period, a_{ji} and a_{ji}^m are the domestic and import input coefficients for the base year, $a_{n+1,i}$ and g_i are the labour coefficient and proportionate tax in the base year and w_i^t is the wage rate in the ith industry in the tth year. It may be recalled that from this residual an entrepreneur has to meet the cost of interest payments on his stocks, depreciation, as well as returns on the fixed capital, if any. No estimates of the interest rates on stocks have been attempted.

This does not support the hypothesis that with the same capital equipment the productivity of labour might be increasing over the years. That will imply that the wage rate of labour is increasing without profits or the interest rate decreasing in the industry. This is obviously not the case in this instance. The tables A and B at the end clearly show that the residual portion goes on becoming progressively negative. The alternative conjecture, that the income of labour is increasing at the cost of profit, is again not borne out. As can be seen from those tables, the income of labour in more recent years has increased in many cases by more than the sum of labour and profit in the base period. The rate of obsolescence seems to have vastly increased in the period 1968 to 1973.

From these tables, we see that different technologies become non-feasible at different times. Whenever this residual becomes negative, it definitely implies non-feasibility. We see that some processes become non-feasible even after only one year. In the table below, the number of processes becoming non-feasible after each number of years is given.

Numbers of non-feasible processes found in different years for firms with 1963 and 1968 average technologies

Year	1964	1965	1966	1967	1968	1969	1970	1971	1972	1973	Total no. of processes
Average 1963 technology	1	5	7	3	10	21	33	31	35	44	70
Average 1968 technology	–	–	–	–	0	9	18	18	27	44	90

The beneficial effect on older firms of devaluation in 1967, and of the floating pound in 1971, is apparent from the table.

It will be noticed further that as soon as an industry becomes non-feasible it remains, by and large, non-feasible for all future years. This corroborates with the theoretical structure given above.

If we look at these two tables as a whole we see that 60 out of 70 commodity groups show a more or less continuously declining profitability for the technique of 1963 average vintage over the years 1963 to 1973. For the technique of 1968 average vintage the figure is 77 out of 90. Though this continuity is broken in many cases by the reversal in 1966 and 1971 under the stimuli of devaluation and of Barber's relaxing of the price code respectively. Mining and energy industries also show the effect of various well-known national and international factors.

The profitability of other industries does not decline over the period, but shows only random fluctuations. They are primarily Agriculture, Forestry, etc., Road and rail transport, Construction, and miscellaneous industries. It is clear that in these industries prices are not primarily determined by the cost, and therefore a given technique of production does not gradually become obsolete with technological advance. While for the rest of the commodities prices are being determined by the cost of production of the appropriate technique of production, as explained above, and therefore we can observe the gradual encroachment of obsolescence. These thus reflect the characteristics of Hicks' fix-price commodities, while the former reflect those of flex-price ones. Hicks observed 'The fact surely is that in modern (capitalist) economies there are, at least, two sorts of market. There are markets where prices are set by producers; and for those markets, which include a large part of the markets for industrial products, the fix-price assumption makes good sense. But there are other markets, flex price or speculative markets, in which prices are still determined by supply and demand' (op. cit., p.23). We have seen above how Professor Hicks' insight is vindicated by our study.

The above implies that an economy-wise disaggregative analysis should rather combine a demand-based price analysis of flex-price commodities with the determination of the input—output based price structure for fixed-price commodities by using equation (17). For the latter, also, a marginal input—output table has to be constructed by choosing one technique for each industry that is on the verge of obsolescence, viz. earning no profit. In its turn, this analytical and empirical framework would be able to provide a firm enough base for analysing the effects of various policy alternatives in sufficient depth on income and its growth, rate of obsolescence and unemployment, and the balance-of-payments and inflationary pressures.

Table A   Residual* as a proportion of the total value of the commodity when produced with the technology of 1963 average vintage

	1963	1964	1965	1966	1967	1968	1969	1970	1971	1972	1973
1 Agriculture	0.3089	0.3176	0.3279	0.3048	0.3300	0.3392	0.3292	0.3180	0.3672	0.3597	0.3270
2 Forestry and fishing	0.2983	0.3203	0.3074	0.3283	0.3264	0.3164	0.3514	0.3031	0.3861	0.4140	0.4799
3 Coal mining	0.1289	0.1232	0.0938	0.1227	0.1133	0.0781	0.0172	0.0195	0.1011	0.0805	0.0089
4 Other mining and quarrying	0.1831	0.1909	0.1784	0.0965	0.1212	0.1002	0.0370	−0.0273	−0.0080	−0.0388	−0.0784
5 Grain milling	0.0801	0.0473	−0.0208	−0.0122	0.0749	0.0433	−0.0095	−0.1995	−0.1310	−0.1093	−0.3560
6 Other cereal foodstuffs	0.0648	0.0681	0.0305	0.0410	0.0600	0.0561	0.0052	−0.0153	−0.1085	−0.1341	−0.1625
7 Sugar	0.0389	0.0748	0.1233	0.0619	0.0882	0.0482	0.0315	0.0187	0.0614	−0.0401	−0.1216
8 Cocoa, chocolate and sugar confectionery	0.1206	0.1051	0.1129	0.0883	0.0923	0.1104	0.0949	0.0828	0.1058	0.1075	−0.0445
9 Other food	0.0623	0.0642	0.0212	0.0220	0.0355	−0.0805	0.0070	0.0525	−0.1167	−0.1536	−0.1574
10 Drink	0.2571	0.2878	0.3170	0.3234	0.3388	0.3135	0.3171	0.2690	0.2399	0.2066	0.0279
11 Tobacco	0.2070	0.2079	0.2517	0.2708	0.2847	0.2472	0.2449	0.0804	0.0932	0.0666	−0.4492
12 Mineral oil refining	0.0381	0.0485	−0.0237	0.0153	0.0554	0.0478	0.1322	0.1847	0.2785	0.3000	0.2525
13 Paint and printing ink	0.1218	0.1073	0.0859	0.0599	0.0499	0.0122	0.0168	−0.0343	0.0021	0.0106	−0.0323
14 Coke ovens	0.0370	0.0231	0.0719	0.0352	0.0457	0.0825	0.0949	−0.0011	−0.0877	−0.1084	0.1101
15 Pharmaceutical and toilet preparations	0.1731	0.1619	0.1073	0.0373	0.0201	−0.0041	−0.0739	−0.0652	−0.0498	−0.1413	−0.2305
16 Soap, oils and fats	0.0807	0.0438	0.0355	0.0590	0.2072	0.2299	0.0866	−0.0288	0.0035	0.0116	−0.1753
17 Synthetic resins and plastics	0.1810	0.1485	0.1005	0.0620	0.0476	0.0255	0.0225	−0.0692	−0.1119	−0.1757	−0.2547
18 Other chemicals and allied industries	0.1340	0.1840	0.1762	0.1779	0.0197	0.1326	0.1071	−0.0892	0.1028	0.0690	0.0018
19 Iron and steel	0.1185	0.0869	0.0643	0.0484	0.0417	0.0230	−0.0037	0.0428	0.0927	0.0524	0.0105
20 Light metals	0.1243	0.0820	0.0763	0.0698	0.0861	0.0161	−0.0053	−0.0146	−0.0042	−0.0335	−0.0593
21 Other non-ferrous metals	0.0940	0.1046	0.0998	0.2131	0.1955	0.2290	0.2804	0.2973	0.2223	0.1933	0.2643

22 Agricultural machinery	0.1235	0.1342	0.1326	0.1121	0.1108	0.1009	0.0589	0.0523	0.0782	0.0438	0.0270
23 Machine tools	0.1549	0.1580	0.1563	0.1289	0.1390	0.1374	0.0890	0.0715	0.1213	0.1049	0.0572
24 Engineers' small tools	0.1369	0.1333	0.1284	0.0935	0.0977	0.0785	0.0722	0.0513	0.0834	0.0792	0.0295
25 Industrial engineers	0.0512	0.0502	0.0425	0.0114	0.0244	−0.0088	−0.0654	−0.0444	−0.0146	−0.0505	−0.0835
26 Textile machinery	0.1150	0.1284	0.1247	0.0992	0.0952	0.0755	0.0380	0.0264	0.0383	0.0597	−0.0172
27 Contractors' plant	0.1300	0.1368	0.1450	0.1363	0.1550	0.1399	0.0959	0.0677	0.0921	0.0744	0.0297
28 Office machinery	0.1220	0.0856	0.0723	0.0061	0.0180	−0.0123	−0.0503	−0.0421	0.0081	−0.0106	−0.1016
29 Other non-electrical machinery	0.1126	0.1190	0.1111	0.0699	0.0769	0.0440	−0.0098	−0.0300	−0.0103	−0.0537	−0.1400
30 Industrial plant and steel work	0.0870	0.0686	0.0501	0.0278	0.0375	0.0110	−0.0267	0.0071	0.0308	−0.0023	−0.0379
31 Other mechanical engineering	0.1233	0.1007	0.0768	0.0415	0.0657	0.0242	−0.0137	0.0358	0.0569	0.0326	−0.0269
32 Scientific instruments	0.1337	0.1397	0.1350	0.1149	0.1276	0.1622	0.1089	0.0950	0.0909	0.0598	−0.0171
33 Electrical machinery	0.0872	0.0821	0.0737	0.1065	0.1014	0.1117	0.0428	0.0968	0.0872	0.0307	0.0508
34 Insulated wires and cables	0.0697	0.0688	−0.2165	−0.0312	−0.2009	−0.3622	−0.4651	−0.6123	−0.4068	−0.3454	−0.6044
35 Radio and tele-communications	0.1387	0.1238	0.0788	0.0456	0.0455	−0.0076	−0.1120	−0.1755	−0.1662	−0.1682	−0.2249
36 Other electrical goods	0.1216	0.0914	0.0466	0.0151	0.0175	0.0140	−0.0440	−0.0831	−0.0948	−0.1845	−0.3765
37 Cans and metal boxes	0.0733	0.1188	0.1121	0.0756	0.0760	0.0368	0.0224	0.0074	0.0349	0.0065	−0.0496
38 Other metal goods	0.1206	0.1239	0.1112	0.0788	0.1088	0.0770	0.0351	0.0320	0.0954	0.0746	0.0059
39 Shipbuilding and marine engineering	0.0305	0.0102	0.1004	−0.0276	0.0013	0.0363	0.0062	−0.0280	−0.0603	−0.0641	−0.1590
40 Motor vehicles	0.0853	0.0875	0.0963	0.0847	0.1067	0.0982	0.0792	0.0563	0.0806	0.0516	0.0254
41 Aircraft	0.0969	0.0881	0.0962	0.0821	0.0881	0.0979	0.0646	0.0449	0.0811	0.0533	0.0046

Table A   Residual* as a proportion of the total value of the commodity when produced with the technology of 1963 average vintage

	1963	1964	1965	1966	1967	1968	1969	1970	1971	1972	1973
42 Other vehicles	0.0402	0.0138	0.0089	−0.0029	0.0155	0.0165	0.0140	−0.0573	−0.0008	−0.0715	−0.1141
43 Production of man-made fibres	0.3224	0.2862	0.2446	0.1250	0.1536	0.0998	0.0378	−0.0276	−0.0665	−0.1306	−0.2200
44 Cotton, etc., spinning and weaving	0.0894	0.0752	0.0966	0.0986	0.1016	0.1411	0.1494	0.1526	0.1528	0.1085	0.1380
45 Wool	0.0326	0.0026	−0.0921	−0.0775	−0.1375	−0.1876	−0.2135	−0.3754	−0.4290	−0.1910	−0.3210
46 Hosiery and lace	0.0999	0.1812	−0.1795	−0.2323	0.0589	0.0028	−0.0388	−0.0708	−0.0379	−0.2128	−0.2421
47 Textile finishing	0.1161	0.1000	0.0670	0.0472	0.0345	0.0131	−0.0197	−0.0649	−0.1155	−0.0771	−0.1095
48 Other textiles	0.1058	0.1000	0.0579	0.0467	0.0336	−0.0100	0.0161	−0.0225	−0.0328	−0.0070	−0.1466
49 Leather, leather goods and fur	0.0624	0.0180	0.0200	0.0672	0.0517	0.0318	0.0455	−0.0523	−0.0499	0.0730	−0.1267
50 Clothing	0.0717	0.0340	0.0314	0.0213	0.0267	−0.0201	−0.0427	−0.0673	−0.0618	−0.1349	−0.2714
51 Footwear	0.0621	−0.0515	0.0648	−0.0771	−0.0609	−0.1189	−0.1774	−0.2116	−0.1967	−0.2510	−0.3092
52 Cement	0.2166	0.2260	0.2087	0.1862	0.1765	0.1760	0.1478	0.1814	0.2348	0.2181	0.1545
53 Other building materials	0.1354	0.1067	0.1021	0.0741	0.0659	0.0664	0.0388	0.0050	0.0199	−0.0020	−0.0249
54 Pottery and glass	0.1357	0.0379	0.0365	0.0364	0.0354	0.0110	−0.0437	−0.0845	−0.0531	−0.1800	−0.1922
55 Furniture, etc.	0.0838	0.0570	0.0810	0.0698	0.0553	0.0273	0.0132	−0.0047	−0.0069	−0.0262	−0.0983
56 Timber and miscellaneous wood manufacturing	0.1089	0.0545	0.0432	0.0189	0.0351	0.0017	−0.0517	−0.0515	−0.0163	−0.0461	−0.0104
57 Paper and board	0.1187	0.0799	0.0720	0.0564	0.0525	0.0565	−0.0189	−0.0242	−0.0250	−0.0467	−0.0965
58 Paper products	0.1269	0.1068	0.1234	0.0818	0.1141	0.0844	0.1186	0.0617	0.0609	0.0585	0.0395
59 Printing and publishing	0.1210	0.1051	0.2877	0.0492	0.0492	0.0386	−0.0043	−0.0103	−0.0079	−0.0567	−0.1114
60 Rubber	0.1110	0.1415	0.1244	0.1165	0.1212	0.0801	0.0648	0.0408	0.1004	0.0714	−0.0489
61 Other manufacturing	0.1258	0.1403	0.1143	0.1115	0.0749	0.0391	0.0304	−0.0447	−0.0199	−0.0533	−0.1289
62 Construction	0.1065	0.0909	0.0898	0.1173	0.0693	0.0766	0.0366	0.0359	0.0265	−0.0310	−0.0079
63 Gas	0.1052	0.1042	0.0978	0.0634	0.0406	0.0738	0.0574	−0.0573	−0.0979	−0.1312	−0.2161
64 Electricity	0.3436	0.3663	0.3851	0.3484	0.3663	0.4007	0.3686	0.2960	0.2582	0.2381	0.1759
65 Water supply	0.3449	0.3615	0.3722	0.3865	0.3701	0.3530	0.3099	0.2261	0.2189	0.1870	0.1356

	0.1995	0.2023	0.2210	0.2439	0.2487	0.2692	0.2692	0.2454	0.2770	0.2444	0.2183
66 Road and rail transport											
67 Other transport	0.1677	0.4928	0.4804	0.4728	0.4778	0.4772	0.4234	0.3796	0.4254	0.3551	0.3197
68 Communication	0.2055	0.1596	0.2055	0.2234	0.2288	0.2651	0.2461	0.2146	0.1282	0.0695	0.0267
69 Distributive trades	0.2630	0.2882	0.2680	0.2805	0.2030	0.1916	0.1913	0.0235	−0.1741	−0.2556	−0.4165
70 Miscellaneous services	0.2165	0.2384	0.2348	0.2412	0.2934	0.2408	0.2576	0.2511	0.2534	0.2336	0.2197

* Its residual after the cost of indigenous, as well as foreign inputs, wages and government, is deducted. This should provide the cost of interest on stock as well as depreciation and returns, if any, on fixed capital.

Table B   *Residual* as a proportion of the total value of the commodity when produced with the technology of 1968 average vintage*

	1968	1969	1970	1971	1972	1973
1 Agriculture	0.3018	0.2891	0.2821	0.3225	0.3139	0.2916
2 Forestry and fishing	0.3451	0.3013	0.3249	0.3967	0.4228	0.4849
3 Coal mining	0.0906	0.0321	0.0295	0.1098	0.0891	0.0170
4 Stone, slate, chalk, sand, etc. extraction	0.1907	0.1465	0.0960	0.1271	0.1097	0.0628
5 Other mining and quarrying	0.3063	0.4025	0.3472	0.3699	0.3605	0.2826
6 Grain milling	0.1077	0.0194	−0.1615	−0.1042	−0.0735	−0.3001
7 Other cereal food	0.0650	0.0462	0.0003	−0.0858	−0.1000	−0.1685
8 Sugar	0.0573	0.0141	−0.0038	0.0366	−0.0568	−0.1365
9 Cocoa, chocolate and sugar confectionery	0.0800	0.0511	0.0500	0.0650	0.0677	−0.0582
10 Oils and fats	0.0500	−0.0072	−0.1792	−0.1187	0.0237	−0.1559
11 Other food	0.0464	0.0853	0.0830	−0.0301	−0.0710	−0.0914
12 Soft drinks	0.0866	−0.0061	0.0002	−0.0048	−0.0090	−0.0905
13 Alcoholic drink	0.3293	0.3004	0.2508	0.2190	0.1876	−0.0172
14 Tobacco	0.1565	0.1751	0.0130	0.0096	−0.0267	−0.5253
15 Coke ovens and manufactured fuel	0.0567	0.0793	−0.0146	−0.1011	−0.1180	0.1006
16 Mineral oil refining, lubricating oils items, etc.	0.0601	−0.0092	0.0403	0.1379	0.1686	0.1015
17 General chemicals	0.1517	0.1374	0.1091	0.1065	0.0822	0.0153
18 Pharmaceutical chemicals and preparations	0.1972	0.1700	0.1809	0.1907	0.1284	0.0637
19 Toilet preparations	0.1233	0.0708	0.0906	0.0769	0.0818	0.0340
20 Paint	0.1669	0.1201	0.1063	0.1292	0.1393	0.0955
21 Soap and detergents	0.0563	−0.1290	−0.2400	−0.2524	−0.2606	−0.3593
22 Synthetic resins, plastic materials and synethetic rubber	0.1564	0.1330	0.1005	0.0573	0.0098	−0.0644
23 Dyestuffs and pigments	0.1514	0.1785	0.1953	0.2414	0.2065	0.1376
24 Fertilizers	0.0625	0.0237	0.0231	−0.0249	0.0408	−0.0069
25 Other chemical industries	0.0978	0.0845	0.0531	0.0516	0.0614	−0.0201
26 Iron casting, etc.	0.0619	−0.0137	0.0053	0.0516	0.0027	−0.0339
27 Other iron and steel	0.0422	0.0141	0.0690	0.1059	0.0834	0.0512
28 Aluminium and aluminium alloys	0.0351	0.0091	0.0045	0.0138	−0.0080	−0.0315
29 Other non-ferrous metals	0.0593	0.0929	0.1482	0.0386	−0.0008	0.1232
30 Agricultural machinery	0.1024	0.0529	0.0526	0.0764	0.0479	0.0297
31 Machine tools	0.0992	0.0506	0.0408	0.0848	0.0736	0.0292
32 Pumps, valves and compressors	0.1091	0.1048	0.0917	0.1219	0.1275	0.0844
33 Industrial engines	0.0842	0.0347	0.0547	0.0764	0.0551	0.0308
34 Textile machinery	0.1283	0.1148	0.1054	0.1136	0.1008	0.0699

Table B   *Residual* as a proportion of the total value of the commodity when produced with the technology of 1968 average vintage*

	1968	1969	1970	1971	1972	1973
35 Construction and mechanical handling equipment	0.1676	0.1265	0.1062	0.1245	0.1108	0.0669
36 Office machinery	0.1046	0.0854	0.0762	0.0921	0.0851	0.0315
37 Other non-electrical machinery	0.1069	0.0646	0.05023	0.0503	0.0198	−0.0519
38 Industrial plant and steel work	0.1948	0.1652	0.1973	0.2124	0.1837	0.1493
39 Other mechanical engineering	0.1017	0.0776	0.1167	0.1415	0.1171	0.0674
40 Instrument engineering	0.1125	0.0573	0.0496	0.0434	0.0112	−0.0673
41 Electrical machinery	0.1180	0.1012	0.0985	0.0882	0.0345	0.0615
42 Insulated wires and cables	0.0532	−0.1068	−0.1714	−0.0499	−0.0064	−0.1652
43 Electronics and telecommunications	0.1025	0.0306	−0.0203	−0.0101	−0.0101	−0.0543
44 Domestic electrical appliances	0.0805	0.0104	−0.0232	−0.0233	−0.0590	−0.1697
45 Other electrical goods	0.1284	0.0794	0.0449	0.0401	−0.0348	−0.1943
46 Shipbuilding and marine engineering	0.0855	0.0583	0.0217	−0.0116	−0.0154	−0.1249
47 Wheeled tractors	0.0921	0.0892	0.0946	0.0959	0.0980	0.1061
48 Motor vehicles	0.0439	0.0284	0.0064	0.0268	−0.0028	−0.0317
49 Aerospace equipment	0.0261	−0.0004	−0.0170	0.0181	−0.0050	−0.0544
50 Other vehicles	0.0046	−0.0029	−0.0702	−0.0195	−0.0843	−0.1282
51 Engineers' small tools	0.1405	−0.0142	−0.0206	0.0469	0.0209	−0.0712
52 Cutlery and jewellery	0.0822	0.0031	0.0119	0.0813	0.1403	0.0167
53 Bolts, nuts, screws, etc.	0.0964	0.0545	0.0488	0.0994	0.0685	0.0115
54 Wire and wire manufactures	0.0499	0.0104	−0.0094	0.0664	0.0371	−0.0557
55 Cans and metal boxes	0.0627	0.0491	0.0333	0.0596	0.0336	−0.0163
56 Other metal goods	0.1032	0.0762	0.0723	0.1133	0.0890	−0.0078
57 Production of man-made fibres	0.2232	0.1846	0.1423	0.1076	0.0600	−0.0163
58 Cotton, etc. spinning and weaving	0.0518	0.0677	0.0757	0.0764	0.0817	0.0733
59 Woolen and worsted	0.0429	0.0222	−0.0795	−0.1362	0.0452	−0.0256
60 Hosiery and knitted goods	0.1176	0.0836	0.0619	0.0258	−0.0821	−0.1366
61 Carpets	0.0845	0.0572	0.0298	−0.0033	−0.0555	−0.0748
62 Household textiles and handkerchiefs	0.0259	0.0476	−0.0072	0.0486	0.1573	0.0140
63 Textile finishing	0.1129	0.0746	0.0325	0.0230	0.0192	−0.0073
64 Other textiles	0.1062	0.1171	0.0951	0.1024	0.0968	−0.0060
65 Leather, leather goods and fur	0.0659	0.0730	−0.0007	0.0001	0.1158	0.0113
66 Clothing	0.0521	0.0303	0.0133	0.0196	−0.0453	−0.1766
67 Footwear	0.0709	0.0248	−0.0067	0.0001	−0.0326	−0.0881

Table B   Residual* as a proportion of the total value of the commodity when produced with the technology of 1968 average vintage

	1968	1969	1970	1971	1972	1973
68 Bricks, fireclay and refractory goods	0.0615	0.0133	−0.0393	−0.0291	−0.0632	−0.1172
69 Pottery and glass	0.0970	0.0538	0.0183	0.0439	−0.0213	−0.0725
70 Cement	0.1304	0.0958	0.1290	0.1799	0.1626	0.0949
71 Other building materials, etc.	0.1063	0.0539	0.0272	0.0166	0.0113	0.0032
72 Furniture and bedding, etc.	0.0750	0.0406	0.0261	0.0289	0.0159	−0.0634
73 Timber and miscellaneous wood manufacturing	0.0761	0.0004	0.0026	0.0357	0.0118	0.0537
74 Paper and board	0.1086	0.0253	0.0181	0.0119	−0.0094	−0.0672
75 Packing products of paper, board, etc.	0.0848	0.0594	0.0567	0.0630	0.0619	0.0434
76 Other paper and board products	0.1546	0.1150	0.1107	0.1321	0.1309	0.1079
77 Printing and publishing	0.1613	0.1227	0.1184	0.1211	0.0792	0.0337
78 Rubber	0.1249	0.1135	0.1036	0.1493	0.1204	0.0274
79 Plastic products n.e.s.	0.1297	0.1021	0.0720	0.0638	0.0242	−0.0297
80 Other manufacturing	0.1274	0.1079	0.0867	0.0894	0.0757	−0.0072
81 Construction	0.1241	0.1095	0.1043	0.0947	0.0484	0.0729
82 Gas	0.1389	0.0760	−0.0233	−0.0461	−0.0594	−0.1778
83 Electricity	0.3877	0.3620	0.2929	0.2520	0.2280	0.1745
84 Water supply	0.3623	0.3213	0.2525	0.2365	0.2067	0.1584
85 Railways	0.2546	0.2737	0.2402	0.2686	0.2527	0.1956
86 Road transport	0.1925	0.1076	0.1235	0.1849	0.1664	0.1156
87 Other transport	0.1310	0.0963	0.0686	0.1023	0.0866	0.0607
88 Communication	0.2084	0.2285	0.2050	0.1303	0.0758	0.0377
89 Distributive trades	0.2627	0.2648	0.1143	−0.0627	−0.1376	−0.2839
90 Miscellaneous services	0.1856	0.2100	0.2040	0.2061	0.1861	0.1697

*Its residual after the cost of indigenous, as well as foreign inputs, wages and government, is deducted. This should provide the cost of interest on stock as well as depreciation and returns, if any, on fixed capital.

n.e.s. = not elsewhere specified.

Notes

1   Mathur, P.N. 'Karl Marx's Two Theories of Value — An Interpretation', *Artha Vijnana*, 10 (1968).
2   Schumpeter, J. *The Theory of Economic Development*, New York, 1961, p. 153.
3   Solow, R.M. 'Competitive Valuation in A Dynamic Input—Output System', *Econometrica*, 27 (1959).
4   Hicks, J.R. *Capital and Growth*, Oxford, 1965, Chapter VII.
5   Leontief, W.W. *The Structure of the American Economy*, New York, 1953.

6   This is, as shown by the author elsewhere, given by $\bar{\pi}$, where $\bar{\pi}$ is the reciprocal of the largest eigen value of the matrix $(I - A)^{-1}B$. Mathur, P.N. 'A Modified Leontief Dynamic Model and Related Price System', *Econometric Annual of the Indian Economic Journal*, vol. XIII, no. 3, 1965. See also 'Economic Analysis in Input–Output Framework' (edited by Mathur, P.N. and Bharadwaj, R.), Poona, India, 1965, pp. 10–12.

7   For macro implications of this, see P.N. Mathur 'The Rate of Interest in a State of Economic Flux' in *Essays in Modern Economics*, M. Parkin (ed.), Longmans, London, 1973.

8   Given the upper limit to the value of r given in footnote 6, the matrix $(I - A^v - r^w B^v)^{-1}$ will be a positive matrix, each of whose elements will increase or decrease with r. Hence, each element of vector $p_0^{-1}\{P\}$ will have its minimum value when $r = 0$.

9   A technology here is understood as a combination of n techniques, one belonging to each industry.

10 Hicks, J., *The Crisis in Keynesian Economics*, Basil Blackwell, Oxford, 1975.

11 Dr M. Dadi of Baroda University, India, has been of immense help to me in carrying out this study. I am thankful to the British Council, which made his stay in Aberystwyth possible.

12 Dr M. Dadi of Baroda University, and Mr Y.A. Suliman, have been mainly responsible for the preparation of these tables.

4

LINKAGES, KEY SECTORS AND DEVELOPMENT STRATEGY

JAMES W. MCGILVRAY

Introduction

Recently, the concept of 'linkages' has attracted considerable interest, as a means of identifying 'key sectors' in a strategy of industrial development. Although discussion of linkages usually relates to developing countries, the idea has also been taken up by regional economists, who see it as a means of identifying industries or sectors which might be suitable for selective promotion within the context of a regional industrial development programme. In either case, it is believed that if resources (especially capital and entrepreneurial skills) can be concentrated on these key sectors, output and employment in the country or region will grow more rapidly than if these resources were allocated in some alternative way.

Now, it is obviously true that some patterns of resource allocation are more efficient than others, in the sense that they will result in higher rates of growth. For reasons which will be referrred to below, it is also plausible to argue that, over any particular time period, an optimal pattern of growth will comprise significantly different sectoral rates of investment and output growth, particularly in a small country or region. If for some reason the market cannot be relied upon for this allocative function, then it is useful to be able to identify *ex ante* these potential high growth sectors, and to try to channel resources into them.

The purpose of this paper is to assess the usefulness of measures of linkage as a means of identifying such key sectors. Although the discussion is general, it is couched particularly towards small open economies, for the simple reason that most developing countries, and virtually by definition all regions, are of this type.

The first section of this paper defines measures of linkage and their use in identifying key sectors. The second section looks at the theoretical and empirical basis of linkages as a guide to resource allocation and reviews some of the empirical work on linkages. In the light of this evaluation, the concluding section assigns a more modest role to the use of linkages as an empirical tool in the formulation of development policy.

Measurement of linkages and identification of key sectors

Linkages are descriptive measures of the economic interdependence of industries. The most commonly-accepted method of measuring sectoral linkages is based on the inverse of an open static input–output model. For an n-industry system, denote the elements of the inverse matrix by r_{ij} $(i, j = 1, 2, \ldots, n)$. Define

$$R_{.j} = \sum_{i=1}^{n} r_{ij} \quad (j = 1, 2, \ldots, n) \tag{1}$$

so that $R_{.j}$ is the sum of the elements in column j of the inverse. Now, each element in column j measures the direct and indirect impact of an increase of one unit in the final demand for industry j on each of the n industries. Typically these elements are defined in terms of gross output values, and $R_{.j}$ is then the aggregate or economy-wide gross output generated by an increase of one unit in final demand in industry j.

For comparative purposes, it is the relative magnitude of $R_{.j}$ which is important, and the measure can be normalised as

$$V_j = \frac{1}{n} R_{.j} \bigg/ \frac{1}{n^2} \sum_{i,j} r_{ij} \tag{2}$$

The numerator is the average value of the elements in column j. The denominator is the average value of all elements of the inverse. This measure, which is independent of the units of measurement, is called an *index of backwards linkage*. Values of $V_j > 1$ are taken to indicate high backwards linkage, in the sense of generating above-average response in other sectors.

Another measure of linkage can be defined by reference to the rows of the inverse. Thus

$$R_{i.} = \sum_{j=1}^{n} r_{ij} \quad (i = 1, 2, \ldots, n) \tag{3}$$

measures the output which would be generated in sector i if final demand in each sector were to increase by one unit. Again, this measure can be normalised as

$$U_i = \frac{1}{n} R_{i.} \bigg/ \frac{1}{n^2} \sum_{i,j} r_{ij} \tag{4}$$

and this is called the *index of forwards linkage*. Values of $U_i > 1$ indicate high forwards linkage, in the sense that these sectors display above-average dependence on the output of other sectors.

These measures were first devised by Rasmussen [5], as the 'Index of Power of Dispersion' (corresponding to the index of backwards linkage) and the 'Index of Sensitivity of Dispersion' (forwards linkage). It is worth noting that these measures pre-dated ideas about the role of linkages in industrial development strategy, and were simply regarded as useful summary measures of the structural interdependence of an economy.

Key sectors are defined as those in which both V_j and U_i exceed unity. A key sector is therefore a sector which generates above-average input require-ments from other sectors, and whose output is widely used by other sectors. Familiarity with the basic structure of input—output tables suggests that key sectors would be found to occupy an intermediate position in the hierarchy of sectors from primary to final. Once identified, it is suggested that these key sectors be given priority in investment allocation and in industrial promotion strategy.

Before reviewing the theoretical basis of the linkage argument, two important points should be noted. First, measures of linkage should not be confused with sectoral (income or employment) multipliers. Sectoral multipliers are designed to measure the impact of an increase in final demand on income or employment.[1] Measures of linkage are designed to measure the impact of an increase in final demands on *gross outputs*. A high value for V_j or U_i does not imply a corre-spondingly high value for the income or employment multiplier, a point over-looked by some writers who seem to assume that high linkages mean a high domestic value-added content.

Secondly, it is important to distinguish between measures of linkage based on the existing technology of a country's or region's structure of production, and measures of linkage based on the existing interdependence of domestic sectors of production. In the latter case V_j and U_i measure the impact of a unit increase in final demand on domestically-supplied inputs and outputs, and the appropriate matrix for calculating linkages is $(I - A_d)^{-1}$, where A_d is the matrix of domestic flow coefficients. In the former case, measures of linkage are based on the technology matrix $(I - A)^{-1}$, where A is the matrix of total (domestic plus imported) flow coefficients. Hence, in this case, V_j and U_i measure the impact of a one unit increase in final demand on total supply, rather than gross output.

We return to this point in the following section. Meanwhile, it is obvious that if technology were identical across countries, technology-based measures of linkage would lead to a unique ranking of sectors. If only the domestic-flow matrix is used, the sectoral values of linkages, and their rank ordering, will differ between countries, depending on the level and structure of imports in the economy. The question of which matrix is the most appropriate for measuring linkages is an important issue which will be discussed below.

An evaluation of linkages as a guide to development strategy

Although Rasmussen devised the measures, the idea of using linkages as a means of identifying key sectors was first mooted in a famous book by Alfred Hirschman [3], who, in the light of the interpretation put upon his ideas, may now regret this venture into input—output economics.

Two important features underlying Hirschman's argument are that in most developing economies (*a*) there are imperfections in factor and product markets, and (b) there is a shortage of entrepreneurial talent. It is also implied that resources are not centrally allocated but depend largely upon the atomistic responses of entrepreneurs. In these circumstances, investment opportunities will be missed and increases in demand will probably be met by a rise in imports. To overcome this, Hirschman suggested a form of disequilibrium development strategy, in which the economy would experience a sequence of severe shortages and/or excessive supply in particular product markets. Faced with these strong market signals, local entrepreneurs would be induced to invest, either to supply products which are scarce, or to utilise products which are in excess supply.

In this process, key sectors play the leading role in creating disequilibrium, and indicating investment opportunities. With respect to backwards linkage, key sectors generate above-average input requirements from other sectors, and therefore (it is argued) there is a greater probability of induced investment in the supplying sectors (to expand existing plant and/or to replace imports). With respect to forwards linkage, the mechanism is less direct but hinges on the probability of investment in sectors in which the product of the key sector is a major input (e.g. plentiful supplies of cotton yarn may induce investment in cotton textile production). Thus, by initially stimulating a rapid growth of output in the key sector(s) there is a greater prospect of generating a sequence of induced investment decisions and an active growth process, in conditions of scarce entrepreneurial talents. Both in Hirschman's book, and in the subsequent literature, rather more weight has been given to backwards linkages than to forwards linkages.

As a basis for an industrial development strategy,[2] the linkages/key sector approach has a number of major defects. The first of these concerns the actual measurement of linkages and the identification of key sectors. Bharadwaj [1] pointed out – a qualification also noted by Hirschman himself – that induced investment will depend on the *level* of demand for inputs (in the case of backwards linkage) and the level of supply of inputs (in the case of forwards linkage). In turn this would depend on the postulated level of output in the selected key sector.

To try to deal with this point, Hirschman suggested a weighting scheme in the construction of the backwards linkage index, where the weights are based on the ratio of the demand for each (commodity) input to the output of that commodity at minimum economic operating capacity. These ratios are taken to approximate to probabilities (and are thus constrained to be $\leqslant 1$); the higher the ratio, the greater the probability that the induced expansion will be forthcoming. Thus derived demand for steel would have to be quite substantial to induce investment in a steel mill, whereas a quite modest demand for protective clothing might justify investment in a protective clothing factory.

Applying this idea to the measure of linkages would give something like

$$V'_j = \frac{1}{n} \sum_{i=1}^{n} w_{ij} r_{ij} \bigg/ \frac{1}{n^2} \sum_{i,j} w_{ij} r_{ij} \tag{5}$$

where the w_{ij} correspond to Hirschman's probability weights, and might well cause a different rank ordering of sectors than that given by formula (2). Note that the matrix of weights $\{w_{ij}\}$ is a function of the levels of output assumed for each sector, and will change as sector outputs change.

However, this modification still leaves open the question of exactly what output weights should be used to determine w_{ij} and hence V'_j, since w_{ij} is a function of $a_{ij}X_j$ and is therefore dependent on the assumed scale of output in sector j. In algebraic terms,

$$V'_j = f(r_{ij}, w_{ij})_i \tag{6}$$

and

$$w_{ij} = g(a_{ij}X_j, K_i)_i \tag{7}$$

where K_i is minimum economic operating capacity in sector i and X_j is the level of output in sector j.

One solution suggested by a number of writers is to use actual final demands or outputs to calculate the w_{ij} values in (7). The trouble here is that measures of linkage based on this weighting system will reflect the actual or *ex post* linkages in the economy (and hence the investment opportunities already available), rather than the *ex ante* or potential linkages created by a concentrated development of certain key sectors, and the (*ex ante*) market disequilibria created by this selective expansion. Thus the question of the scale of expansion of the key sectors (and incidentally the question of how the expansion of the key sectors is to be induced) remains unresolved, despite the fact that the modified sectoral linkages, and their rank ordering, depend upon the assumed scale of output in the key sectors. In summary, while linkage measures based on the *ex post* level and pattern of production may be useful in summarising the interdependence of sectors at the current level of development, they are not necessarily very useful in the context of the type of growth sequence envisaged by Hirschman.[3] These criticisms, though methodological, must at least cause some doubts about the reliability of linkages as a means of identifying key sectors in the development process. A more fundamental criticism is the complete absence of any considerations of comparative advantage. The majority of developing countries (and of course regions) are small and highly trade dependent, and decisions about investment (however financed) can rarely ignore comparative cost criteria. Sectoral rankings provided by measures of linkage take no account of comparative advantage and of the choice between imports and domestic production, despite the fact that the linkage hypothesis relies heavily upon import substitution in the development process. Nor is there any reference to export possibilities which, despite restrictive effects of tariff and non-tariff protection, have been an important impetus to growth in many developing countries.

Conflict between the prescriptions of trade theory and growth theory as applied to the development process is not unfamiliar. With notable contributions by Chenery [2], there has been considerable progress in synthesising elements of both, particularly by means of programming models which involve shadow prices.

While these models emphasise interdependence and growth, the patterns of production and trade which are determined incorporate principles of dynamic comparative advantage. Choice between imports and the domestic production of intermediate goods is determined, and traded and non-traded goods can be distinguished.

The theoretical basis of programming models lies in general equilibrium theory, and resource allocation according to comparative advantage follows from an extension of the model to include trade. Resource allocation is consistent with a balanced growth approach to development, using the term 'balanced growth' to mean *ex ante* equilibrium in product and factor markets. The linkage-based model, however, implies an unbalanced (disequilibrium) growth sequence which is quite distinct from that implied by programming models and cannot be incorporated in them. Thus if the Hirschman argument is accepted and a disequilibrium growth process is prescribed, some alternative means must be sought to account for comparative advantage in the measures of linkage and the identification of key sectors.

This dilemma is reflected in the question, raised in the previous section, of whether to use the domestic flow matrix $(I - A_d)^{-1}$ or the technology (total flow) matrix $(I - A)^{-1}$ in computing measures of linkage. The domestic flow matrix will provide measures of linkages based on the existing interdependence of production in the country or region. However, since the purpose in calculating linkages is to identify potential areas of investment, including import-substituting investment, the technology matrix is more suitable. However, this might well yield a ranking of sectors which is quite unrealistic in terms of comparative advantage, particularly where natural-resource-based industries are concerned. What is perhaps required is some hybrid matrix which includes only potentially-replaceable imports. Unfortunately, it is not easy to determine this *a priori.* Even if possible, we have now moved a long way from the rather simple measures of linkage described above.

Finally, it is important to clarify some misunderstanding about the relation between linkage-based development and the often-confusing controversy over balanced versus unbalanced growth. In an extensive piece of empirical research, Yotopoulos and Nugent [6] attempt to test the hypothesis that countries which follow the Hirschman strategy of unbalanced growth experience higher rates of growth than countries which pursue an alternative strategy of balanced growth.[4] Countries which pursue the Hirschman strategy are identified by the degree to which relative sectoral growth rates are positively correlated with a unique set of sectoral linkage indexes. Thus, a country whose sectoral growth rates are positively correlated with the indexes of sectoral linkages is said to comply with the Hirschman strategy. If countries which pursue the Hirschman strategy also experience higher overall growth rates, this supports the argument for linkage-based (Hirschman-type) development.

This is an inadequate test of the linkage hypothesis, for two reasons. First of all, the linkage hypothesis does not imply that key sectors will necessarily grow faster than other sectors; if the strategy is successful, the fastest-growing sectors may be those which are most closely linked to the key sectors, not the key sectors themselves. These sectors may have relatively low indexes. For example, suppose a country posseses a pulp milling industry and this has a very high linkage index and is therefore identified as a key sector. An expansion in this sector may induce investment in a paper and board-making industry, where these products were previously imported. The import-replacing paper and board industry would experience a faster rate of growth than the pulp-milling industry, though the latter has a higher linkage index. Hence, correlating sectoral growth rates with sectoral indexes of linkages is not an adequate measure of compliance with the Hirschman strategy.

Secondly, while the Hirschman strategy certainly implies uneven sectoral growth rates, the reverse argument does not apply. In the Hirschman sense, 'unbalanced growth' does not mean simply that different sectors grow at different rates. It means a process of growth characterised by continuous *ex ante* disequilibria, which in turn induce investment. Correspondingly, it is not sufficient to identify 'balanced growth' as meaning proportional growth in all sectors, a totally unrealistic paradigm of an alternative development strategy. In the Hirschman sense, balanced growth means a development process in which there is *ex ante* equilibrium in inter-industry supply and demand, and is quite consistent with, say, an export-based growth strategy in which the international and national sectors experience quite different rates of growth. This indeed has been the experience of many developing countries in the last two decades, in which comparative advantage (particularly natural-resource-based advantage) and the supply of imported technology have played the major roles. There is no necessary connection between this form of 'unbalanced' growth and that implied by Hirschman-style linkage-based development, and it is therefore incorrect to assume that variations in sectoral growth rates demonstrate a linkage-based development strategy.

Conclusions

The conclusion of this review of the 'linkage hypothesis' is that, whatever may be thought of the Hirschman-type development strategy, the various measures of linkage described above are altogether too crude as an empirical device for the identification of key sectors and, *a fortiori,* as a basis for empirical analysis of the role of linkages in the development process. Moreover, this scepticism is supported by the observation that, in the actual experience of developing countries, patterns of international trade and international competitiveness, natural resources, and endowments of skill and technology appear to exercise the dominant role in development. Yet none of these factors are given explicit recognition in the linkage-based development process.

It is regrettable that an original and valuable contribution to an understanding of economic development processes has been emasculated and oversimplified, a victim of the tendency to subordinate economic hypotheses to the restrictive requirements of elementary regression and correlation analysis. Thus measures of linkage have been reduced to the mechanical computation of index numbers.

Both Hirschman's theory, and the various measures of linkage described, have a useful role to play in the understanding and practice of development planning, at national or regional level. Input—output tables, and the various measures of structural and trade dependence which can be derived from them, give a valuable insight into the interdependence of different sectors of an economy, and can be used as a first step in the identification of potential areas of project development and evaluation. It is altogether too naive, however, to suppose that this complex process of analysis and evaluation can be reduced to a rank ordering of index numbers.

Moreover, once the key sectors or projects have been selected, whether or not a Hirschman-type strategy is pursued to induce the desired allocation of resources is a separate (though related) issue, which depends *inter alia* on political and institutional considerations. It is quite feasible to envisage a 'balanced' development strategy based on a higher-than-average growth of certain key sectors, as distinct from the 'unbalanced' sequence envisaged by Hirschman. In either case, different sectors would experience different rates of growth.

Notes

1   See for example McNicoll [4].
2   Linkages are not confined to industrial sectors, but service sectors have low linkages and would not qualify as key sectors.
3   Another curious feature of these linkage measures is that capital goods sectors, which sell their output to final demand, will always have very low forwards linkages and will therefore never emerge as key sectors.
4   This study suffers from all the defects listed earlier in this paper, as well as some others. For comments on the paper, and a rejoinder, see the *Quarterly Journal of Economics*, May 1976.

References

[1]   Bharadwaj, K.R., 'A Note on Structural Interdependence and the Concept of a Key Sector', *Kyklos,* vol. 19, 1966.
[2]   Chenery, H., 'Comparative Advantage and Development Policy', *American Economic Review,* March 1961.
[3]   Hirschman, A.O., *The Strategy of Economic Development,* Yale, 1968.
[4]   McNicoll, I., *The Shetland Economy,* Research Monograph No. 2, Fraser of Allander Institute, 1976.
[5]   Rasmussen, P.N., *Studies in Intersectoral Relations,* Amsterdam, 1956.
[6]   Yotopoulos, P. and Nugent, J., 'A Balanced-Growth Version of the Linkage Hypothesis', *Quarterly Journal of Economics,* May 1973.

GOVERNMENT POLICY AND THE STRUCTURE OF THE ECONOMY

V.H. WOODWARD

Introduction and summary

The post-war period has seen a steady rise in living standards and a consistently low unemployment rate (until the 1970s) unparalleled in British history. But the performance of the British economy relative to other advanced industrialised countries has not only been very poor – relative decline actually accelerated in the 1960s and early seventies since the growth of manufacturing output was well under 50 per cent of the rate of all other OECD countries combined compared with 60 per cent in the fifties. The poor performance of manufacturing industry is central to the policy problem since it provides the bulk of export earnings needed to pay for imports of food and raw materials. Yet the relative decline has been allowed to go unchecked resulting in both a worsening balance of trade and declining employment in manufacturing.

The importance of the declining contribution of manufacturing in the last decade to the major targets of policy, employment and the balance of trade, was overlooked because of excessive concentration on macroeconomic aggregates in economic decision taking. The overall balance of trade did not worsen as might be expected through the decline in manufacturing over the last decade partly because of growing net exports of services. This has led to the suggestion that we can pay our way by expanding exports of services and that the declining contribution of manufacturing does not matter. But the expansion of services cannot possibly fill the gap – a large part of the improvement in net exports of services has been due to commission on rapidly growing imports of manufactured goods (relative to exports) and this cannot be allowed to continue. The importance of the declining employment in manufacturing in the last decade was overlooked because the overall unemployment rate did not worsen significantly owing to rapid expansion of employment by the government. The preoccupation with macroeconomic aggregates, and the instruments of macroeconomic policy, whether monetary or fiscal policy or the exchange rate, has concealed the nature of the policy problem, which is increasingly structural. Consequently, there is no solution through policies on the demand side alone.

The key policy problem is relatively low investment per worker, which is both a consequence and a cause of slow growth. We have had relatively slow growth

Table 1   *The trade balance and employment in manufacturing 1963−75 − a summary*

	Average level			Change	
				Average 1963−5 to Average 1972−4	
	Trade balance			Trade balance	employment
	1963−71	1972−74	1975	(£m. 1970 prices)	(thousands)
Group A Trade-gaining industries	1266	1832	1853	710	−132
Group B Trade losers, employment gainers	720	200	425	−540	184
Group C Trade losers, employment losers	737	275	265	−538	−566
All manufacturing*	2723	2307	2543	−368	−514

n.b. Industries classified to the above groups according to change in employment and trade balance, average 1963−65 to average 1972−74.
*Defined to exclude food, building materials, non-ferrous metals, timber and paper.

partly because of external and long-run institutional factors. But an important factor has been the erroneous demand-management policies which led to stop-go. This resulted in a series of short-run capacity constraints and so a large and permanent increase in import penetration on each upswing. This is an important explanation for the relatively slow increase in investment per worker, both directly and indirectly. The direct effect was that investment did not precede demand on an adequate scale because the increase was shown to be short-lived in successive booms and the trend growth in demand, particularly in investment goods industries, was almost zero. Indirect effects occurred because slow growth understandably made trade unions resist redundancies since there were few alternative job opportunities and because management had less incentive to be efficient.

Slow growth is a major, but not the only explanation for decline. The poor record of innovation in British industry is another. Despite the British tradition of inventions and scientific discoveries there is a growing gap in the exploitation of technology. Certain industrial sectors have experienced a strong underlying growth in demand yet investment has been inadequate. Table 1 shows the deterioration of the trade balance of these industries (group *B*) was even larger than in industries experiencing a slow growth in demand (group *C*). The failure of group *B* industries to generate more employment to offset declining employment in the slowest growing sectors, which they would have done if they were internationally competitive, is a major cause for concern. The industries are relatively labour intensive. The successful manufacturing industries (Group *A*) tend to be more capital intensive.

The policy problem is therefore partly a structural one. The deterioration in the manufacturing trade balance in the last decade was partly explained by poor trade performance in growth sectors which are expected to offset losses in declining sectors if the market mechanism is functioning properly. This structural factor explains why the depreciation of sterling failed to improve the overall balance of trade in manufacturing 1971—74. The contribution of this factor to net employment change in manufacturing was reinforced by the tendency for the successful manufacturing industries to be relatively more capital intensive than the less successful.

There is no solution to the policy problem through the unaided workings of the market mechanism. The structural problem is not the only reason. Capital stock per worker is now so low relative to that in other countries that it is unlikely the backlog can be made up through market forces; even if it could there would be a massive policy problem in the redeployment of redundant labour. But, because of this historical experience there must be serious doubts that adequate investment will be forthcoming ahead of demand, even with sensible demand management; this is of crucial importance over the next decade.

While there is no possibility of halting relative decline without government intervention a necessary condition for successful intervention is continuity of policy. But while consensus policies are a necessary condition if relative decline is to be halted they are not sufficient. The availability of North Sea oil provides the one opportunity in the foreseeable future to do something about it.

But neither major political party has any firm proposition on how this asset is to be used to arrest Britain's economic decline; moreover, the permanent civil service is traditionally too preoccupied with the short-term economic situation to make any concrete proposals. The crucial time period is 1980—85 when the North Sea oil will be making a growing contribution to the balance of payments. It is a feasible policy option to steer these resources into productive investment but not without a major government initiative — to do this will require extensive organisation and preparations must begin now. If no positive action is taken the growing contribution of North Sea oil to the balance of payments will be absorbed primarily by consumption. If this happens further deindustrialisation can be expected after 1985, when stabilisation of oil production is achieved, with dire consequences for employment.

Investment subsidies operating primarily through the market mechanism 1980—85 would appear to have a good chance of success, provided consistent policies were pursued on the demand side. Selective subsidies might be available for all investment by technologically-backward industries, particularly those facing a strong trend growth in demand. Selectivity on these grounds contrasts with the official policy of 'backing winners' since the industries concerned typically have poor external trade performance. But there is a limited justi-fication for selective subsidies by industrial sector. General subsidies are proposed which would be available to all other manufacturing industries but only to the extent that their investment was increased over some past average level — these subsidies would be aimed at inducing investment ahead of demand. The combined effects of the proposed subsidies should raise investment in manufacturing 1980—85 by at least one third and prevent greatly increased import penetration.

The policy problem

The relationship between investment, the balance of payments and employment is central to the policy problem. Studies based on aggregate data often fail to find a close association because structural change masks the inadequacy of investment in certain sectors. This inadequacy is both a cause and consequence of poor trade performance and it leads to relatively low employment generation even in sectors facing a strong underlying growth of demand.

A detailed analysis of trade and employment performance was carried out for 58 manufacturing industries for the period 1963—75, usually at minimum list heading level; summary figures are given in Table 2. A list of the constituent industries is given in the Appendix. In Table 2 industries have been allocated to one of four groups[1] — those which *gained* employment and whose trade balance (1) deteriorated or (2) improved and those who *lost* employment and whose trade balance (3) improved or (4) deteriorated. Gains or losses in employment or trade were judged by the change in the average position 1963—65 to 1972—4 — since the beginning and end periods broadly cover the same stage in the trade cycle any underlying trends should be revealed. The year 1975 is included in the tables to demonstrate that the effects of the 1972/73 boom do not appear to be reversible.

The movement in the overall trade balance 1963—71 is broadly explicable in terms of changes in domestic and external demand and relative prices. The sterling exchange rate was fixed 1963—66 while the devaluation in 1967 apparently succeeded in significantly improving the trade balance 1968—71. The puzzle is what happened after 1971 when the trade balance deteriorated markedly despite the maintenance of competitiveness after 1971, achieved by the downward float of the £.

The division of industries into the four groups shown in Table 2 is revealing because it suggests there are underlying trends affecting each of the groups which have a significant effect on the aggregate outcome and which, in the last few years, have over-ridden the effects of relative prices on the overall competitive position. Looking at the two groups which improved their trade performance first, shown in the second and third rows of Table 2, there appears to be nothing unusual about their figures 1963—75. Their trade balance does not show a marked deterioration 1972—75. The deterioration in the overall trade balance 1972—75 is explained almost entirely by the worsening performance of the categories in the first and fourth rows of Table 2. This shows that in the last decade there was a significant structural problem, certain sections of industry either not responding or responding in an unexpected way to macroeconomic measures influencing domestic demand or external competitiveness.

Table 2 *The trade balance and employment in manufacturing 1963–75**

	1963	1964	1965	1966	1967	1968	1969	1970	1971	1972	1973	1974	1975
Trade balance (£ million 1970 prices)													
(1) Employment gainers, all trade losers *except motor vehicles*	713 151	735 130	770 157	741 148	610 106	712 114	866 126	689 18	646 1	269 −136	82 −327	246 −288	425 −120
(2) Employment and trade gainers	452	442	446	450	409	464	609	677	796	722	701	764	786
(3) Employment losers, trade gainers	724	601	696	840	659	675	782	764	912	941	1147	1220	1067
(4) Employment and trade losers	848	730	862	747	572	616	770	731	760	443	259	123	265
Total manufacturing†	2738	2508	2773	2777	2250	2467	3028	2861	3114	2375	2188	2353	2543
Employment (thousands)													
(1) Employment gainers, all trade losers *except motor vehicles*	1083 639	1159 687	1197 711	1221 733	1185 726	1221 758	1267 777	1305 796	1300 796	1294 804	1350 840	1347 850	n.a. n.a.
(2) Employment and trade gainers	957	979	1014	1033	1023	1023	1055	1076	1072	1027	1028	1054	n.a.
(3) Employment losers, trade gainers	2358	2380	2418	2433	2382	2331	2356	2348	2268	2187	2192	2220	n.a.
(4) Employment and trade losers	2598	2597	2574	2549	2414	2343	2347	2287	2153	2036	2014	2011	n.a.
Total manufacturing†	6996	7105	7203	7236	7004	6918	7025	7016	6793	6544	6584	6632	n.a.

*Classified by group according to change in employment and balance of trade from average 1963–65 to average 1972–74. See Appendix for a list of constituent industries.
† As defined in Table 1. Includes groups 1 to 4.
Source: Overseas Trade Accounts, Department of Employment Gazette.
n.a. = not available.

Table 3   *Changes in investment, the trade balance and employment by the four groups 1963–74*

	Trade balance (£m. 1970 prices) average		Employment (thousands) average		Change 1963–65 to 1972–74		Growth 1963–74 — Index 1974 (1970 prices, 1963 = 1.00)						
	1963–65 / 1972–74	1972–74	1963–5	1972–74	Trade balance (£m. 1970 prices)	Employment (Thousands)	Home market	Home output	Exports	Imports	Total output	Import penetration	Invest-ment–output ratio†
(1) Employment gainers, *all trade losers except motor vehicles*	739	199	1146	1330	−540	184	2.01	1.61	1.95	7.33	1.70	3.65	0.77
	146	−250	679	831	−396	152	2.55	2.11	2.70	6.70	2.22	2.63	0.82
(2) Employment and trade gainers	447	730	983	1036	283	53	1.64	1.35	2.50	4.05	1.60	2.47	1.13
(3) Employment losers, trade gainers	674	1103	2385	2200	429	−185	1.42	1.25	2.27	2.80	1.44	1.97	1.01
(4) Employment and trade losers	813	275	2586	2020	−538	−566	1.21	1.01	1.41	2.95	1.08	2.44	1.17
All manu-facturing*	2673	2305	7101	6587	−368	−514	1.46	1.23	1.95	3.50	1.38	2.40	1.01

*As defined in Table 1.
†Index 1963 to average 1972–74.
Source: Overseas Trade Accounts, Department of Employment Gazette, Census of Production, own estimates.

The lower half of Table 2 shows the employment in each of the groups of industries corresponding to the trade balance figures just discussed. Employment in manufacturing overall increased by two hundred thousand 1963–66. It fell by two hundred thousand in 1967 and by another hundred thousand in 1968. The boom which peaked in 1969 saw an increase in employment of only one hundred thousand 1969–70. But by 1974 employment was 380 000 less than in 1970. Although the groups which gained or lost trade did not correspondingly gain or lose employment there is in fact an important connection between changes in the trade balance and employment. This is demonstrated by Table 3 which shows the growth of domestic and external demand and fixed investment for industries in each of the groups.

If the balance of trade for industries facing a rapid growth of demand substantially deteriorates this must be largely explained by poor management (or that the interests of management diverge from the national interest). The impact of government demand-management policies must be of less importance to these industries than those facing a slower growth in demand and trade union resistance to change must be less because jobs are being created and not lost. The industries which lost trade but gained employment during the sixties, group 1, experienced a very rapid growth of the home market, averaging 6.6 per cent a year (8.9 per cent a year excluding motor vehicles). Excluding motor vehicles, the growth of exports was also faster than for other groups, averaging 9.4 per cent a year compared with only 6.3 per cent for manufacturing overall. But imports grew much more rapidly than exports, averaging nearly 20 per cent a year (18.9 per cent excluding motor vehicles). Import penetration grew more rapidly for this group than for any other. Why was this the case? The explanation is ultimately bound up with investment decisions. Apart from motor vehicles the industries concerned are primarily part of chemicals and electrical engineering. Table 3 shows that investment by industries in group 1 has grown much more slowly than the growth of output – the investment ratio actually fell during the sixties compared with an increase for all other groups. The level of investment appears to have been inadequate. In the case of chemicals poor performance appears to be explained by concentration of investment in basic chemicals at the expense of downsteam chemicals which are more labour intensive. This was actually encouraged by government policy since substantial investment subsidies, which the chemicals industry enjoyed, were given in development areas without any regard to job creation. In the case of electrical engineering the explanation for inadequate investment appears more complex. It is partly explained by a technology gap (e.g. electronic computers). It also seems to be partly explained by the diversion of the attention of management towards takeovers and rationalisation rather than the expansion of capacity. The increasing proportion of components imported from the Far East is another explanation. Is this solely because of cheap labour? It is notable that industries with worsening trade performance (groups 1 and 4) are significantly more labour intensive than groups 2 and 3. A factor influencing relative decline may be that British management is relatively poor at managing labour-intensive industries. This would be compounded by a general deficiency in the growth of investment per worker, since the effects on trade performance are likely to be greater in labour-intensive industries than capital-intensive industries because labour costs per unit of output are higher. Another factor is the role the City has played in providing capital for the development of labour-intensive industry in the Far East.

The poor investment performance of industries in group 1 has wider significance than the resulting deterioration in the trade balance. If there is to be no overall decline in manufacturing employment the growth of employment in industries experiencing a fast growth of demand has to offset the loss of employment in industries experiencing a slow growth in demand. Apart from the growth of demand, industry technology is an important factor influencing employment growth. Industries which gained trade, groups 2 and 3, either generated little extra employment or lost employment — although this is partly explained by a slower growth of demand compared with group 1. Employment generation was smaller because the trade-gaining industries were more capital intensive. On balance the trade gaining industries lost 132 000 jobs. But industries losing both trade and employment lost 566 000 jobs in the 1960s. The principal explanation for employment loss was the slow growth of domestic demand, which averaged only 1.8 per cent a year. But because these industries, notably textiles, clothing and footwear, are labour intensive employment is particularly sensitive to changes in their trade balance. But the marked deterioration in the trade balance only began in 1972 so the employment effects are unlikely to have shown through fully in the period covered by Table 3.

The rapidly worsening trade balance of labour-intensive industries since 1970, whether employment gainers or losers, raises questions about the maintenance of tolerable levels of employment if free trade continues, given that trade-gaining industries are relatively capital intensive. Estimates of the direct effects of trade on employment can be made by calculating what output would have been if there had been no change in net exports 1963–74 for each of the 58 manufacturing industries for which statistics are available and by adopting the relationships between output and employment which actually occurred. Over the period 1963–74 the direct effect of the improvement in the trade balance of trade-gaining industries was a gain of 112 000 jobs compared with a loss of 253 000 jobs in trade-losing industries. The net loss of jobs due to the direct effects of trade was therefore 141 000 compared with an overall decline in manufacturing employment of 514 000. But the indirect effects of this notional loss of jobs due to free trade must have been considerable. For example, if the trade balance in clothing deteriorates it reduces potential output and so employment in labour-intensive textiles as well as in clothing. Apart from these indirect effects there are dynamic effects on employment through the decline in national income. The overall effect of free trade 1963–74 may have been to reduce potential employment in manufacturing by as much as three hundred thousand compared with an overall decline of five hundred thousand jobs. Most of this is attributable to the deterioration in the trade balance 1970—74 although the full effects on employment had not shown through by 1974.

While the relative decline of UK manufacturing industry was initiated by domestic factors (whether institutional or erroneous demand-management policies) resulting in a slow growth of domestic demand, a factor of growing importance in the last decade was free trade owing to the cumulative effects of decline on relative productivity levels. It is likely to become increasingly important. Inflation is an additional, but related factor influencing relative decline. The UK is likely to be less successful in resisting the effects of inflation, which may be initiated by external factors, such as a rise in prices of primary products, because of dissatisfaction with past economic performance. Investment, and so the growth of industrial capacity, is adversely affected by a fall in profitability relative to that in countries more successful in controlling inflation. In the period 1970—75 the investment—output ratio in UK manufacturing industry has fallen much more than in Germany and France, partly owing to faster inflation, and the effects of this on relative trade performance, and so employment, are bound to be felt in the next few years.

Policies to raise the level of investment

There has never been more uncertainty about prospects for the economy over the next few years than at the time of writing. On the one hand there are predictions of strong export-led growth and on the other highly pessimistic projections for the balance of payments. The outcome will probably be somewhere between these two extremes — if OECD countries grow by 5 per cent 1975—80 the UK will probably achieve 3 per cent. Unfortunately unemployment is likely to remain high by post-war standards since the weak balance of payments position will prevent faster growth. But this may be regarded as acceptable provided preparations are seen to be made over the next few years which present a real prospect of faster growth and full employment in the 1980s.

With a political consensus and appropriate policies, it may be possible to influence the underlying growth of the economy 1980—85 in a way that seems unlikely to occur with existing policies through the market mechanism, although miracles cannot be expected. But even if the result was to add only 1 per cent a year to sustained growth, it would be worth while. There is also a real possibility that the employment situation will actually get worse if policies of the type to be proposed are not adopted.

The significance of the period 1980—85 is that North Sea oil will at last be making large and growing contributions to the overall balance of payments. This will temporarily allow a faster growth in domestic expenditure than otherwise possible until stabilisation of oil production is achieved around 1985. Whether or not the oil has more than a temporary effect on the growth of the economy depends on the extent to which the resources it represents are channelled into investment rather than public or private consumption.

If the opportunity is taken to increase investment substantially, projects are sensibly chosen and the whole-hearted cooperation of the trade unions is obtained there is a good possibility of breaking out of the pattern of past relative decline. The alternative, to allow the present political divisiveness to determine how these extra resources should be spent, could well be disastrous. Labour would allow a relatively high proportion to be absorbed by public spending. Conservatives would effectively cut taxes to allow a rise in consumer demand, hoping thereby to stimulate investment. No double the latter course of action would result in a modest investment boom — but past experience suggests investment would be inadequate and there would be a flood of imports. The end result of both Labour and Conservative policies could well be a further absolute decline in the size of the manufacturing sector in the mid 1980s since the sterling exchange rate would be buoyant owing to oil revenues and this would make exports of manufactures less competitive than would otherwise be the case. Holland has experienced deindustrialisation of this kind through the exploitation of natural gas reserves although starting with a more competitive manufacturing sector than the UK.

The year 1980 is not far away and if a substantial investment drive is to be made preparations must begin now. What are the practical problems involved in raising the level of investment? First, objectives will be considered and then policies aimed at achieving them will be discussed; the policy proposals are made with the requirements of a political consensus in mind.

Objectives

The objective of raising the level of manufacturing investment is not based on the belief that there is an automatic connection between investment and growth. It is because North Sea oil will allow a relatively fast growth in demand and it is in the national interest to ensure as large a part as possible is met by an expansion of domestic output. A substantial increase in investment, however, will not only provide capacity in the medium term, it will help change attitudes of both management and workers and perhaps lead to faster sustained growth. Thus the central objective is not growth itself but to raise the level of profitable investment in manufacturing industry — the distinction is important because past initiatives on the supply side have put growth first without ensuring the necessary expansion of capacity.

It might be thought that the sole criteria for raising investment in manufacturing (apart from obvious ones such as profitability) should be the contribution to the balance of trade — employment in manufacturing can decline since the balance of trade gain would allow the government to increase the pressure of demand and so maintain full employment through the transfer of labour to non-manufacturing industries. However, while the employment level in manufacturing does not necessarily have to remain stable, there should be concern if the composition of output moves significantly away from labour-intensive industries for other than technological reasons. This happened in the 1960s as labour-intensive electrical engineering and chemicals industries failed to generate the employment they might have done owing to lack of capacity and competitiveness. Employment in labour-intensive textiles and clothing industries has been increasingly threatened by a marked deterioration in net exports since 1970. These industries have long been in decline because of the slow growth of domestic demand but the extent to which decline through external trade should be allowed to go, as well as the acceleration in the rate of decline, must be a matter for serious consideration. The employment loss in these industries and their supplying industries puts additional pressure on an industrial strategy which must essentially be concerned with raising investment per worker in sectors with growth prospects. For even in growth sectors a substantial investment drive may lead to redundancies and resistance to redundancies from trade unions would, quite naturally, be greater the higher the level of unemployment.

Industrial policy should therefore be specially concerned with labour-intensive industry. An industrial strategy which has the sole objective of improving the balance of trade in manufactures may be difficult to carry through owing to resistance by trade unions. Such a strategy would also reinforce past trends towards a manufacturing sector with a capital-intensive structure. This is undesirable because there would be a loss of industrial skills in the labour force and consequently manufacturing industry may have difficulty in adapting to longer-run changes in demand.

Coordination of policies

The experience of the past shows clearly that any initiative on the supply side must be accompanied by consistent policies on demand. Consensus policies will only succeed if the objectives are clear and limited. A policy of raising investment involves restraining consumption. However, the slow growth of private consumption in the last decade and high marginal rates of taxation must have influenced productivity through reducing incentives and also had some influence on the rate of inflation. Growth of private consumption is also desirable to stimulate productive investment and this will involve restricting the growth of public expenditures in real terms over the next decade, other than required to maintain present standards. In practice this might involve an increase in expenditure, dependent on demographic trends, to maintain the real value of pensions and because of relative price changes but there could perhaps be an overall ceiling of 1 per cent a year. Given agreed plans for public spending, assumptions about underlying growth and resources needed for investment, the allowable growth of private consumption can be determined. To ensure this does not get out of line incomes policy, as well as fiscal and monetary policies, must become a permanent institutional feature. External demand would be regulated by exchange-rate changes to ensure exports were always highly competitive. The incomes policy will minimise the depreciation necessary but a useful once-for-all incentive to exports, without raising import prices, may be gained by reducing taxation on profits earned from exporting — Hufbauer[2] has shown effective tax rates are higher in the UK than in many other industrial countries.

Given these policies on demand, the problem is to ensure a substantial increase in investment actually takes place in the appropriate industrial sectors. The nature and extent of the selection process is an important factor.

Selective incentives

There is a growing emphasis on selectivity in industrial policy. This is a key feature of Labour's White Paper on Industrial Strategy.[3] where the policy of assisting sectors with most 'potential' was laid down. It is reflected by the increasing number of selective investment schemes for which aid has been given under the 1972 Industry Act. Selective schemes are popular with the permanent civil service since the objective, installing investment, is clear-cut and attainable and the burden on the exchequer is not open-ended. Priority can be given to the most urgent cases. The overall contribution of selective schemes to raising the level of investment above what it would have been otherwise in the years 1974–76 was, however, probably insignificant.

The case for selective investment subsidies by sector within manufacturing industry is finely balanced. The advantage is that a higher level of aid can be given out of limited resources than if assistance was available for all industries. The expertise in central government is very limited and selectivity reduces the work burden. Selectivity also presents the possibility of coordination of policy measures. But there are no satisfactory criteria for selection by industrial sector. Good past performance is no guarantee of future performance – it may have occurred simply because of fast growth in demand which will not be repeated as saturation levels are reached. Companies vary in efficiency within industrial sectors. There is little justification for discriminating in favour of inefficient companies in growth sectors at the expense of successful companies in declining sectors.

But selectivity by industrial sector should be an important part of industrial policy. Selective investment subsidies should be extended and be adopted for sectors when large-scale restructuring is required. In these cases, involving substantial reorganisation, the subsidy, or part of the subsidy, would relate to all investment rather than increases in investment over past levels and would be conditional upon the reorganisation taking place. This might involve mergers on government recommendation and would probably require coordination of government policies e.g. retraining, regional policy. But selection on these grounds is a different matter from the philosophy of 'picking winners' which appears to lie behind the industrial policy White Paper. This strategy involves concentrating assistance on a group of industries selected on various criteria based on past performance because they were supposedly successful. But obviously successful sectors are very few and to select a sufficient number of sectors to have an overall impact requires arbitrary methods of selection.

General incentives

The main policy instrument for raising the level of investment, apart from the extension of selective schemes, should be cash grants payable only to the extent that investment was raised above the average level for, say, the past five years. Existing investment incentives could be retained in their present form. The justification of new incentives of this type is that in the past investment has not come through in advance of demand on the necessary scale. These incentives would apply only to manufacturing industry and because of their restricted coverage and conditional nature, applying at the margin not the average, they could be granted on a very generous scale. Allied with the certainty of a relatively fast growth of demand 1980—85 and consensus policies on the composition of that demand it would be surprising if a very substantial investment boom was not generated and this would reduce the potential for greatly increased import penetration, although a considerable proportion of investment goods would continue to be imported. In order to ensure that profits earned from this state-financed investment were reinvested measures would be desirable to deter distributions of company income.

The allocation of a new investment subsidy

The allocation of resources between selective and general subsidies would be based on very detailed analysis of industrial performance and prospects at sector level. Such an analysis would assess the past and potential contribution of each sector to the main targets of policy, employment and the balance of trade. The criteria for choosing sectors for selective investment subsidies would be mainly poor trade performance. The analysis of past performance summarised in Table 2 provides a starting point, taking industries allocated to groups 1 and 4 as potential candidates for selective subsidies, although a consideration of prospective performance might modify the list. The objective of investment subsidies is to improve UK competitiveness and capacity relative to advanced industrialised countries. Trade-losing industries are relatively labour intensive and we cannot compete on equal terms with third world and East European countries. Trade in manufactured goods with these countries should therefore be closely regulated by a battery of quotas, tariffs and administrative controls. At the very least the UK should maintain parity with other EEC countries on import penetration of manufactured goods from third world countries.

Table 4 shows the trade balance 1970—74 for industries with the largest absolute deterioration in their trade balance (judged over the period 1963—74) — these are the major candidates for *selective* subsidies. First priority sectors are those facing a relatively rapid growth in demand and which are consequently potential employment generators; there is less danger that investment subsidies would lead to excess capacity than in other sectors. The sectors involved are the synthetic resins and plastic processing parts of the chemicals industry, a large part of the electrical engineering industry and motor vehicles. Second priority sectors are those facing a slow growth in demand and are consequently losing employment. Here the case for selective investment subsidies is less pressing. Mechanical engineering industries included have faced a slow growth of demand in the last decade because of the slow growth of domestic investment but the

Table 4   *Major potential candidates for selective subsidies**

MLH (1968 SIC)	Industry	Trade balance (£m. 1970 prices)				
		1970	1971	1972	1973	1974
First priority						
276,496	Chemicals (part)	27	26	9	−17	−33
363−366, 368−9	Electrical engineering (part)	0	−31	−156	−345	−308
381	Motor vehicles	670	644	404	408	533
Second priority						
412−6 418, 421−9, 441−50	Textiles, clothing footwear (part)	20	−75	−110	−154	−168
332,339	Mechanical engineering (part)	194	226	108	66	103
361	Electrical engineering (part)	63	86	86	52	35

*See table 5 for full list.
Source: Overseas Trade Accounts, own estimates.

strategy of raising investment would improve their prospects. The prospects for textiles, clothing and footwear industries would be improved by more closely controlled trade with third world and East European countries.

A possible allocation of investment subsidies is shown in Table 5. The total resources available 1980−85 would be approximately £500 million per year at 1975 prices − this assumes the contribution of North Sea oil to the balance of payments 1976−79 would be used to pay off accumulated debt or build up currency reserves. The allocation between selective and general subsidies (arbitrarily) assumes the former consists of a cash grant of 40 per cent of capital expenditure and the latter consists of a cash grant of 40 per cent of the increase in capital expenditure over the previous five years. Motor vehicles and all nationalized industries are excluded on the grounds that funds are already earmarked. The figures for possible investment before and after subsidy 1980−85 should be regarded as orders of magnitude only. No allowance has been made for dynamic effects on the level of investment after subsidy. No precise estimates can even be made of the direct effects of such subsidies on investment. Evidence for the past suggests only about 20 per cent of an increase in investment subsidies resulted in an increase in investment.[4] But there are several reasons for expecting the proposed subsidies would be vastly more effective.

First, the prospects for the growth of demand would be unusually predictable. Second, the subsidies should be accompanied by measures to discourage distributions relative to retentions of income by companies. Third, less resistance to new investment would be expected from trade unions if an explicit long-run strategy existed. Fourth, the marginal principle would apply as far as possible.

Investment-incentive schemes have had disappointing results in the past

Table 5   *Possible allocation of new investment subsidies 1980–85*

	Fixed investment (£m. 1975 prices)				New invest-ment sub-sidy (£m. 1975 prices)
	average 1970–74	likely average 1975–79	possible average 1980–85		average 1980–85
			before subsidy	after subsidy	
Selective subsidies:					
first priority*	364	412	490	790	120
second priority†	456	535	610	810	80
General subsidies‡	1550	1659	2000	2410	300
All manufacturing§	2370	2606	3100	4010	500

*All industries in group 1 of Appendix except motor vehicles.
†All industries in group 4 of Appendix except iron and steel.
‡All industries in groups 2 and 3 of Appendix except aerospace and shipbuilding.
§As defined in Table 2. n.b. Food manufacturing is excluded from discussion throughout because it cannot be considered in isolation from general issues of agricultural policy which are beyond the scope of this paper.
Source: Census of production, own estimates.

because of their unconditional nature – although no assistance is given unless investment takes place, it is received whether or not the investment level is increased or reduced. It has been assumed in Table 5 that £200 million a year would be used for selective subsidies and the balance for general subsidies. The incidence of selective subsidies would be much greater than general incentives but so would the effect pound for pound on the level of investment since they would be conditional on the installation of capacity which would be unlikely to occur otherwise. A major part of the selective subsidies would go to the electronics industry. Assuming 100 per cent effectiveness of both types of subsidy at the rates proposed, the result would be to raise the annual level of investment in manufacturing by about one third for six successive years.

Appendix   Classification by the four groups

No.	1968 SIC MLH	Industry
(1) Employment gainers, trade losers		
14	276.1	Synthetic resins and plastic materials
15	276.2	Synthetic rubber
36	363	Telegraph and telephone apparatus and equipment
37	364	Radio and electronic components
38	365	Broadcast receiving and sound reproducing equipment

No.	1968 SIC MLH	Industry
39	366	Electronic computers
42	369	Other electrical goods
45	381	Motor vehicles
48	390	Engineers' small tools and gauges
60	472–473	Furniture and bedding, etc.
66	496	Plastic products (not elsewhere specified)

(2) Employment and trade gainers

10	272	Pharmaceutical chemicals and preparations
11	273	Toilet preparations
25	333	Pumps, valves and compressors
28	336–337	Construction and mechanical handling equipment
31	341	Industrial plant and steelwork
33	351–354	Instrument engineering
40	367	Radio, radar and electronic capital goods
50	411	Man-made fibres
53	417	Hosiery and knitted goods
54	419	Carpets
65	491	Rubber

(3) Employment losers, trade gainers

5	231–239	Drink
6	240	Tobacco
8	271.2	General chemicals – organic
9	271.1 and 271.3	– other
12	274	Paint
16	277	Dyestuffs and pigments
18	279	Other chemical industries
21	321	Aluminium
26	334	Industrial engines
27	335	Textile machinery
32	342,349	Other mechanical engineering
43	370	Shipbuilding and marine engineering
46	383	Aerospace industry
49	391–399	Other metal goods
56	431–433	Leather, leather goods and fur
64	485–489	Printing and publishing

(4) Employment and trade losers

13	275	Soap and detergents
17	278	Fertilisers
19	313	Iron castings
20	311–312	Other iron and steel
23	331	Agricultural machinery
24	332	Machine tools

No.	1968 SIC MLH	Industry
29	338	Office machinery
30	339	Other machinery
34	361	Electrical machinery
35	362	Insulated wires and cables
41	368	Domestic electrical appliances
44	380	Wheeled tractors
47	382,384, 385	Other vehicles
51	412−413	Cotton spinning and weaving
52	414	Woollen and worsted
54	415,416, 418,421− 429	Other textiles
57	441−449	Clothing
58	450	Footwear
67	492−495, 499	Other manufacturing
63	482−484	Other paper and board products

Notes

1 Note that in Table 1: group A = groups 2 and 3; group B = group 1; group C = group 4.
2 Hufbauer, G.C., 'The taxation of export profits', *National Tax Journal*, vol. XXVIII, no. 1.
3 *An approach to industrial strategy*, Cmnd 6315, HMSO, 1975.
4 Lund, R.J., 'The econometric assessment of the impact of investment incentives', in *The Economics of Industrial Subsidies*, A. Whiting (ed.), Department of Industry, HMSO, 1976.

6

USE OF AN INPUT–OUTPUT FRAMEWORK FOR MONITORING CURRENT DEVELOPMENTS IN THE ECONOMY

O. NANKIVELL

Introduction

The themes of this paper are as follows. First to argue that confidence in input–output work – at least in this country – is at a low ebb. Second, to argue why this unhappy situation cannot be accepted despite the factors working against the use of these techniques. Finally it shall be argued there is a way forward which is likely to be both effective and capable of implementation without excessive demands on very scarce resources.

The current state of input–output analysis

To begin on a pessimistic note, the proposition will be examined that there has been a singular lack of achievement among input–output practitioners in the UK and that, worse still, there are signs that the situation is worsening with diminishing support and interest in the approach. This proposition will be argued along three lines:

(a) The first is simply to draw attention to the paucity of information available to researchers and analysts. Most readers will be familiar with the data problems involved in compiling input–output tables, and these will be returned to at greater length later. However, it has to be acknowledged that the statistical base for carrying out input–output analysis is very small especially when compared to the Keynesian macroeconomic national accounts system which both in the amount of detail provided and the frequency with which it is published provides a base of information for researchers to study which is largely lacking for the input–output specialist. It is only, for example, since 1970 that the UK has begun to produce and publish annual input–output tables. Prior to 1970 input–output tables were published at infrequent intervals. Planning work, for example in 1967, relied on 1963 input–output tables used in conjunction with those for 1948 and 1954. Thus even when they appeared, besides all the problems of interpolation, the 1963 tables had to be extrapolated and

The author wishes to acknowledge that this paper is covered by Crown Copyright and that it is reproduced with the permission of the Controller of Her Majesty's Stationery Office made consistent with the national accounts figures for the years from 1963 to 1966. This inability to generate a steady and adequate stream of data on an input–output basis has been arguably the largest single inhibiting factor in the use of input–output analysis in Britain.

(*b*) The second argument which supports the proposition relates to the analytical use that has in fact been made of the technique. There has been an unhappy history of seeking to use an input–output based forecasting model for planning purposes in the United Kingdom. Despite all its attractions for this purpose and the great deal of good will existing among industrial planners both in Government and industry – especially in industry – it must be admitted that so far the gains have been limited. The reasons for this are many and include the problems relating to data, the lack of timeliness of the results as well as many communication problems between industrialists and economic planners. But the fact is that, as yet, it is difficult to point to any area where it can be said that input–output analysis and forecasting has proved its value. It may yet come but it is a long time coming and others can be forgiven for finding the waiting period too long.

(*c*) The third argument is that the subject of input–output analysis and its associated disciplines has over the years attracted relatively little theoretical interest among the academic community. The field, of course, contains areas of great interest and the possibilities, especially of using an input–output approach for constructing effective forecasting models, offer an enormous opportunity to academics. Of course, there have been a substantial number of distinguished contributors but one is still left with the feeling that when compared with the much greater output and interest in all other aspects of economic theory, particularly the Keynesian system, there is something very disturbing about the small size of the effort going into this subject.

The second set of comments about the present situation relate to the issue of whether on reflection the main thrust of input–output work has gone in the right direction; whether in fact some of the work has been based on false premises. Here again the proposition will be expanded in three ways.

(*a*) The first is that some people have always assumed that one of the great advantages of input–output analysis is that by working at detailed levels of disaggregation and specialising on measuring inter-industry transactions the system will in some sense measure what is really happening in industry in contrast, for example, to the Keynesian macroeconomic system which, the argument runs, is an abstraction mainly for the benefit of economists and is rarely recognisable as the real world to businessmen. There is a great deal of truth in this proposition. However, two observations can be made on areas where in practice the proposition falls to the ground somewhat. The first is that input–output coefficients, or for that matter most of the ratios that can be derived from input–output tables, are very

odd animals — being neither fish nor fowl. It is known in principle what is
happening in industry, e.g. whether new technology is being introduced,
whether short- or long-term subsitutions are taking place and whether the
effects are directly or indirectly felt. The trouble is that only a very
laborious analysis can give even limited information about what is actually
happening in coefficient terms — all too often the values observed simply
pick up an amalgam of these changes. These coefficients are therefore at
best a very rough proxy for items of primary interest and this must therefore detract a great deal from the potential value of the work if the claim
is to be sustained that the movement in these coefficients is the principal
area of interest. Worse still it is an almost impossibly bad wicket on which
to bat for planning purposes since the task of explaining actual or
unexpected movements in coefficients to businessmen, as has to be done
in, for example, planning exercises, presents an almost superhuman task.
This probably is the rub of the whole matter since at the point when
input—output forecasting becomes most interesting, i.e. when the attempt
is made to insert in the projections industrial views about the changes in
technology or the effect of changing the relative prices of factor inputs,
it becomes clear that there are little or no means of communicating with
industrialists who are expected to provide the basic industrial information
required for such an exercise. The point made at this stage is to comment
sadly on the fact that in practice the approach appears at its weakest when
it was expected to be at its strongest.

(*b*) The second argument to back this pessimistic proposition further is to
comment on the claim made by many input—output practitioners that
they are in business to observe changes in the structure of industry. Leave
the cyclical movements in the economy (runs the argument) to the
Keynesians (or perhaps now to the Friedmanites) of this world and instead
concentrate on the things that really matter in the long term, i.e. the slow
but inexorable change in the structure of industry which is what long-term
growth is all about. This is perhaps why, in practice, throughout the world
short-term models are macro-economic and longer-term models are of an
input—output type. Few would dissent from this statement as one of the
basic objectives of input—output work though as already stated it has its
problems. What is challenged is whether this is a sufficient condition upon
which to embark on input—output analyses. To those engaged in this work
such an approach has two basic weaknesses. The first is that since it is a
long-term phenomenon there is a real danger that those who wish to look
at it get tucked away in research and lose what fragile fingerhold they had
on the policy scene. Those who have been involved with policy whether in
industry or in Government, will know that the first rule of the game is to
get in where the action is and to resist those, what may be called, centri-
fugal forces which others seek to generate, that throw weaker brethren out
to the perimeter and leave the centre of the stage for themselves. It is a

very sad but true fact that when planning activities are at their height those who have nailed their flag to basic fundamental analyses – however important and relevant they might in fact be – are frequently left out of the scene.

The second observation is that while admitting the value of input–output work for observing changes in structure, to offer input–output analysis solely as a means of studying these phenomena is a great underuse of the vast wealth of information which is contained in a series of input–output matrices. The point is that viewed in retrospect input–output practitioners have probably been misguided in the emphasis they have put on the value of their techniques for measuring changes in structure at the expense of seeing to what other uses the techniques can be put.

(c) The third argument to substantiate the proposition that effort has been misdirected relates to the question of data. It seems that input–output compilers, and therefore the analysts, have fallen into the trap of a particularly vicious circle. They have become accustomed, at least this is the case in the United Kingdom, to the fact that the preparation of an input–output table is a massive data operation and this has led to three generally accepted conventions. The first is that until recently it was only expected that input–output tables be constructed at infrequent intervals in view of the demands for data required to produce them. The second is that if the job is done infrequently then it had better be done for a year when the fullest amount of information is available, i.e. when a full census of production is being taken or (nowadays) when a purchases inquiry is being held; in other words a year with the maximum amount of information. The third convention, which is perhaps the most unsatisfactory of them all, is that if the job is lengthy and if it needs the fullest amount of information then best choose a normal year otherwise, since the structure may be distorted in one way or the other, it will not be a good year to analyse. And so years avoiding major industrial disturbances or other oddities are preferred. While there may be or may have been in the past some merit in each of these arguments, when they are all put together what remains is a statistical product which in fact entraps and leaves no alternative but to look rather leisurely and in a very limited way at what are asserted to be structural changes. More important, an approach is adopted which fails to contribute through its measure of inter-industry activity to the daily problems of economic policy. The point is that conventions appear to have been adopted about the compilation of input–output tables which overly constrain the way in which the tables are constructed and, therefore, compound the other problems which have already been described.

The final remark under this section is again related to data problems and there the remarks can only strictly speaking relate to UK experience. The fact is that conventional data sources for compiling input–output tables in some respects are getting weaker rather than stronger. Whereas in the past the policy was to hold massive censuses of production every five years or so which collected detailed analyses of sales and purchases, the policy now is to steamline the collecting system and to build it primarily around short snappy sales inquiries on a quarterly basis supplemented by much slimmer annual inquiries to give benchmarks at which to place the quarterly system and less frequent detailed inquiries into purchases. While the case for this system is very strong, for other purposes it has the incidental disadvantage of weakening the conventional approach to compiling input—output tables particularly because the sales and purchases data are not necessarily for the same years of return. If to this is added the increasing reluctance of businessmen to complete the very detailed inquiries and the increasing cost of carrying out the larger inquiries the problem becomes very serious.

The second point is that it was thought for a while that the annual reference framework in which to set input—output analyses could indeed be improved by making use of interpolative techniques such as the RAS method. Unfortunately experience in the UK, which will shortly be published, is that the RAS method is a very poor way of extending input—output tables and while it is still valuable to continue compiling annual tables incorporating these techniques, the accuracy of the procedures is causing increasing concern. Certainly far more direct information needs to be imposed on the system than it is possible to do at the moment if the quality of the annual tables is to be kept at a high enough level to warrant publication.

The argument so far has been that there are very serious and justified causes for concern about the current state of play on input—output work, the methods of compilation and the uses to which it has been put as well as the underlying research backing to the work. I now want to go on to refute the tempting argument that in the light of all these qualifications it is best to forget about input—output work or at best relegate it to an academic activity for those who are not able to hold their own among the macroeconomic and monetarist schools of economics!

The present case for input—output analysis

In this country, particularly, the framework for the consideration of economic policy continues to be dominated by the Keynesian approach. It follows that by and large the basic information system on which policy decisions are based is one which attempts to quantify the Keynesian framework. However, increasingly it is felt that this does not give a sufficient picture of what is happening and that, in particular, it fails to provide a detailed and timely measure of inter-industry activity. The demands therefore for good and consistent measures of industrial activity which are listed below and which cannot start anywhere else than in the compilation of an input—output matrix must lead us to find a way of reviewing the effort to construct an input—output system.

(*a*) The policy interest in looking at the economy in this way is steadily increasing. Ever since the National Plan in 1965 the emphasis has shifted more and more to a recognition that the economic problems facing this country end up as problems of detailed industrial and management planning. The present UK position embodied in the Industry Act 1972 and the planning agreements associated with it represents the latest form of industrial planning following a variety of experiments since the War.

(*b*) One reason for this increased emphasis is of course the recognition that it is industry that creates wealth and that most of the issues requiring resolution are microeconomic problems. Somehow the analytical ability must be brought to the point where it is possible to identify specific issues and assist in their solution.

(*c*) Whereas in the past the constraint on handling a vast amount of information involved in industrial analysis was a very real one the development of computer techniques has much improved the position. While it is too early to say that the problem has been mastered, at least it is possible to see the many ways in which computers can be used not only to store, handle and retabulate information but also be used as a monitoring device to identify and draw attention to the significant changes out of the manifold variations taking place in an inter-industry matrix.

(*d*) It is now clear that there are many more things than structural change to be gleaned from input—output which has an as yet barely tapped potential for the analysis of movements during the cycle. For example it is possible that frequent and timely input—output tables over the past two years in the United Kingdom could have helped study the changes in industry surpluses and deficits as shown by them. Secondly in a period of severe depression an ability to have been able to follow through, as it were, the detailed industry effects of both the cycle, and specific events such as the rise in oil prices, the effects of incomes policy, etc., would have been invaluable.

(*e*) Finally the value of using timely input—output tables as a means of exercising quality control on the whole variety of estimates going into the national accounts has been underestimated. Indeed in some countries input—output tables are used as their benchmark for national accounts.

And so the argument is that the present atmosphere is one which is extremely conducive and encouraging for industrial activity analysis and that, provided the objectives of input—output work are redefined, it is an opportunity to be seized to great advantage. Moreover it is clear that with the advent of computers the ability to offer a valuable tool is greatly improved. What remains, however, is to see whether the data system itself is capable of producing industry analyses quickly and in detailed enough form to support this sort of activity as well as the conventional input—output analysis. The concluding section will describe a way of responding to this current situation.

The current approach to the compilation of input—output tables

Practitioners in the UK as in any other country are in a sense prisoners of their data system, which determines the way problems are approached. A Norwegian would be discussing entirely different problems and, particularly at this stage, offering a variety of alternative solutions. However, as far as the United Kingdom is concerned the crucial question is whether — in order to respond to current policy needs and to enable input—output analysis to realise its full potential — timely input—output tables can be constructed which will allow the trade cycle to be tracked throughout. If this can be done accurately enough then a place in the policy arena will be ensured by being timely, contributions to many more issues than the main one of structural change will be possible and hopefully, by providing this information system, a much broader and more fruitful base for the academic community will be achieved. To deal first with the data problems. One task of the compiler of an input—output matrix is to establish the commodity composition of the components of final demand. It is an area that is always limited by data constraints — for example in the UK the commodity analysis of stockbuilding or for that matter public expenditure is very limited indeed. The signs of hope, however, are that for the main areas such as consumers' expenditure and capital formation the recent conversion of the compilation of the Central Statistical Office's national accounts onto a computerised system, with data entry taking place via terminals as the information arises, means that commodity converters of some sort for these components are immediately available once the quarterly national accounts are compiled. Secondly, of equal importance, a computerised method of converting data for imports and exports onto a producer-industry classification ready within the time scale of the production of the quarterly national accounts has been devised. Thirdly there is the question of compiling an inter-industry matrix — if possible on a quarterly basis. Here the new system of industrial statistics which has effectively replaced the large benchmark operations of the past must be considered. Over the past 7 or 8 years in the UK a system of quarterly sales inquiries which now effectively covers the whole of the industrial sector has been steadily introduced. These inquiries, among other things, measure total sales and give a commodity analysis of these sales. In fact some 4000 different commodities are identified in these inquiries. This substantial new field of data offers the prospect of an alternative source for an input—output matrix and one that is available very quickly on a quarterly basis. The working assumption is that a commodity analysis at this level of detail will uniquely determine a sufficiently large proportion of the cells by specific inputs to enable us to tackle the number of residual cells with determination and with a real prospect of creating the whole matrix. The gaps will, of course, be around the generalised inputs such as fuel but in many of these cases other information is available which should enable the project to proceed without undue difficulty. It is fortunate that some of the information from the Business Statistics Office can be transferred in computerised form to allow the deadlines for the timely quarterly input—output work to be met.

These developments mean that a number of possibilities for data analysis are now open which hitherto have not been available and the attempt is being made to take advantage of this position — in the first instance, experimentally of course — but with high hopes of establishing additional valuable approaches to analysing the economy. There are two projects which although being pursued independently at the moment will ultimately merge into a single approach: the creation of production accounts for a number of selected industries and the construction of the input—output tables for the most recent period possible.

A production account brings together estimates of the total supply of the products of an industry/commodity to match against the various demands for that industry/commodity. To do this estimates of both the domestic output and imports are needed to give total supply. Against this estimates of final demand need to be created; for example, consumers' expenditure, exports for the industry/commodity as well as, if appropriate, intermediate demand.

The resultant production account will fill an important gap in UK economic statistics. The National Accounts for the United Kingdom are compiled by using a large disparate set of sources, rather than data from a unified system as in some other countries. This means that the separate measures of GDP, i.e. from the output, expenditure and income sides, do not exactly match. It also means that it is not easy to interpret events by a speedy and easy reconciliation of movements in supply and demand. There is thus a great potential advantage in any development which not only provides a broad and consistent view of economic activity in a particular sector but also improves the ability to track down the possible causes of the often disparate movements in the alternative measures of GDP.

If this is to be useful for current policy purposes it needs, of course, to be available as quickly as possible for the latest possible period. Furthermore, if a number of such production accounts are carefully selected to be representative of national output and expenditure then a composite production account can be constructed to explain the movements between supply and demand at national aggregate level. It will be clear that these production accounts bear a close resemblance to an input—output matrix and the natural step will be to proceed to create the full matrix. However, the production accounts matrix is valuable in its own right. Its value lies in its ability to explain events by reference to the cells inside the matrix in contrast to conventional analysis which is normally either in terms of an analysis of the industrial composition of total output without reference to destination or an analysis of total expenditure by component of demand without reference to source, in the latter case ignoring the effect of intermediate demand.

The second experimental project is taking the form of an attempt to construct an input—output matrix for the latest possible quarter. This project is being carried out in addition to the work on the annual input—output tables, although it is an area where both exercises feed on each other to mutual advantage; the techniques of the more systematic work on the annual accounts are in the main capable of being adopted for quarterly accounts while the need for speed on the quarterly basis has led to computer innovations which can be adapted to advantage for the more detailed annual work.

The rewards of success in this project are potentially very great since it would make available the fullest possible analysis of industrial activity and be sufficiently soon after the event to be useful in policy formation. There are, however, formidable data problems to crack, many of which have already been referred to. There remain as well many other imponderables which will have to be resolved. An important item is the question of distribution margins and data on services on which UK data like that of many countries are notoriously weak anyway. The approach on this is to work on two assumptions. The first, obvious, one is to see what information is available. Fortunately the work of the Price Commission is yielding a great deal of information which hitherto was not available. The second is – bearing in mind the lessons learnt from attempting to apply the RAS method – that in these areas it will be wrong to rely entirely on a mechanical method. Rather it would be preferable to set up a monitoring group who will impose intuitive views on the unknown variables so that at least it can be said that the input–output tables compiled along these lines are based on a particular view of changes in margins. It is hoped that time and new information will guide and allow modifications so that the process is gradually improved.

Conclusions

The purpose of this paper has been to argue that a new effort is required now, lest the input–output work of the last 20 years in this country loses steam. In order to regain the initiative it has been argued that it is time to recast the approaches radically, both to the purposes to which input–output analyses should be put and to the means of constructing the input–output matrices themselves. The case has been argued confidently in the light of the increasing demands for this type of analysis for policy purposes and because there are already sufficient signs of success.

7

CONTROLLING URBAN CHANGE: MODELS OF THE URBAN ECONOMY

W.I. MORRISON *and* T.A. BROADBENT

Introduction

The optimism of the white heat of the technological revolution of the mid 1960s has been followed by considerable disillusionment about the ability of science and the application of science to solve social problems. This is especially apparent in the urban planning field, where the new systems technology, which was embraced wholeheartedly in the late 1960s, subsequently failed to solve many problems of urban decay and decline — and suffered a backlash in consequence. To one school of sociologists the 'systems' approach to analysing cities is synonymous with a 'status quo' view of society, the so-called functionalist theory in which all existing institutions and social groups have their allotted place and function, cooperating together in a harmonious system. To others, the brave new 'computer models' of cities, of traffic flows, and of urban economic structure have often helped to reinforce the negative aspects of urban change. They have helped to justify massive motorway developments, legitimised the redevelopment of town centres, and at the same time have failed to solve the vast urban problems pointed out in the twenty or so 'Structure Plans' so far produced by local county councils in England. Unemployment rates go up to 25 per cent in inner Liverpool, for example and in the whole of Merseyside almost one third of the housing stock lacks an amenity or is sub-standard in some way.

This paper tries to show that it is the way new methods are used rather than the methods themselves which should be blamed for planning failures, and that systems techniques can provide new perspectives on urban structure and can clarify some of the fundamental economic forces which promote urban decay. The paper briefly describes the main features of the national economy, noting its relative decline, homogeneity and integrated nature, and its 'maturity', suggesting it is an 'over-developed' economy, faced with barriers to further extensive growth. We then outline recent trends in urban development, the patterns of urban concentration, growth and decentralisation — and stress the openness of urban economies and their dependence on the national economy.

The national, regional and urban planning systems are described, together with the instruments available to control or mitigate urban change within the constraints imposed by the national economic system. The overall picture is one of short-term response, with powers which are negative rather than positive, and an increasing evidence of incapacity to control urban change effectively in spite of an increased number of instruments and powers at all levels. The argument essentially follows that elaborated in more detail in Broadbent (1977).

The paper concludes with a description of the input—output and activity analysis models being used and developed on Merseyside and other areas, recognising that they are only two of a whole range of techniques being used in urban planning. However, they exemplify the systems approach and can be used to analyse national, regional and urban issues.

The national economy and economic management

OECD data (1974) shows that the UK growth of GNP has averaged 2.8 per cent from 1965 to 1973, compared with over twice this figure for France, Italy, Spain and West Germany. The UK is well and truly at the bottom of the growth league. The UK economy declined from 120 per cent the size of that of France in 1963 to about 80 per cent in 1972; from 100 per cent of the West German economy to 60 per cent in 1972. The OECD figures for 1972 show the UK per capita GNP as one of the lowest of the comparable countries.

The UK economy is a very centralised, homogeneous and concentrated structure. Some of its key characteristics can be noted as follows:

(i)   Ninety-five per cent of the working population are employed for a wage or salary, there being fewer non-employees (small farmers, own-account workers, etc.) than in other Western countries.

(ii) There is a great deal of social and economic inequality — see the Diamond Commission (1975) or Atkinson (1973), and this is reflected in large local inequalities within individual urban areas. Thus the overall unemployment rate of unskilled workers on Merseyside is 20 per cent, and unemployment rates in some areas of the city are more than three times the rate in others.

(iii) Despite this pattern of inequality, differences between regions are smaller than in comparable economies and obvious measurable differences, for example in unemployment rates, have been decreasing recently. Scotland and the North of England now have roughly twice the unemployment rate of the South East compared with nearly three times the South East rate ten years ago.

More and more goods and services are produced in some sense for a national or even an international market. At the same time there is an increasing degree of *interdependence* between different parts of the economy so that, for instance, manufacturing firms are becoming increasingly dependent on outside agencies, both public and private, for capital finance. The greater degree of dependence by the producing sectors, especially manufacturing, on the financial sectors (banks, finance houses, etc.) is mirrored within the public sector by the increasing dependence of local government on central government for finance, with only 30 per cent of local income now coming from local sources.

Manufacturing firms or *central government offices* which happen to be located within particular urban areas are part of the local system only in some very restricted sense, principally through their employment of local *labour*. For many other purposes they may best be regarded as part of the wider national economic system. Thus, though very important for the planning of a local area, the trend of employment in a major manufacturing firm will be decided by processes and agencies outside that local area. This means that the local planners will be in the position of having to 'forecast' such changes, rather than directly influencing them, taking into account as far as possible the influences of these outside forces.

Concentration

The structure of the private sector has changed radically during the past two decades. In 1950 the top one hundred manufacturing firms produced 20 per cent of industrial output; by 1970 this had risen to nearly 50 per cent. If this increasingly concentrated *structure of production* was reflected uniformly in all local areas, the average urban area would be faced with a basic employment structure which was very largely dependent on large national or multinational enterprises. The Merseyside Structure Plan explicitly mentions the major firms in its area (e.g. Ford, Unilever, Plessey), while Cleveland is another extreme example where the British Steel Corporation and Imperial Chemical Industries employ a very significant proportion of the total labour force.

One clear implication of this concentration of production is a large degree of *specialisation*, i.e. of the concentration of the local industrial base in one or two sectors. Thus steel and chemicals are concentrated in Cleveland; vehicles, glass and foods on Merseyside; engineering in Wolverhampton; textiles in North East Lancashire; services and tourism in East Sussex. Many Structure Plans thus argue for a *diversification* of the local economic base through the growth of new sectors, thereby increasing the employment of skilled labour. Interestingly, several areas consider that their economies are growing towards the national average, which usually means that the broad balance between services, distribution, manufacturing, etc. is becoming similar to the national average, even though *within* manufacture the economy may still be very much concentrated in single industries or even single plants.

Significant interrelationships do exist between the major firms in an area and other smaller local firms. Several Structure Plans discuss the need to strengthen these local economic links through local sub-contracting. For despite increasing concentration of production, there are still a very large number of small firms, even though they may not be as important in employment terms. Merseyside has upwards of 20 000 small firms (mainly in the service sectors), while other areas such as Wolverhampton have a definite 'small firms' structure to their local economy.

Aggregate measures such as 'employment' may be useful as preliminary indicators of economic structure, but for explaining economic changes and processes they are likely to be insufficient. Total employment by sector may be significant where the total is a statistical average of many small firms, but where the employment is concentrated in large enterprises the analysis should recognise these as individual units.

Restructuring

There has been in the last few years a slight decline in national employment in *manufacturing* and a more noticeable increase in *service* employment. Since wage and salary payments are the major economic input into a local area, these changes in employment have more immediate direct relevance for the local Structure Plan area than the equivalent changes in output. Manufacturing employment declined from 36 per cent of total employment in 1966 to 35 per cent in 1974, and output declined from 33 per cent to 29 per cent of GNP. Services increased as a percentage of total employment over the same period; with education, insurance, banking etc. and medical services showing especially large increases, while 'leisure' and public administration took a smaller percentage increase. It should be remembered, however, that many parts of the service sector (especially financial, retailing and public administration) are themselves major units within the national economy, undergoing just the same process of concentration as the manufacturing sector.

In real terms (i.e. in payments for real goods and services as distinct from transfer payments) there has been a steady growth in the *public sector,* which accounted for 32.4 per cent of GNP in 1974 compared with 26.3 per cent in 1961. This represents the real size of the public sector. (On the other hand transfer payments, i.e. money which passes through government (e.g. pensions, subsidies to industry etc.), have increased more rapidly so that total 'public spending' now amounts to around 60 per cent of GNP). Central and local government employment represents some 10 per cent of the total labour force.

Although this is not the place to analyse the reasons for these changes, or their wider economic significance, it is clear that such employment changes are very important at the local level. For instance the decline of manufacturing often occurs in smaller, older establishments in the inner areas of cities, while the new larger units employing fewer workers are located on the periphery or in neighbouring towns. Conversely, financial services, local government and other types of office employment may be concentrated in the central area, through redevelopment schemes. The analysis will need to decide at how fine a level of detail to specify the sectors of industry and services which are undergoing restructuring, bearing in mind particularly the *spatial and land-use implications* of these changes. Office employment uses less land and is more concentrated than manufacturing, while manufacturing firms which are shedding labour may still need more land. These overall trends, which are occurring in varying degrees across the whole country, highlight the need to analyse some of the subjects together, rather than separately. Thus the changing structure of inner-city employment from manufacturing to services (including retailing, which is often regarded as a separate subject) can be seen as a result of a single underlying process.

A plethora of short-term instruments is available to the Treasury. This is another unique feature of the UK economy: far more effort has been put into stabilisation policy in the UK than in other comparable countries. None of the measures was specifically directed to changing the structure of the economy, and only recently have these more fundamental issues come to the centre of political debate. The emerging pattern is one of increasing difficulty in handling the short-term situation — as evidenced partly by the increasing number and sophistication of controls and more frequent budgets, and partly by the increasing levels of unemployment, inflation and trade deficits. Kennedy (1974) notes a continual increase in the sophistication of the techniques of short-term management over the last thirty years.

It would be fully consistent with the arguments outlined earlier that, while short-term economic management was becoming more necessary and more difficult, business and politicians should become more interested in longer-term planning, something which would help to sustain a smooth growth path and avoid some of the negative effects of the 'short-term' fetish. A whole panoply of new institutions and procedures was introduced in the 1960s. But these did not affect the exercise of direct economic power by the public sector. This remained almost exclusively harnessed to the needs of the short-term management. The new institutions were essentially exhortatory bodies — with no powers to alter the underlying structure of the economy. Regional policy was an extension of this approach, with a progressive refinement of areas (principally in the North) designated as development areas, special development areas and intermediate areas. The total resources involved in regional 'policy' (for it was not planning) were relatively large — £2000m. between 1967 and 1974. Its success has been debatable — most of the grants have gone to a few large firms who would probably have made their investments anyway. Moore and Rhodes (1973) suggest that the policy was reasonably successful — moving 220 000 jobs to development areas. Certainly regional discrepancies have been reduced, although not necessarily because of the policies. Others see the policy as 'empiricism run mad'. Conventional criticisms tend to cite its lack of selectivity and its inability to parcel together bundles of investment specifically geared to a region's problem.

The national pattern of population and employment change

The most obvious fact about the national spatial pattern of population and employment is its extreme *concentration*. Almost half the population live within the eight Metropolitan Counties of Tyne and Wear, Greater Manchester, Merseyside, West Yorkshire, South Yorkshire, West Midlands, Greater London and Strathclyde (a Scottish 'region'). This large proportion of the national population is therefore covered by just seven Structure Plans. This raises an immediate question with respect to the powers and responsibilities of Structure Plan authorities. In the two-tier system of local government these Metropolitan Counties have at their direct disposal far fewer *resources and powers* to directly influence development than do the lower tier, non Structure Plan Metropolitan District Councils. It is these Districts which control education, the largest item of local authority current expenditure, and housing, the largest item of capital expenditure and the one which dominates the physical pattern of urban development and land use. But are these Metropolitan concentrations in any sense meaningful? Do they function in some sense as metropolitan units, and if so, how do they relate to the national system of economic and urban development?

Studies undertaken by Hall *et al.* (1973) and Drewett *et al.* (1976) provide a convenient perspective from which to describe the salient features of national urban change. Each of their areas is identified as having a central core, defined in employment terms as either having more than 5 workers per acre or over 20 000 jobs. The population of each area is a least 70 000. It is apparent that many of the administrative county boundaries more or less encompass at least one Standard Metropolitan Labour Area, although in nearly all cases there are awkward mismatches at some points. Some Structure Plans draw attention to these mismatches.

Three quarters of the population live within the urban areas defined in SMLAs by Hall *et al.* (1973) This means that most Structure Plan problems are 'urban' problems. The consistent pattern during the thirty years up to 1961 was one of *urban growth* coupled with the *decentralisation* of population from inner areas to the suburbs. Thus the total population of the larger urban centres grew by five million over this thirty year period, with the majority still living in the cores of these urban areas.

Employment is more concentrated than population, even at this broad aggregate level of the Hall and Drewett studies. Thus the urban cores have 60 per cent of total employment, there having been a decline of 3 per cent between 1961 and 1971. Their results suggest that employment 'follows' population in decentralisation.

The overall recent pattern of urban change is as follows:

Accelerating decline:	largest cities (e.g. London, Liverpool, Newcastle)
Decelerating growth:	a broad band of cities in Yorkshire and East Central Scotland
Decelerating growth:	new towns; other towns close to London; Midlands cities (e.g. Birmingham, Coventry); outer regional growth centres
Accelerating growth:	outer South East; towns near conurbations; 'free standing' towns

Thus regional urban population and employment growth in the decade 1951–61 occurred largely in the South East, followed by the West and East Midlands. In the 1960s the urban population of the South East did not grow, but this region experienced large-scale internal changes due to decentralisation from London. While nearly all urban areas are experiencing decentralisation it is only with the very largest, e.g. London, Manchester and Liverpool, that the trend is really marked, developing into large-scale overspill and promoting the growth of surrounding urban centres.

The two most obvious results of the decentralisation of urban areas have been longer journeys to work and increased social segregation. The population of the outer areas of cities has tended to contain an increasing proportion of the upper socioeconomic groups, while the declining cores have an increasing proportion of the lower groups. This phenomenon has been crystallised in recent debates as the 'Inner City Problem', in response to which various policies have been proposed for revitalising urban cores.

Aspects of these broad trends are recognised in many Structure Plans. Merseyside's whole draft strategy is concerned with revitalising the run down of under-used city fabric that has resulted from a continuing high out-migration, leaving a high concentration of lower social groups in inner areas. As the converse of the same process, Wolverhampton is concerned with West Midlands overspill and East Sussex with containing urban growth in an outer Metropolitan centre (Brighton). However, having recognised the aggregate scale and nature of population and employment change in its area, it is necessary for the Structure Plan analysis to appreciate the *causes* of these changes before they can be influenced by the Plan. The sections below therefore identify some of the processes in the national economy which impinge to a greater or lesser degree on all local areas, and which often form the crucial driving force behind local urban change.

The whole economy is being gradually incorporated inside large firms, in contrast with the neoclassical perfect market model, where all the significant processes occur *between* firms. This process is even more significant for the urban system described above. Mapping the set of firms on to the set of urban areas tends to suggest that a given urban area (defined as a labour area) is often only a small 'labour-consumption' appendage of a branch plant of a large firm. Thus the division of functions within firms becomes just as significant for the economic base of an urban area as the division of functions in the economy as a whole. Keeble (1969), Warneryd (1968), Westaway (1974) and Goddard (1975) discuss this in terms of specific functions (research, production, levels of control, and short-term management and long-term strategic planning). Pred (1973) notes the non-local multiplier effects of investment in the modern economy.

These effects, together with the progressive integration and interdependence of the national economy at the national level, mean that *the only significant processes left at local level are those which flow through households*. These are the wage and consumption payments which turn the commuting area into a spatial-economic area. In input—output terms, viewed through the first-round payments and receipts of the household sector, the urban labour area appears relatively closed. Other inter-sector transactions are very small.

Local government and planning

While total public spending has risen as a proportion of GNP, local government spending has done so even faster. Whereas public spending in money terms rose by 120 per cent during the 1960s, local authority spending in the UK increased by 170 per cent (twice the growth of GNP). Local spending amounted to about one third of total public spending or nearly 15 per cent of GNP in 1973. We might therefore see in local government an exaggerated version of what is happening to central government — with all the contradictory implications of the growth of the public sector magnified. Note however that this total spending includes some transfer payments and when these are excluded, local government took 12 per cent of GNP in 1973 (8.9 per cent in 1963).

Thirty per cent of local government spending is capital expenditure (5 per cent for central government), and it spends the greater proportion of all public capital spending (£3100 million in 1973—74 as compared with £834 million for central government).

Local government is overwhelmingly concerned with 'social consumption'. Looking at Figure 1, education dominates local spending and has grown massively since the war. The major item is teachers' salaries, and one recent growth element has been the expansion of further education. The trading functions have declined — the utility services have been absorbed into national public corporations. Housing is the dominant sector in capital spending.

In the two-tier system of local government which emerged in England and Wales in 1974 (and in Scotland in 1975), the way spending is apportioned between the two tiers in the major English conurbations is different from that in the rest of the country. The so-called non-metropolitan areas outside the conurbations are 'top-heavy'; each of the forty or so English and Welsh counties take up about 90 per cent of all spending, with only housing of the major services undertaken as a lower-tier district function. In the conurbations the 'metropolitan counties' are the upper tier, and they spend only 20 per cent of the total. Highways and transport are their major function. It is a weird system indeed, with a huge variation in size between the lower-tier non-metropolitan districts (24 000 to 42 000) and also among the metropolitan districts (173 000 to over 1 million). The non-metropolitan, upper-tier counties also vary from 99 000 to 1.4 million. Local urban and rural structure plans are prepared and submitted by the upper-tier county councils.

The post-war planning systems — plans without powers

The 1947 Planning Act essentially created the whole planning system of the UK as it exists today. It instituted very effective control on development in some ways, e.g. the green belts (Hall *et al.*, 1973). It can be argued, and indeed it is essential to the arguments put forward in this paper, that the key to its success in these areas is to be found in the way it made a comprehensive, once and for all change in property rights. It effectively nationalised the right to decide whether land should be developed. We would argue that another fundamental revision in

Figure 1. *Revenue and capital expenditure of local authorities in England and Wales*

	1947–48				1972–73			
	Rev-enue £m.	%	Capi-tal £m.	%	Rev-enue £m.	%	Capi-ital £m.	%
Education	209	(21.8)	10	(3.3)	2903	(36)	385	(14)
Housing	59	(6.1)	213	(70.1)	1400	(18)	838	(30)
Trading	279	(29.0)	54	(17.8)	498*	(5)	205	(7)
Police and fire	44	(4.6)	1	(0.3)	573	(7)	47	(2)
Highways	70	(7.3)	5	(1.6)	476	(6)	267	(9)
Public health	62	(6.5)	7	(2.3)	447	(5)	289	(10)
Industrial health	19	(2.0)	1	(0.3)	164	(2)	16	(1)
Welfare, aged and children	–	–	–	–	391	(5)	51	(2)
Other	218	(22.7)	13	(4.3)	1242	(16)	697	(25)
Total	960	100%	304	100%	8004	100%	2795	100%

*Water supply has since been removed to water authorities.
Sources: Hepworth (1971) Local Government Financial Statistics 1972–73

property rights in land is now required. From 1947 onwards, all landowners only owned rights to the *existing use* and the *existing value* of their land (although the value provision was later rescinded). Any development required first of all 'planning permission'; secondly, developers had to pay 100 per cent of the increase in the value of the land resulting from the development.

Urban growth created conflicts between large cities, such as London and Birmingham, and the surrounding areas. Between 1930 and 1966 the car-ownership rate rose from one household in ten to one in two. In the 1950s central government encouraged all local authorities to make green belts, and in the absence of effective regional coordination several of the larger cities lost major planning inquiries in their attempts to expand into neighbouring rural counties. Large slum-clearance programmes were started again in 1955. Around 1960, it was stated that many big cities had simply 'run out of land' (Cullingworth, 1972). In the metropolitan ring around London the net growth of population in the 1950s was 800 000, one third of the total in Britain. To meet these problems, a series of *ad hoc* subregional studies were undertaken during the 1960s (e.g. Leicester, 1969; Notts–Derby, 1969). Hall shows that most of these reports continued the Howard–Barlow–Abercrombie formula of planned decen-tralisation of conurbations, green belts, and new towns, with an overall emphasis on housing policy.

In 1968 a new Town Planning Act brought in a two-tier system of plan making. The aim was to reduce the amount of detail in the plans which were submitted for central-government approval. 'Structure Plans' would be submitted to the ministry containing the main, broad policy proposals in outline for a large area. Detailed land-use maps would then be solely the responsibility of the local authority.

At the time of writing, the planning system remains essentially as it was laid down in the 1947 Act (with its financial provisions removed by the Conservative government of the 1950s). As we have seen, the control exercised by planning authorities is essentially one of negative response to private initiative. The plan is not implemented by the planning authority itself. To be practical, therefore, it can only attempt to channel the forces already operating in the land market, in the demand for space and in the demand for locations, into what it perceives to be desirable directions.

Effects and operation of the system

Hall *et al.*'s (1973) *The Containment of Urban England; Volume 2* is probably the most ambitious attempt to make an overall assessment of the impact of the UK urban-planning system. It is not a rigorous econometric or statistical analysis and its conclusions are at least open to question, especially as to how much of the pattern of change in urban development has been due to planning as such, rather than to the market. Hall sees the major success of the system as the 'containment' of urban sprawl through the green belts. It is seen to be less successful over the planned expansion of large towns (other than London). The system was designed with a 'no-change' situation in mind and it has therefore slowed the rate of change, especially the decentralisation of employment and services from the town centres. It has helped to promote 'apartheid' through increased geographical separation between home and work. It may also have helped to increase land prices overall because of its 'drip-feed' attitude to land release for development. The gainers from planning are seen to be 'rural residents'. Commuting owner-occupiers have made questionable gains, with their long journeys to work and poor housing-space standards. However, more recently this result has been challenged. The 'Second Land Use Survey' is a mammoth and detailed exercise to examine the local, microscopic details of land-use change which has occurred in specific local areas. The survey seems to indicate that planning has not been at all successful in stopping piecemeal urban fringe development which is wasteful of land.

Free-market-critics of the planning system (e.g. IEA, 1974) suggest that what is good about the system is largely due to the market, and that planning has essentially reduced the rich interplay of ('micro') market forces which produced natural, organic, 'untidy' cities and towns by a rigid bureaucratic simplistic planning image with its 'zones', 'neighbourhoods', 'precincts', etc.

Ambrose and Colenutt (1975) forcibly point out the failures of urban planning to curb the power of developers, owing to the fact that the whole system of development control is *ad hoc*. The 1968 Act has failed as yet to achieve a coverage of up-to-date legally approved plans across the country. This must surely be a central failure of the system within its own terms, since the development plan is the only real 'positive' aspect to the system. In the next two years more authorities will have approved Structure Plans, but this will still mean that many areas will have to rely on plans that are several years out of date.

The current use of techniques in urban planning

Planning at national and local level is becoming more pervasive. The public sector bears more of the costs of production and planning tries to regulate market processes which are becoming more and more difficult to control. The instruments brought to bear at both levels are limited to those which do not threaten the working of the private market. The public sector tries not to compete directly with the private sector — and thus its instruments of control remain of a 'passive response' or 'incentive' nature. There are, for instance, grants and taxes at national/regional level, and negative development control at local level. These instruments are not harnessed to the planning function, which tends to be carried out as a separate activity; there is a gap between plans and powers.

This situation is paradoxical — it gives rise to a dual and contradictory need for planning techniques. There is a genuine need to increase understanding of the processes promoting development and change so that, at the urban level, planning can perform its passive response task. On the other hand, the restricted power of planners means that many social goals cannot be achieved, and so techniques are sometimes used to justify an existing situation or to obscure the planners' inability to promote change.

The present state of employment of formal techniques in Structure Planning is interesting; not primarily because particularly advanced techniques are employed: it is the way the techniques are used, the way they are connected to the concrete problems faced, the selection of methods and the way partial techniques are linked together which is of interest.

This is because local authorities cannot choose to isolate a specific process or subject to study — they are faced with a complex set of problems. Although there are a host of sophisticated partial and general, static and dynamic techniques from which to choose, relatively few of the comprehensive methods are feasible to use — in terms of the data available. There is therefore typically a series of partial analyses related together in some kind of *ad hoc* comprehensive and often contradictory way.

The typical development process specified by Structure Plans usually pinpoints an autonomous set of fundamental factors which reflect the openness of the local economy. The economic base and the natural increase of the resident population are generally the 'independent' causal factors. These interact with each other through the labour market (in an often unclear manner) and with a land constraint. They in turn influence a set of dependent factors — the labour-adjusting factors of migration and commuting and the various services — housing (which sometimes is seen to affect migration), retail, other services and transport. The local authority is seen to have some influence over these latter factors and their location. The labour supply/demand interaction with its associated problems of labour-area definition, migration and commuting levels and the housing supply/demand interaction (again interacting with migration) tend to be the weakest points in the analysis and often lead to a kind of circular reasoning.

With the fundamental economic driving force specified, Structure Plans display a concern with their competitive position not by analysing the large firms which dominate their economies, but by using simple coefficients (location quotients, specialisation coefficients, shift and share analysis) to measure their performance or prospects for future growth. There is indeed something of an obsession with performance and competitive prospects, especially in the larger metropolitan areas which tend to suffer the largest problems of unemployment, up to 20 per cent in certain areas, and housing where up to one third of the stock may be substandard. Only one or two areas have begun to use input–output and linkage analysis, and one has used a dynamic simulation economic model.

Most 'techniques' in the labour-supply area tend to involve disaggregated activity-rate analysis. The population is forecast with cohort-survival matrix techniques almost universally and migration is either trend analysis or regression of housing and employment variables. Housing is usually seen as dependent on population via disaggregated headship-rate analyses. In some areas a static supply/demand allocation is examined using techniques to pinpoint hidden households, overcrowding, and the mismatch between households and housing sizes. In general there is an almost complete absence of socioeconomic disaggregation in the treatment of household and population analysis and there-fore an inability to distinguish the distributional effects of policies.

For spatial analysis only occasionally are formal activity-allocation models used, although retail-location models are employed more frequently. Factor/ component analysis is used by several of the larger conurbation authorities to pinpoint key social areas. The transport component of the plans tends to be based on a separate study, using the standard transport techniques of gener-ation, distribution, modal split and assignment. As is to be expected, questions of spatial design, zoning systems, and market areas are treated very informally although there is sometimes an attempt to define explicit intersecting labour areas.

The picture of the use of formal models is one largely of trending, simple data and accounting analyses using coefficients, backed up with a small set of more formal techniques – linear transformation/allocation methods, social area component analyses, cohort survival/migration models and a very occasional 'sophisticated' activity-allocation model and an input–output analysis.

The plethora of 'trending' reflects the lack of direct powers in the Structure Plan as well as the technical shortcomings of the analysis. Even where the more formal techniques are used they tend to be employed for 'forecasting' rather than planning, again reflecting the openness of Structure Plan areas and the lack of direct planning control over the basic driving forces of development.

Viewed by the researcher, this picture might seem disappointing, but it is also fair to point out that Structure Planners are often faced with the difficult task of cobbling together in an empirical manner a large set of partial techniques into some kind of *ad hoc* general-equilibrium framework – for which research carried out so far has failed to provide an adequate conceptual framework. It is precisely in the domain of integrating separate, partial analyses into a common framework that accounts-based techniques have most to offer.

Accounts-based models and urban planning

The concept of planning as a cyclical and continuous process is now too well known to require much elaboration (McLoughlin, 1969; Boyce *et al.*, 1970; Massey and Cordey-Hayes, 1971). The planning process is accepted as encompassing a number of stages in an attempt to explore and understand 'the effects and implications of diverse objectives, assumptions, plans and policies' (Boyce *et al.*, 1970, p.7). The stages — formulation of objectives, setting of standards, assembling data, outlining and elaborating alternatives, evaluation and decisions, monitoring and review — take place in parallel and in sequence as successive improvements are made to the data base and as the underlying processes become more fully understood.

Within this context models can serve a useful role, especially when the impact of alternative strategies is being considered. Here the formal representation of theories about the way in which the system operates can permit analysis of the options available in a consistent way. However, we need to be extremely careful about the way in which models are used in the planning process. Because planning is a continuous process it should ideally not be based on methods which are essentially one-off exercises. Such approaches are wasteful of time and money, especially if there is a large data requirement, and also pose difficulties when attempts are made to integrate the separate studies into a consistent whole.

Ideally what is needed is some form of model-based information system, which can be used to link the different parts of the planning process. We must accept at the outset that the complexity of the process is such that attempts to develop an all-embracing model will not be particularly useful, and that mechanical applications of models are sterile exercises. The kinds of models required in urban planning need to be sufficiently flexible to encompass variations in the amount and the nature of data (quantitative/qualitative) but at the same time should be capable of shedding fresh light on key relationships in the system under consideration and being used as a basis for forecasting. Especially important is the requirement, stressed by Stewart (1975), that models at this spatial scale should include an examination of the urban political economy — the actions of central and local government institutions, of private and public sector industries, of the components of the labour and property markets, and of those managing the allocation of public-sector resources.

Accounts-based models are able to fulfil many of the requirements of an information system needed by the urban planner. By explicitly representing the major relationship between the component parts of the system in *matrix form*, accounting models prevent double-counting of entries and enable consistency to be achieved, and the more complex the system the greater the value of the consistency. A strategic-level information system can be logically built up on accounting principles, and the data collection and organisation can be related to the degree of explanation required. Consistent organisation of the data means that further analytical techniques can be used.

The precise characteristics of the accounting model adopted in any particular situation will clearly depend to a large extent on the specific nature of the problems faced. The central or core account of an information system should ideally consist of an input–output or activity–commodity representation of the economic system, since the economic health of a particular area has such a crucial bearing on all other issues of interest to the planner. There should also be a number of subsidiary accounts, which can be seen as side calculations which incorporate additional information (e.g. on the behaviour of particular sectors) and which would link in with the main account. Again, the nature of the subsidiary accounts would depend on local circumstances, but they might include local government, housing, education and health, for example.

A major advantage of accounts-based models is that if formulated correctly they can provide a starting point for subsequent disaggregation. Disaggregation can thus be concentrated on particular problem areas or sectors, can be included as a series of side calculations and can provide a means whereby micro-studies of individual producers can be linked to the overall structure of the economy. The overall process is one of progressive adaptation, in which early versions may require only limited data but where later and more complex versions and their associated data are justified, designed and constructed on the basis of preliminary results from the early version.

The input–output and activity-analysis models which we have been constructing in the Planning Research Applications Group at the Centre for Environmental Studies are essentially models of the kind just outlined, and have been developed with applications in operational planning in mind.

The Merseyside economy

Merseyside is above average on most counts of urban deprivation and although it has managed to improve its economic structure, its main industries do not have very good growth prospects. The draft Structure Plan shows that up to one third of the housing stock is substandard, and that this problem is especially acute in the inner area. The planners further maintain that there is underutilisation of infrastructure in these inner areas as a result of population dispersal to the periphery. A recent Planning Research Applications Group study showed that there is also considerable polarisation of social areas (Webber, 1976). There is a permanent problem of unemployment, with some 80 000 workers currently out of a job (from a population of 1.656 million). Most of these are male and un-skilled, and so a major task involves considering the kinds of industries that might be promoted in the area in order to alleviate this high level of unemployment, much of which has been created as a direct result of the subregion's continued overdependence on certain activities such as those related to the port. Moreover, many of the unemployed workers live in the declining inner areas of the conurbation, whereas most of the newer industrial development has taken place on green-field sites on the urban fringe. This is now a cause for concern in the local authority, especially as the planners are only too well aware of their inadequate powers. For example, the county planning officer recently pointed out that the planning profession is much less able to deal with decline or no-growth in an economy than with growth, a situation which needs to be remedied with haste (Lees, 1976).

The strategy embodied in the draft Structure Plan involves directing invest-ment back into the inner areas, and since the County Council has few means of implementing such a policy the plan exhorts central government to change its policy of favouring new settlements. Recently the government announced its intention of doing that very thing.

Of the two exercises described below, the first was a joint exercise between Planning Research Applications Group and the Merseyside County Council, aimed at the construction of a working input—output model which focussed in some detail on the linkages within the local economy, and especially within the manufacturing sectors. The second is a more experimental exercise being under-taken as part of a project funded by the Department of the Environment to investigate the techniques used in Structure Planning (see Barras and Broadbent, 1975). Both exercises involve the use of an accounting approach, but the input—output model concentrates on the industrial transactions whereas the activity-analysis model concentrates more on the household sectors, the production and consumption of labour, and the use of capital stock.

The input—output model

Given the Merseyside background, it was felt that an inter-industry model could make a useful contribution to the kinds of problems being faced, and that it could provide the overall framework for economic analysis and a means of relating individual sectoral studies to the economy as a whole.

The model developed was a version of the RAS or biproportional models suggested originally by Leontief (1951) and later developed as part of the Cambridge Growth Project by Stone and others (Department of Applied Economics, University of Cambridge, 1962; 1963; Bacharach, 1970). This model was selected since earlier work involving one of the authors (Morrison and Smith, 1974; Smith and Morrison, 1974) had shown that the model could be used to simulate the transactions between industries located in a particular region, if estimates of the proportions of local sales and purchases made by regional sectors could be obtained together with estimates of sectoral output figures. These data are used as row and column constraints in the model, and are applied to a matrix of national technical transactions to give a simulated matrix of intra-regional transactions (see de Kanter and Morrison, 1976).

The Merseyside model includes more constraints than the traditional RAS model. If for any Merseyside sector local sales exactly balanced local output, the row entries in the intra-regional transactions matrix were set equal to the row entries of the technical-transactions table. A second type of constraint relates specifically the use of the RAS model at the regional scale, where the table to be produced is quite likely to be for a year very similar to, or the same as, the base year of the technical data. This implies that the amount of technical change which will take place will be limited, or non-existent, and hence it is necessary to assume that the entries in the original technical-transactions matrix represent an upper bound on the value of the relationship between any pair of sectors.

Algebraically, we define:

$A = (a_{ij})$ = national matrix of technical transactions

$B = (b_{ij})$ = matrix of regional technical transactions derived from partial adjustment of the national table during the calculations

$R = (r_{in})$ = matrix of regional technical transactions data derived from national tables

$T = (t_i)$ = vector showing total regional sales by regional industries

$Z = (z_j)$ = vector showing total regional purchases by regional industries

r_{i*} = summation of r_{ij} along row i

b_{*j} = summation of b_{ij} along column j

The model involves several repeated stages; each stage is labelled with the index k.

For $k = 1$, set $r_{ij}^k = a_{ij}$. $\qquad$ (1)

Sum along rows:

$$r_{i*}^k = \sum_j r_{ij}^k. \qquad (2)$$

If $r_{i*}^k = t_i$, put $r_{ij}^{k+1} = a_{ij}$ for all j. $\qquad$ (3)

Adjust coefficients according to sales:

$$b_{ij}^k = \frac{t_i}{r_{i*}^k} r_{ij}^k. \qquad (4)$$

Sum along columns:

$$b_{*j}^k = \sum_i b_{ij}^k. \qquad (5)$$

Adjust coefficients according to purchases:

$$r_{ij}^{k+1} = \frac{z_j}{b_{*j}^k} b_{ij}^k. \tag{6}$$

If $r_{ij}^{k+1} > a_{ij}$, set $r_{ij}^{k+1} = a_{ij}$. $\tag{7}$

Repeat to stage (2) until final convergence.

The constraints prevented a final exact convergence. The aggregate error $(\sum_i t_i - \sum_i r_{i*})$ was less than 0.8 per cent of total regional outputs $(\sum_i t_i)$, and differences in individual sectors were also small in absolute and percentage terms (less than 2.5 per cent), and so the results were regarded as acceptable. However, work is in progress involving consideration of alternative solution methods, possibly involving a programming approach as suggested by Arrow and Hoffenburg (1959) and Matuszewski, Pitts and Sawyer (1964).

The model contains 67 sectors, most of which consist of manufacturing activities since the choice of sectors is defined by the structure of the national tables. The major assumptions made were that the technical structure of individual industries on Merseyside is the same as in the UK as a whole, and that output per employee was also the same as in the UK. Data on local sales and purchases were obtained by a 'Delphi' method. Individuals with some direct knowledge of the economy made estimates of the percentage local sales and purchases of the Merseyside sectors, and the final figures were decided in discusion. Differences were in fact small, and were highest in those sectors which are least important in the region. Clearly, obtaining data in this way is potentially hazardous, but it is our view that major errors have been avoided, and that the table produced for Merseyside at least represents a first step which can give results of relative if not absolute importance.

So far, the results of the model have consisted of the usual set of input—output applications — output, income and employment multipliers, sectoral forecasts and impact studies, analysis of imports, attempts to identify major linkages and key sectors in the economy. The aim, however, is to combine the input—output model with a wider forecasting model currently being developed, and also to extend the input—output work to include analysis of the kinds of economic issues which appear to be especially significant at the regional level. These issues consist essentially of those aspects of the behaviour of individual establishments which influence the pattern of linkages over time — the impact of corporate growth and associated changes in external control, the impact of product cycles, and the importance of information flows to the firm. What this implies is that we do not regard the input—output model as a mechanical technique for forecasting the local economy but instead see it as a starting point and integrating framework for further studies of the economy.

Work to date has involved the identification of sectors which possess strong links at the Merseyside level (particularly food and chemicals), a detailed evaluation of the importance of the port to the local economy, an analysis of those sectors making a large number of local purchases, and a preliminary estimate of the potential impact of a major development scheme which was refused planning permission. As a result of the analysis undertaken Merseyside County Council established a task force designed to stimulate the activities of firms, especially small firms, in certain key sectors (food, chemicals, mechanical engineering), and to increase the awareness of firms in these sectors of grants and support available from government sources.

Activity analysis

Elementary aggregate model

The data for this model is shown in Figure 2, a study of which will help to demonstrate the general structure of the more complex models. Basically, this elementary model has no spatial structure, and simply treats the Merseyside economy as a single unit. It is divided into 15 column-sectors, of which three are households, and two relate to journey to work. Three sectors produce exports (primary, manufacturing and offices). The remaining sectors are locally consumed public and private services including transport activities and construction (which is regarded as a *given* level of activity).

Each column in the table represents one of these activities, and the actual entries in the columns represent the relative quantities of the commodities produced (positive sign) and consumed (negative sign). Each row of the table then gives the total pattern of production and consumption for a single commodity. All the activities except one produce only one commodity in this simple model. The final column of constraints shows the overall balance of the total input and output of each commodity. Thus for the commodities like retail goods and labour, production and consumption balance and the constraint is zero. For the export activities the constraints show how much of each output is exported, and in manufacturing for example this is 250 000 units, the measuring units in this case being the numbers employed in the activity.

It is helpful to trace through the causal links in the table. Looking down the 'Non-manual household' column, we can see that this activity produces 1.36 non-manual workers, consumes 0.97 units of education for its children, and 0.16 units of retail goods. It produces a total of 2.97 individuals as its contribution to the total population of the area, and it also contributes one household unit to the total number of households in the area. Finally it consumes 0.07 units of local government services and 0.03 units of other utility services.

We can trace through what happens to the output of this household. The non-manual worker produced is consumed by a journey-to-work activity, which consumes in its turn 0.09 units of the commodity transport, and which outputs this non-manual worker 'at work', where he or she can be consumed by one of the various production activities along the 'non-manual labour at work' row. Similarly, the education consumed by this household is produced by an education

Figure 2. *Merseyside: data for elementary aggregate model*

Activities / Commodities	Primary	Manufacturing	Construction	Utilities	Transport-Producing	Retail	Office	Local Government	Journey-to-work Non-manual	Journey-to-work Manual	Education	households Non-manual head	households Manual head	households Retired head	Slack	Constraints
Non-manual (work)	0.21	0.23	0.18	0.19	0.38	0.83	0.59	0.66	+1		0.50					0
Manual (work)	0.79	0.77	0.82	0.81	0.62	0.17	0.41	0.34		+1	0.50					0
Non-manual (home)									−1			+1.36	+0.25		x	0
Manual (home)										−1			+1.23		x	0
Children											+0.61	−0.97	−0.97	−0.16		0
Retail						+1.0						−0.16	−0.16	−0.16		0
Population												+2.97	+3.23	+2.25	x	+1 494 400
Households: non-manual												+1.0				+157 940
manual													+1.0			+317 360
retired														+1.0		52 380
Transport: non-manual					+1.0				−0.09			−0.07	−0.07	−0.7		0
manual					+1.0					−0.09		−0.03	−0.03	−0.03		0
Local Govt.								+1.0								0
Utilities				+1.0												0
Construction			+1.0													+46 480
Primary	+1.0															+6 740
Manufacturing		+1.0														+25 000
Offices							+1.0									+162 700
Floorspace: manufacturing		−0.39													x	−98 391
retail						−0.27									x	−22 695
office							−0.10								x	−10 104

Coefficients negative unless otherwise stated.
Note: For equation system see Figure 4.

activity, which in turn uses quantities of manual and non-manual labour in equal proportions. This model is shown in equation form in Figure 4.

Three-zone model

The second, more complex, model introduces the spatial dimension, by using those commodities which are *explicitly transported* in the aggregate model. It was stated earlier that the most important economic flows in an area are those passing through households. These flows are the wage payments, and the subsequent spending of wages on consumer goods. Consequently, we look first at transport of the commodity labour. It is well known that the journey to work essentially determines the pattern of demand for transport in an urban area, and that accessibility to employment has an influence on the demand for housing in different residential zones.

The three-zone model therefore describes the trade in the commodity labour between three concentric zones (the district of Liverpool, the 'outer ring' of districts, and the outside world). It means in essence setting up two tables similar to Figure 2, one for the City and one for the outer area. The outside world is represented by a modified set of constraints. A modification of this model brings out an additional table, related to one of the deprived inner areas. This would be one of the social areas referred to above, and the table would focus solely on the residential activities, but would specify them in much more detail.

Fully-disaggregated model

The above two models are essentially approximations for a fully-detailed model which allows for a very fine breakdown of spatial detail, and a large number of zones. This fully-disaggregated model is best described by the equations set out below (see page 107) and diagramatically in Figure 3. These equations allow for any of the commodities produced to be transported about the area, but in order to make such a model viable it is necessary to make some further assumptions ('laws of behaviour') to simplify the problems created by the fact that there are now innumerable different goods being produced at a large number of different places. This kind of general spatial economic equilibrium problem has previously proved very intractable. For this reason, in the detailed model (part 2 on page 107) it is assumed that the production of local goods and services is for Merseyside *as a whole,* and not for consumption at any *particular* place in Merseyside. This reduces the problem of calculating all the *individual* flows of commodities between all pairs of zones to one of determining the 'market centre' for each commodity, or the 'mean point of production or consumption' for the whole Merseyside system. In the equations shown, this is done by synthesising the coefficients for the transported commodities through the use of a gravity-type model.

Figure 3 *Fully disaggregated model with implied intrazonal flows*

		Production activities X_i^l									Transport activities T_{ij}^k								
		Activity 1			Activity 2			Activity N			T_{ij}^1			T_{ij}^2			T_{ij}^3		
Production																			
Com-	$z1$	+1									−1−1−1								
modity	$z2$		+1									−1−1−1							
1	$z3$			+1									−1−1−1						
Com-	$z1$				+1									−1−1−1					
modity	$z2$					+1									−1−1−1				
2	$z3$						+1									−1−1−1			
Com-	$z1$							+1									−1−1−1		
modity	$z2$								+1									−1−1−1	
N	$z3$									+1									−1−1−1
Consumption																			
Com-	$z1$	$-a_1^1$			$-a_1^2$			$-a_1^N$			+1	+1	+1						
modity	$z2$		$-a_1^1$			$-a_1^2$			$-a_1^N$		+1	+1	+1						
1	$z3$			$-a_1^1$			$-a_1^2$			$-a_1^N$	+1	+1	+1						
Com-	$z1$	$-a_2^1$			$-a_2^2$			$-a_2^N$						+1	+1	+1			
modity	$z2$		$-a_2^1$			$-a_2^2$			$-a_2^N$					+1	+1	+1			
2	$z3$			$-a_2^1$			$-a_2^2$			$-a_2^N$				+1	+1	+1			
Com-	$z1$	$-a_N^1$			$-a_N^2$			$-a_N^N$									+1	+1	+1
modity	$z2$		$-a_N^1$			$-a_N^2$			$-a_N^N$								+1	+1	+1
N	$z3$			$-a_N^1$			$-a_N^2$			$-a_N^N$							+1	+1	+1

Note: z = zone.

Figure 4

Merseyside: spatially aggregate model – equation system (example)

Labour at work: $-\sum_l a_\lambda^l E^l - \sum_s a_\lambda^l S^l - {}_g a_\lambda G + J^\lambda - {}_t a_\lambda T = 0$ $\lambda = 1, \ldots, \Gamma$

Labour at home: $\sum_l b_\lambda^l R^l - J^d - U^\lambda = 0$ $\lambda = 1, \ldots, \Gamma$

Children (education): $-\sum_l {}_r a_c^l R^l + C = 0$

Households (population): $\sum_l {}_r b_P^l R^l = P$

Transport: $-\sum_\lambda {}_j a J^\lambda + T = 0$

Services: $S^m - \sum_l {}_r a_s^l R^l = 0$ $m = s = 1, \ldots, M$

Basics: $E^l = \hat{E}^l$

Floorspace: $-\sum_l {}_e a_f^l E^l - \sum_s a_f^l S^l - a_f^l G + U_f = 0$ $f = 1, \ldots, F$

notes: (i) For notation, see list on p. 108.
(ii) There is only one technique of production for each activity.

Equation system

1 Fully disaggregated model with implied interzonal flows
Production of commodity k by all activities l with different production techniques t in zone i is:

$$\sum_l \sum_t {}^t b_k^l \; {}^t X_i^l - \sum_j T_{ij}^k \geqslant B_i^k \qquad\qquad \begin{aligned} k &= 1, \ldots, K \\ i &= 1, \ldots, I \end{aligned} \qquad (8)$$

Consumption of commodity k in zone j:

$$-\sum_l \sum_t {}^t a_k^l \; {}^t X_j^l + \sum_i T_{ij}^k \leqslant B_j^k \qquad\qquad \begin{aligned} k &= 1, \ldots, K \\ j &= 1, \ldots, J \end{aligned} \qquad (9)$$

2 Model with production for whole urban market, with interzonal flows aggregated into flows (T_{i*}^k) to and from the market centre.
Production:

$$\sum_l \sum_t {}^t b_k^l \; {}^t X_i^l - T_{i*}^k \; B_i^k \qquad\qquad \begin{aligned} k &= 1, \ldots, K \\ i &= 1, \ldots, I \end{aligned} \qquad (10)$$

Consumption:

$$-\sum_l \sum_t {}^t a_k^l \; {}^t X_j^l + \sum_i A_i^k \; T_{i*}^k \; f_{ij}^k B_j^k \qquad\qquad \begin{aligned} k &= 1, \ldots, K \\ j &= 1, \ldots, J \\ I &= J \end{aligned} \qquad (11)$$

where $A_i^k = 1/\sum_i f_{ij}$ $\qquad\qquad\qquad\qquad\qquad\qquad\qquad$ (12)

f_{ij} = function of distance between zones i and j.

Notation

Indices:
  i, j zones
  l, m activity type
  t type of production technique
  k commodity
  $*$ indicates summation over an index

Activities:
  ${}^t X_j^l$ level of activity of type l operating technique t in zone j
  T_{ij}^k level of transport activity carrying commodity k between zones i and j.

Technical coefficients:
  ${}^t b_k^l$ amount of output of commodity k produced by a unit output of activity l using technique t
  ${}^t a_k^l$ amount of input of commodity k needed to produce a unit output of activity l using technique t.

For the equations (Figure 4) of the spatially aggregated model (Figure 2), the general activity X is divided into major groups of activity:

E — basic employment (*exports*)
G — local *g*overnment services
C — education (of *c*hildren)
R — *r*esidential (labour producing) activity
S — *s*ervices (largely retail)
J — *j*ourney to work (transport activity)
T — production of *t*ransport.

Similarly, some of the commodities are also distinguished through the indices:

λ — labour
c — education
s — services
g — local government services.
f — floorspace

Each of these indices can take on several values, e.g. in figure 2, there are two types of labour.

The technical coefficients are also disaggregated:

$$^t_g a^l_k$$ amount of commodity k consumed by unit activity of group g, type l, using technique t.

The constraints are also divided into types:

U — unemployment
P — total population
$\hat{E}$ — exports of basic goods.

Conclusion

This paper has outlined the context within which formal models of urban areas are being used in the planning process in the UK. The situation is generally one in which the local planners are attempting to cope with the consequences of often unexpected events determined by forces outside the area, and beyond their control. This is why local authorities are so often interested in techniques which 'predict' or 'forecast', or which test the impact of some external change. The paper has also tried to show how accounting methods can help to provide a comprehensive and exhaustive framework for analysing the interactions and linkages in a local economic system. The argument has been illustrated by reference to practical applications, initiated by local authorities and by central government.

It is suggested that the public sector will become more and more intimately concerned with the management and control of the economy at both national and local levels. Whether this means an increasing need to respond to events or the establishment of more direct control, the demand for effective techniques which reveal the processes promoting urban change will continue to grow.

References

Ambrose, P. and Colenutt, R. (1975), *The property machine*, Penguin.

Arrow, K.J. and Hoffenberg, M. (1959), *A time-series analysis of interindustry demands*, North-Holland, Amsterdam.

Atkinson, A.B. (ed.) (1973), *Wealth, income and inequality*, Penguin.

Bacharach, M. (1970), *Biproportional matrices and input−output change*, Cambridge University Press, London.

Barras, R. and Broadbent, T.A. (1975), *A framework for structure plan analysis*, Planning Research Applications Group Technical Papers TP8, Centre for Environmental Studies.

Boyce, D.E., Day, N.D. and McDonald, C. (1970), *Metropolitan plan making*, Regional Science Research Institute, Philadelphia, USA.

Broadbent, T.A. (1977), *Planning and profit in the urban economv*. Methuen

Cullingworth, J.B. (1972), *Town and country planning in Britain*, Allen and Unwin.

Department of Applied Economics, University of Cambridge (1962), *A computable model of economic growth. A programme for growth*, Number 1, Chapman and Hall, London.

   (1963), *A programme for growth, Part III: input−output relationships 1954−66*, Chapman and Hall, London.

Diamond Commission (1975), *Royal Commission on the Distribution of Income and Wealth*, Report No. 1, Cmnd 6171, HMSO.

Drewett, R., Goddard, J. and Spence, N. (1976), *British cities. Urban population and employment change, 1951−71*, Research Report No. 10, Department of the Environment.

Goddard, J.B. (1975), *Organisational information flows and the urban system.*

Hall, P., Gracey, H., Drewett, R. and Thomas, R. (1973), *The containment of urban England, I and II*, Pelican.

Hepworth, N. (1971), *The Finance of Local Government*, Allen and Unwin (2nd edn).

Institute of Economic Affairs (1974), *Government and the land*, Institute of Economic Affairs.

de Kanter, J. and Morrison, W.I. (1976) *The Merseyside Input−Output Study*, Paper presented to Regional Science Association, British Section, September.

Keeble Lewis (1969), *Principles and practice of town and country planning*, Estates Gazette.

Kennedy, M.C. (1974), 'The economy as a whole' in Prest, A.R. and Coppock D.J. (eds.), *The UK economy: a manual of applied economics*, Weidenfeld and Nicolson.

Lees, A. (1976), 'Decline and decentralisation', *The Planner,* 129−30.

Leicester City Council and Leicester County Council (1969), *Leicester and Leicestershire Sub-Regional Planning Study*, Leicester City Council, and Leicester County Council.

Leontief, W.W. (1951), *The structure of the American economy, 1919−39*, Oxford University Press, New York.

Massey, D.M. and Cordey-Hayes, M. (1971), 'The use of models in structure planning', *Town Planning Review*, **42**, 22−44.

Matuszewski, T.I., Pitts, P.R. and Sawyer, J.A. (1964), 'Linear programming estimates of changes in input-coefficients', *Canadian Journal of Economics and Politital Science,* **30**, 203, 210.

McLoughlin, J.B. *(1969), Urban and regional planning: a systems approach,* Faber and Faber, London.

Moore, B. and Rhodes, J. (1973), 'Evaluating the effects of British regional economic policy', *Economic Journal,* **83**, 87–110.

Morrison, W.I. and Smith, P. (1974), 'Non-survey input–output techniques at the small area level: an evaluation', *Journal of Regional Science,* **14**, 1–14.

Notts–Derby Sub-Regional Planning Unit (1969), *Notts–Derby Sub-Regional Study,* Notts–Derby Sub-Regional Planning Unit.

Organisation of Economic Cooperation and Development (1974), *National accounts of OECD countries 1962–1973,* OECD.

Pred, A. (1973), 'The growth and development of cities in advanced economies' in Pred, A. and Tornquist, G., *Systems of cities and information flows,* Lund Studies in Geography (B), No. 38.

Smith, P. and Morrison, W.I. (1974), *Simulating the urban economy,* Pion, London.

Stewart, M. (1975), 'The economic planning context', pp. 2–15 of South Glamorgan County Planning Department (eds.), *The urban crisis: economic problems and planning,* Royal Town Planning Institute London.

Warneryd, O. (1968), *Interdependence in the urban system,* Gothenburg.

Webber, R.J. (1976), *Liverpool Social Area Study 1971 Data: Final Report,* Planning Research Applications Group Technical Paper PRAG TP 14, Centre for Environmental Studies, London.

Westaway, E.J. (1974), 'The spatial hierarchy of business organisations and its implications for the British urban system', *Regional Studies,* **8**, 145–55.

REGIONAL INTERDEPENDENCE IN THE UNITED KINGDOM ECONOMY

I.R. GORDON

Introduction

To a detached observer three of the most conspicuous features of British
regional policy might seem to be its essential continuity of direction over a
period of several decades, a lack of visible progress toward its declared objectives
and the virtual absence of real and sustained debate over its aims and strategy. If
these judgements are at all accurate, the particular combination of characteristics
ought to be a cause for concern — not least for professional economists, whose
contribution to the formation of regional policy (the Regional Employment
Premium apart) seems to have been remarkably limited. This is not to say that
good policy-related research has not been undertaken or that its conclusions
have been entirely ignored by policy makers — but rather that its principal function has been to legitimate their existing commitments to a particular type of
regional policy.

One reason for the lack of a more critical debate is clearly an element of self-
selection in the economists with an active interest in regional questions, whose
political assumptions tend not to be representative of the range in the profession as a whole. Within these shared assumptions which are often close to
those of official policy there have, however, been more practical difficulties in
joining issue with the quite direct and straightforward interpretation of the
regional problem on which policy has rested. This has had a strongly empiricist
cast to it, focussing on the evident regional disparities in the pressure of demand
for labour, the legacy of dependence in the peripheral regions on extractive and
heavy industries no longer offering a source of employment growth and the lack
of obvious locational constraints on most of the newer manufacturing industries.
Taken together with the political certainty that the central objective is (on
equity grounds) the removal of regional disparities in unemployment, these
perceptions provide the basis for a dominant theory of regional policy which *can*
be quite sophisticated in its development[1] but which inevitably has a high degree
of face validity. Such a theory accords only a subsidiary role to a range of
factors, including agglomeration economies, the locational preferences of
individuals and the incidence and diffusion of technical progress, which other
economists have argued (both on *a priori* grounds and from micro-observation)

to be critical to the regional growth process — but the importance of which it has been hard to demonstrate at the macro-level.[2] Faced with these alternative perspectives, policy makers might reasonably feel that they are being asked to exchange their present certainties for, at best, a set of uncertainties and, at worst (as perhaps with some of the growth pole prescriptions) for some untested patent nostrum. Neither is an attractive alternative particularly when what is thought to be mainly required is persistence and commitment. Even with the steady improvement in the depth of regional statistics, there are, however, real difficulties in *positively* validating alternative growth models at least with standard econometric techniques — in particular, consistent time series remain short in relation to the length of lags expected in the system, and attempts to introduce inter-regional linkages further eat up the available degrees of freedom. As a means of stimulating debate about regional policy it may therefore be more fruitful at the present stage to concentrate on operationalising as full a version as possible of (what I have called for shorthand) the dominant theory and testing *its* adequacy as an explanation of past performances, before turning to an analysis of residuals.

One central proposition of this dominant theory is, in Arthur Brown's words, that: 'It is the flows of goods and services across regional boundaries that govern regional fortunes in the main'[3] and this is the working hypothesis underlying the inter-regional input—output model recently developed at the University of Kent. Two basic assumptions are involved: that regional performance depends *primarily* on external forces rather than internal processes and that demand rather than supply factors provide the main exogenous variables. Implicit in these two is a broader judgement, that at the start of any period the distribution of economic activity by sector and region is in equilibrium under a prevailing set of supply and demand schedules, which need not therefore be explicitly analysed. Regional responses to shifts in the pattern of demands during any period depend therefore upon a combination of structural and locational characteristics which may be represented by the system of interdependences of an inter-regional input—output model.

In practice, versions of the dominant theory tend to ignore spatial considerations both as they relate to inter-regional relations and to the internal organisation of activity within a region — or rather they are treated as having only historical relevance, as influences on the distribution of activity at the start of a period. Emphasis in explaining current performance is therefore placed firmly on the *structural* characteristics of regions which are treated as 'spaceless subsets of the national economy'.[4] It is, however, far from clear that such basic locational attributes as accessibility to markets are without *direct* effect on regional differentials, while the specific interdependences of particular regions are clearly important in the transmission of economic fluctuations. Even a static application of inter-regional input—output analysis, assuming fixed regional trading patterns, enables us to look at some of the most direct interactions between structural and locational factors resulting from the geographical as well as sectoral specialisation of a region's markets. But it also provides a framework within which changes in those trading patterns and the direct effect of location can be explored.

I want to talk about some of our recent work on the modelling of inter-regional input—output linkages in the UK in the third section of this paper. Before doing so, however, it may be appropriate to discuss some of the ways in which regional interdependences on the supply side appear to influence unemployment rate differentials (as the major concern of regional policy makers) and how a more explicit consideration of these linkages might alter the prevailing interpretation of these variables.

Interdependences in regional unemployment

One of the main results of ignoring significant interdependences between regions is likely to be a biased perception of the forces operating *within* particular regions. A very good example of this danger emerges from a recent study by Thirlwall of the relationship between regional unemployment rates and unfilled vacancy statistics used as an indicator of labour demand.[5] As in other studies, a strong relationship — apparently similar in form — was found between these two rates within each region but in this case significant interdependences were also found between the unemployment rates of different regions. In particular un-employment rates in all other regions appeared to be strongly influenced by the situation in a composite Midlands region[6] (and to a lesser extent by develop-ments in South East England) *as well as* by the level of vacancies in their own region. Since the latter should incorporate all sources of demand for labour in the region, whether direct, indirect or induced, it seems clear that the interdepen-dencies revealed must relate to the supply side of the labour market and most probably reflect the equilibriating role of inter-regional migration among the working population.[7] Thus, for example, an increase in labour demand in the Midlands raising the vacancy rate there without changing it in other regions should draw in additional migrants from all those regions and serve to lower the unemployment rate in each. The effect is extremely simple but — after years of emphasis on the immobility of labour and the ineffectiveness of migration as an equilibriating mechanism — its scale emerges as surprisingly large. Thirlwall produces two sets of estimates of the distribution of labour demand, in terms of vacancy rates, required to bring unemployment rates in each region to a common level of 2 per cent. The first of these, which ignores regional inter-dependencies, suggests that what is required essentially is the elimination of existing differences in vacancy rates: except for the South East region, for which a figure of 0.8 per cent is estimated, the required vacancy rates all fall in the narrow range 1.2 to 1.4 per cent. These estimates are based, however, essentially on the experience of cyclical variations, during which regional unemployment rates move largely in parallel, and understate the difficulty of altering regional relatives. This is seen clearly when regional interdependences are incorporated and the target vacancy rates for all regions are solved simultaneously, leading to estimates of the required shift in vacancy rates which are around three times as large. In other words, even when quite short lags are assumed, it appears that about two thirds of the initial impact on regional unemployment rates gets dispersed through adjustments in the pattern of inter-regional migration. From the point of view of regional policy the problem seems to be not so much that migration is ineffective as an equilibrating mechanism but rather that the equilibrium it tends towards is broadly the existing pattern of differentials.

The other implication of these results is that regional labour markets may differ in character rather more than has usually been supposed when explicit account has not been taken of interdependences. When these linkages are incorporated, the required vacancy rates to equalise regional unemployment rates at 2 per cent appear to differ sharply between regions. At one extreme an apparently negative figure is indicated for the South East, while at the other in the North West and Wales rates of over $2\frac{1}{2}$ per cent seem to be required, which have not been achieved in any region during the last twenty years. A more restricted specification of the interdependences, making regional unemployment rates depend solely upon the level of vacancies within the region and the national average rate, still suggests that vacancy rates of 2 per cent would be required in the North and Wales with a negative rate in the South East.

Both sets of estimates involve linear extrapolations well outside the range of past experience and must be regarded with considerable reserve — but they do apppear indicative of important inter-regional variations in the level of non-demand-deficient unemployment. Previous studies of unemployment—vacancy relationships appeared to show that this component (the sum of structural and frictional elements) varied remarkably little between regions and that regional differentials had to be explained essentially in terms of relative demand pressure.[8] These were again, however, single-region analyses incorporating mainly cyclical experience. In the presence of interdependences on the supply side there is no unique relationship between a region's unemployment and vacancy rates independent of the labour-market situation in other regions. Existing estimates of the non-demand-deficient component of regional unemployment are, in fact, conditional on the maintenance of something like the existing pattern of regional differentials in unemployment — and their similarity probably tells us more about the strength of inter-regional linkages than about the source of these differentials. To get at the latter we probably need to consider the set of rates equating unemployment and vacancies in *all* regions simultaneously, which Thirlwall's analysis suggests will vary significantly between regions.

It may be objected that analyses of recent experience on a region by region basis do in fact cover quite important changes in regional differentials since these are themselves cyclically sensitive. The absolute difference in unemployment rates between Development Areas and the country as a whole has (during the last two decades) averaged around 1 per cent in years of low unemployment but nearer 2 per cent in years of high unemployment. And this type of cyclical variation in the apparent scale of the 'regional problem' seems to have a

noticeable influence on policy makers with the visible commitment to regional
policy fluctuating in sympathy with the unemployment rate. Explanations of
the differences in cyclical sensitivity have concentrated very heavily on the
demand side, focussing first on the direct effects of industrial structure — though
this now seems to have been discounted[9] — and then at the possibilities of differential labour hoarding or discrimination against branch plants. Strangely little
attention seems to have been given to the evidence that *employment* in the
peripheral regions may be, if anything, rather less cyclically sensitive than in the
more central regions[10] — but its clear implication is that their greater sensitivity
in terms of unemployment should be explained mainly from the supply side.
Here two main explanations suggest themselves. Firstly, it is possible that
employers in labour-shortage areas may be more inclined or able to concentrate
adjustments in employment on workers over retirement age who will not then
register as unemployed — the numbers involved seem too small for this to be the
main explanation. Secondly, levels of inter-regional migration (and particularly
the net shifts) may tend to fall off in periods of economic stagnation or contrac-
tion. Since migration is essentially an act of investment, involving immediate costs
for the individual in exchange for an uncertain stream of future benefits, it
would not be surprising if migrants were affected by some of the same expectational and liquidity factors as industrial investors with corresponding cycles of
mobility and immobility. Time-series data on migration is notably weak (and
confounded by fluctuations in overseas immigration) but is not inconsistent with
this hypothesis which also seems to be supported by the tendency to wider
fluctuations in housebuilding rates in the regions gaining migrants. If firmer
evidence could be found that a cyclical sensitivity in migration underlies the
more familiar cyclical sensitivity in unemployment a somewhat different policy
response might be appropriate. First one would question the sense in which
regional problems do actually become 'worse' or 'better' over the cycle and the
need for consequent policy adjustments — though politically these may be
inevitable. But, secondly, consideration could be given to assistance with and
incentives to migration specifically during periods of relatively low activity.
Locational preferences are multi-dimensional and in normal times one should
be sceptical about arguments that prevailing migration levels reflect an irrational
degree of inertia. Indeed, as we have argued earlier, there is some evidence that
migration can be extremely responsive to changes in economic conditions.
Nevertheless at some stages of the cycle, migration may be unnecessarily
inhibited by liquidity or expectational factors and government assistance would
then be an appropriate element in regional policy.

The methodological issue is clearer: cyclical fluctuations in regional unemployment differentials are not simply reflections of changes in relative demand
pressures and so cannot provide direct evidence on the effects of a more equal
distribution of labour demand. Conjectures about these demand a very explicit
consideration of regional interdependences in terms of labour movements. The

preliminary evidence considered here suggests that regional problems will then seem rather harder to solve than when interdependences were ignored.

Inter-regional input—output linkages[11]

Turning to interdependences on the demand side, more exclusive reliance has to be placed on cross-sectional evidence, using the relative magnitudes of existing flows between sectors and regions to indicate the probable strength and implications of inter-regional linkages. Following this approach adds to the familiar limitations of static input—output analysis further restrictive assumptions about the stability of regional trading patterns — and, more specifically, of inter-regional differentials in competitiveness. Off-setting, and potentially out-weighing, these rigidities and lack of theoretical sophistication is the capacity of the accounting framework to accommodate, on a consistent basis, a high degree of disaggregation in the representation of regional specialisation both in commodities and geographical markets. The Kent model distinguishes some 40 sectors in each of the 11 standard regions but the basic building-blocks underlying the base-year flow matrix involved 81 sectors and 62 sub-regions. The rub is that at this level of disaggregation — but equally at any lower level — hard data on regional flows is virtually absent. Thus in most respects regional technologies have to be assumed simply to parallel the national, while the pattern of trade flows has been simulated from an analysis of survey data on commodity flows relating to a small number of sub-regions. A major simplification has also been adopted from the earlier studies of Chenery and Moses, in assuming a region's entire purchases of a commodity[12] to be routed through a single demand pool, irrespective of the particular purchasing sector, thus enabling the full inter-regional matrix to be decomposed into separate sparse matrices of technical and trade coefficients. While the resulting estimates of transactions between individual sectors-in-regions are clearly of limited reliability, the overall pattern of trade flows represented in the model should capture the more important *systematic* aspects of regional interdependence in goods and services. With the broad aim in mind of operationalising and testing a fairly full version of the 'dominant theory' of British regional performance — rather than producing a tool for the planning of industrial complexes — a middle course has been followed between the massive data-gathering exercise undertaken for the Harvard multi-regional model of the United States and the entirely *a priori* approach to trade flows adopted, for example, in Nevin's early Welsh model and a recent Belgian inter-regional model, both of which assume the minimisation of transport costs.[13] The amount of entirely 'new' information in the Kent model is limited — instead the emphasis has been on incorporating the quite considerable amount of information which is already available (if often in fragmentary form) on regional activity, patterns of specialisation and relative accessibility within a consistent logical framework which enables their less obvious second- and third-order implications to be drawn out.

This point perhaps deserves some emphasis at a time when a watershed, or at least a plateau, seems to have been reached in regional economic statistics. After a decade of notable and much-needed improvements in the general range, quality and frequency of official statistics it would now be unwise to expect either that further changes will continue this tendency *or* that longer time series on a consistent basis will develop. Acceptance of this likely situation should not be allowed to rule out the development of more and better econometric analyses of regional performance, though it does make the modelling of such analyses on established practice at the national level obviously impractical as well as inappropriate (which it always had been). In general it might be suggested that advances on this front require rather less *ad-hockery* in theorising but a greater willingness to improvise in the operationalisation and testing of models. This would involve both further efforts at constructing estimates for *relevant* regional variables from indirect sources, following the lead given by Woodward's pioneering set of regional accounts,[14] and also a wider use of imposed coefficients in cases where there is little *a priori* expectation of regional variation or where independent evidence is available, for example from cross-sectional analyses of the flows involved in regional linkages. Needless to say, this type of work is both more time-consuming and less elegant than the direct application of estimation techniques to published time series — but these are concessions which will have to be made if some of the gap is to be closed between the comparative richness of the best informal accounts of British regional performance and the aridity of much of the statistical analysis which has been undertaken so far.

The great bulk of the work involved in developing a first inter-regional input—output model for the UK has been of precisely this painstaking kind, involving the step-by-step disaggregation of the national industry-by-industry transactions matrix, which would be tedious to report here. But there are two aspects with wider implications, both involving regional interdependences. The first of these concerns the estimation of trade coefficients indicating the proportions of a region's purchases of a particular commodity which are drawn from the various producing regions — and by inference the proportions in which additional purchases would be allocated. This represents our most substantial area of direct ignorance, since there are no records which relate at all directly to inter-regional trade, and in the completed model the estimated coefficients for some of the more heterogeneous service sectors provide almost certainly the largest source of direct error. For most of the sectors involved in goods production, however, we were able to synthesise flows with a greater degree of confidence on the basis of an analysis of consignment movements for industrial establishments in five sub-regions of the South West and Wales. The model employed was a variant of the gravity formulation suggested by Leontief and Strout for use in this context, although the particular specification owes more to the recent work of geographers such as Wilson and its use was confined solely to simulating base-year flows.[15] In matching the estimated distributions of demand and of output of a commodity sub-region-by-sub-region it was assumed basically that purchases were allocated randomly, subject to a constraint on total distance costs incurred — and consequently that trade flows tend (*ceteris paribus*) to decline in proportion to some power of physical distance, i.e.:

$$F_{ijp} = O_{ip}D_{jp}A_{ip}B_{jp}d_{ij}^{-\beta_p}$$ (1)

where

F_{ijp} = sales of commodity p produced in area i to purchasers in region j

O_{ip} = output of commodity p in area i

D_{jp} = purchases of commodity p in area j

d_{ij} = distance from area i to j

A_{ip}, B_{jp} and β_p are parameters estimated iteratively.[16]

Estimation of this model for 44 commodities using the consignment survey data yielded values for the distance exponent ranging between near zero and almost 4 but with a clustering of values around 1 and a significant tendency for the low-value—high-weight commoditites to display more sensitivity to distance. The typical inversely proportional relationship corresponds with Leontief and Strout's assumption and with the results of international-trade studies but it suggests a much stronger distance effect than has been assumed in more recent analyses of regional performance. If the distance deterrence equation is interpreted as a derived *demand* function for means of overcoming distance it seems to imply rather large values for the share of distance-related costs and/or the substitution elasticities of traded goods. The typical distance elasticity is, of course, around unity but the corresponding distance *cost* elasticity is probably rather higher — perhaps as much as 3 or 4 for inter-regional trade — while the substitution elasticity in relation to total price would have to be some multiple of this figure, reflecting the ratio of total to distance-related costs. Even for some engineering products, distance cost elasticities of about half this size seem to be indicated. There may be some upward bias to these estimates purely on cross-sectional evidence if, *within* the commodity groups identified, areas tend to specialise in products for which there are specific local demands. Such specialisation itself, however, reflects some of the cost penalties in relation to information acquisition and dissemination or service provision incurred by firms attempting to trade in more distant markets against actual or potential local competition.

Much recent writing on the regional economies has, quite rightly, tended to play down the significance of direct transport costs for a large part of manufacturing industry, particularly within a relatively small country such as Great Britain. Nevertheless even a preliminary analysis of regional interdependences makes it clear that very few regional activities serve an entirely undifferentiated national market and that variations in accessibility still represent one of the most basic influences on regional economies. One reflection of this is seen in the comparative degrees of regional self-sufficiency which, at the aggregate level, seem to have less to do with patterns of industrial specialisation than with the simple facts of size and accessibility — larger and more remote areas both tending to be more self-sufficient. These simple correlations highlight the fact that distance operates as a double-sided barrier, serving *partly* to protect weaker industries with local markets in the peripheral areas from the full force of metropolitan competition. As Caesar pointed out in a paper to another Section of this Association over ten years ago, this must make the *net* effects on regional activity levels of the lowering of these barriers through communications improvements problematic though hardly insignificant.[17] Since then there has been considerable investment, justified at least partly in regional development terms, in the road links of the peripheral regions but there is still no clear evidence as to whether local activity gains or loses as a result. Theoretical results with a single-commodity gravity model suggest that the more peripheral of two regions should increase its market share if distance *costs* between them are reduced equally for both parties[18] — but it is not clear that this conclusion carries over to a multi-commodity situation where the peripheral region is the major producer of some commodities. An early study, reported to this Section by Cleary, of perhaps the most dramatic recent communications improvement, the Severn Bridge, suggested that effects on *industrial* markets and locations were slow to develop.[19] In retrospect this is perhaps less surprising, given that distance costs involve so much more than direct transport costs and are mediated by long established patterns of communication, organisation and product differentiation, but important trade effects should still be forthcoming. Within the framework of the inter-regional input—output model we hope to trace through the longer-term implications of this type of communication improvement by adjusting the trade coefficients to correspond with alternative matrices of effective distance.

I should now like to say something more briefly about the treatment of regional consumption since this links up with some of the issues raised in the previous section. The regional distribution of consumer expenditure has been made largely endogenous in the inter-regional model by introducing a household sector selling principally its labour and generating demands for the outputs of both the private and public sectors. The input-coefficients for this sector clearly reflect financial more than technical determinants and the flows are explicitly treated in monetary terms, with the relatively constant coefficients across regions for inputs of labour representing the equivalent of a Cobb—Douglas production function. But the size of induced consumer demand for particular commodities as a result of increased household income (or output) in a region will vary according to how far this involves additional households (i.e. migration) or higher incomes for existing households. At the national level household numbers seem to be relatively insensitive to income changes — but at the regional level alternative estimates suggest that between a half and 90 per cent of adjustments in total income over periods of a decade or so take the form of changes in household numbers rather than in average incomes.[20] Thus average consumption coefficients provide a better first approximation than do nationally based marginal coefficients for regional household sectors.[21]

The implications of these alternative approaches are really quite substantial even for total output in a region. For a simple household, income multiplier marginal consumption coefficients imply a value of about 1.5 for the country as a whole (or a region closed to inter-regional trade) compared with about 2.0 when average consumption coefficients are used. The inter-regional model suggests that a typical region retains about half the secondary income generated by an initial injection of demand, implying multipliers of around 1.25 and 1.5 for the two sets of consumption coefficients. Thus if average coefficients applied at the regional level but marginal coefficients at the national level there would be no *net* leakage of secondary income out of the originating region. This is an extreme assumption and realistically we must expect some leakage though this may well be out-weighed eventually by the effects on capital-stock adjustment. The important point is that the distribution between sectors and regions of the additional output requirements following regional-policy measures depends critically on the responsiveness of inter-regional migration but that no simple inferences can be drawn about the real resource costs of assistance from this distribution since only a rather small proportion of the additional labour employed in the assisted areas may actually be unemployed.

Conclusions

The development of the basic inter-regional input–output matrix with a full set of coefficients for a single past year (1963) should mark the beginning rather than the end of a programme of research on regional interdependences. The obvious next step is its application to demand patterns in the preceding and succeeding periods to test the combined influence of structural and locational factors on actual regional performance. I would guess that before this exercise is completed the consensus over the basis of regional problems and policy will finally have broken down. Already the combination of a revival of resource-based industries, decline in metropolitan populations and some, probably more temporary, effects of the current recession have transformed the visible certainties of regional performance into a much more complex pattern. And a number of political developments[22] have strengthened the perception that intra-regional imbalances may be at least as important as — though *not* independent of — inter-regional differences. However strong or weak they may have been in the recent past it seems that the independent roles of migration and of the spatial organisation of regions will have to be recognised in explaining current and future trends — and that some of the artificial distinctions between urban and regional economics must go. At the same time it has become clear that many of the major 'urban' issues cannot be tackled outside their national and regional context. It seems thus that the logic of situations, rather than detached economic analysis, is leading us towards a more sophisticated form of spatial economic policy which will be much more concerned with supply factors and with inter-dependences between different levels of aggregation. Coincidentally this is very much the direction in which French regional planning is moving with the development for the *VII*th Plan of the REGINA model which integrates distinct national, inter-regional and urban levels of analysis.[23] The time is probably ripe for a similar initiative in this country — but *certainly* an important shift in direction is required, if the profession is to contribute more to the formulation of regional economic policy in the next decade than in the past three or four. Simply to acknowledge that 'the situation has changed', without reanalysing past experience, is a recipe for more naive empiricism.

Notes

1   As for example in A. J. Brown's *The Framework of Regional Economics in the U.K.* (CUP, 1972)
2   Harry W. Richardson in his *Regional Growth Theory* (Macmillan, 1973) outlines an operational model in which these factors assume a central importance but holds back from quantitative testing for the present on grounds of 'the unfortunate experience of predecessors, shortage of data and the conviction that such testing would be premature'.
3   A. J. Brown, op. cit., p. 201.
4   Richardson, op. cit., p. 86.
5   A. P. Thirlwall, 'Forecasting regional unemployment in Great Britain', *Regional Science and Urban Economics,* 5, 357–74; R. J. Dixon and A. P. Thirlwall, *Regional Growth and Unemployment in the United Kingdom* (Macmillan, 1975), ch. 5.
6   Yorkshire and Humberside, East and West Midlands.
7   Thirlwall suggests that the linkages primarily reflect leakages of demand from region to region. While such interdependences are undoubtedly important in the transmission of employment fluctuations (see above pp. 116–20) they should only affect unemployment in a region *via* its own vacancy rate.
8   E. g. Dixon and Thirlwall op. cit.; P. C. Cheshire, *Regional Unemployment Differences in Great Britain* (NIESR Regional Papers II, CUP, 1973).
9   See Dixon and Thirlwall, op. cit., ch. 4.
10   Linear regression using data on numbers of males in employment and unemployed at mid year 1956–69, together with a time trend, suggested that the North, Scotland and Wales together experienced 28% of the fluctuations in UK unemployment and 15% of the fluctuations in employment whereas their average share of employment was 20% of the national total.
11   The work reported in this section was supported by the Social Science Research Council, to whom grateful acknowledgement is due, under a project originally directed by Professor H. W. Richardson.
12   Strictly, the products of a specific sector, since the model is industry — rather than commodity — based.
13   See K. R. Polenske, *A Multi-Regional Input–Output Model for the United States,* Harvard Economic Research Project, Report No. 21, 1970; E. Nevin et al., *The Structure of the Welsh Economy,* University of Wales Press, 1966; D. Vanwynsberghe, *L'Economie du Brabant dans une Perspective Inter-Regionale et Inter-Sectorelle: Une Approche Input–Output,* Conseil Economique Regional pour le Brabant, 1973.

14   V. H. Woodward, 'Regional Social Accounts for the United Kindom', in *N.I.E.S.R. Regional Papers I,* Cambridge University Press, 1970.

15   The original proposal (W. W. Leontief and A. Strout, 'Multi-Regional Input—Output Analysis', in T. Barna (ed.), *Structural Interdependence and Economic Development,* Macmillan, 1963) redefined the trade coefficients so that trade flows varied in proportion to the changing distribution of regional output as well as to the distribution of demands.

16   For further discussion of the applicability and use of this model for simulation of inter-regional trade flows see: I.R. Gordon, 'A Gravity Flows Approach to an Inter-Regional Input—Output Model of the U.K.' in E. Cripps (ed.), *Space-Time Concepts in Urban and Regional Models,* Pion, 1974, and 'Gravity Demand Functions, Accessibility and Regional Trade', *Regional Studies,* **10,** 25—37, 1976.

17   A. A. L. Caesar, 'Planning and the Geography of Great Britain', *Advancement of Science,* **21,** 230—40, 1964.

18   L. H. Klaasen, 'Energy, Environment and Regional Development', *Foundations of Empirical Economic Research,* Series 1975/1, Netherlands Economic Institute, derives similar results in looking at the related issue of the differential impact of changing fuel prices.

19   E. J. Cleary, 'The Economic Consequences of the Severn Bridge' in G.D.N. Worswick (ed.), *Uses of Economics,* Blackwell, 1972.

20   See I.R. Gordon, 'The Return of Regional Multipliers: A Comment', *Regional Studies,* **7,** 257—62, 1973.

21   With this treatment there are obvious problems of consistency *unless* attention is confined to exogenous changes in demand which are self-balancing at the national level. A better approach would be to extend the regional consumption vectors to include appropriate negative coefficients for consumption in the off-diagonal regions. At present this is ruled out, however, by the very considerable computational advantages of restricting the technical matrix to a block-diagonal form.

22   Including perhaps the current crisis in local government finance, the rise and fall of the various special urban programmes, the debate over devolution and the spread of high unemployment.

23   See R. Courbis, 'The REGINA Model for French Regional—National Planning' in K. Telford (ed.), *Economic Models in Regional Planning,* IBM (Peterlee, 1976).

9

THE SCOTTISH BALANCE OF PAYMENTS – 1973

V. G. BULMER-THOMAS

The balance of payments (BOP) of the United Kingdom has, over the years, acquired overwhelming importance as a measure of economic performance and even of welfare. The announcement by the authorities of a deficit is always greeted with gloom, unless it is a diminished deficit, and a surplus can be said to have the opposite effect.

Much of this importance is misplaced. The BOP can be thought of as an account recording all transactions with foreigners and like all accounts it must balance. A 'deficit', therefore, only makes sense if one or more items is omitted from one or both sides of the account. The balance of trade and the current account of the balance of payments are often for this reason spoken of as being in deficit or surplus. For the world as a whole these deficits and surpluses must cancel, so that the deficit of one nation will be matched by the surpluses of others. Since the distribution of these deficits/surpluses among the nations of the world does not correspond to any accepted notions of economic prosperity, there is no reason to attach welfare significance to a deficit.

This is even more true of a region. Nonetheless, it is very interesting to know what the balance of payments of a region is for various reasons; first, it may help in monitoring economic performance; secondly, it may shed light on the contribution of different sectors to the health of the economy; and, thirdly, as a by-product of estimating it, we may be able to build up a more complete picture of economic activity within the region.

For the UK, as for other nations, the BOP account is a double-entry system in which entries in one part of the account (the current) are matched by corresponding entries in the other (the capital). Since the data are available independently, the deficit on the one part must be matched by a surplus on the other, although there is always a small residual error. Thus if the current account is in deficit, this means the capital account is in surplus, i.e. sources of funds exceed uses and the country is a net borrower from abroad.

For a region such as Scotland, where the available data cannot support a direct estimate of the BOP either in terms of the current or capital account, this suggests an interesting way of estimating the current account of the BOP. If the current account deficit/surplus can be interpreted as net borrowing/lending to

Figure 1.   Simplified four-account social accounting matrix for an open
economy

	Pro- duction	Appro- priation	Accumu- lation	Rest of world	Total
Production	—	500	200	300	1000
Appro- priation	600	—	—	100	700
Accumu- lation	—	100	—	100	200
Rest of world	400	100	—	—	500
Total	1000	700	200	500	

the rest of the world (ROW), then it must be equal to the difference between
gross capital formation and domestic savings.

The best way of showing this is by means of a simplified social accounting
matrix (see Figure 1) in which the four most basic forms of economic activity —
production, consumption, accumulation and foreign transactions — are recorded.
In the row corresponding to the production account, we have traded income
from all sources except that transactions between producers have been consolidated.[1] Thus, 500 of producers' income comes from sales to consumers, 200
from purchases of capital goods and stockbuilding and 300 represent sales to the
ROW, i.e. exports. 400 of this income goes as imports while the remainder is
taken up as factor payments. Factors of production supplement their payments
from producers with 100 of income from ROW which they dispose of as consumption (500), savings (100) and factor/transfer payments to ROW. Finally,
the 200 of capital formation is paid for by 100 of domestic savings and 100 net
borrowing from abroad.

The net borrowing or deficit on current account could have been estimated in
three ways; first by a direct estimate of commodity exports (300), commodity
imports (400) and transfer/factor payments to and from abroad; secondly, by
taking the difference between factor payments (600) and gross domestic expenditure (500 and 200) to obtain the net trade balance and adding to it the net
balance for transfer/factor payments to and from abroad; thirdly, as the difference between accumulation and domestic savings.

When we have completed our input—output tables for Scotland, we will
obtain a direct estimate of the balance of trade. However, this would still leave
transfer and factor payments; since these are dominated by interest received and
paid on financial flows between Scotland and England on which there is no
accurate information, it is clear that the third method must be used to obtain an
estimate of the current account of the balance of payments.

The notion of a current account deficit as representing net borrowing from
abroad also helps to explain why a deficit *per se* has no welfare significance. A
nation will have to borrow from abroad if it seeks to expand at a rate faster than

Figure 2.   Four-account three-sector social accounting matrix for an open economy

| | Pro-duction | Appropriation | | | Accumu-lation | Rest of world | Total |
		House-holds	Govern-ment	Busi-ness			
Pro-duction	–	400	100	–	200	300	1000
Appro-priation:							
house-holds	300	–	100	50	–	50	500
govern-ment	100	25	–	50	–	25	200
busi-ness	200	25	–	–	–	25	250
Accumu-lation	–	25	–25	100	–	100	200
Rest of world	400	25	25	50	–	–	500
Total	1000	500	200	250	200	500	

that permitted by the current level of domestic savings; in this respect it is just like a company which borrows funds in the capital market. Some firms need to borrow to support intelligent investment plans, while others need to borrow to support inefficiency. Whether being in deficit for a region or a nation is desirable depends, among other things, on whether the gross capital formation is in some sense too high or whether domestic savings are too low. One reason for concern with a UK deficit is that a rich nation should be capable of financing what have been only modest rates of investment with internal resources, but this does not apply to a region such as Scotland where it is generally agreed that the rate of investment needs to be higher than that consistent with present levels of income and saving.

Some conceptual and methodological problems

The decision to estimate the balance on current account for Scotland as the residual of the capital account raises many problems which need to be resolved before the work of estimation can begin.

In terms of Figure 1, domestic savings appear as one entry. However, the available data do not take this form and instead we must subdivide the appropriation account in terms of those sectors for which data are available. Since sector savings are the difference between sector incomings and outgoings on appropriation account, we need a sectorisation scheme for which data on incomings and outgoings can be obtained and for Scotland this must be households, government and business. The implicit social accounting scheme, therefore, being used is that of Figure 2 in which all accounts are consolidated except the appropriation account which divides into three sectors.

Each of the accounts shown schematically in Figure 2 will be considered in more detail below. At this point it is only necessary to say that deconsolidating the appropriation account makes both incomings and outgoings more complicated, but the total for domestic savings is simply the sum of sector savings.

The balance of payments is usually taken to refer to all transactions between residents and non-residents. An alternative formulation limits it to actual flows across the borders. The difference can be illustrated by the case of a foreign tourist making a commodity purchase in Scotland: in the first case the transaction corresponds to an export, while in the second it does not. The former seems the more appropriate interpretation and is therefore adopted here.

This means, however, that 'residency' must be defined for each sector. In the case of households, this is straightforward since the Inland Revenue definition can be used; this assumes that a person is resident if he spends more than six months of the year in question in the country. Thus, for example, foreign technicians working on oil rigs for less than six months are non-residents so that their wages and salaries represent imports of factor services. In fact, the use of national insurance cards by the primary data source on wages and salaries and the choice of 1973 as the year of estimation means that this problem is unlikely to occur. The problem of cross-border traffic, i.e. Scots working in England and living in Scotland and vice versa, will also disappear, since Inland Revenue data allocate income from employment to each region according to residency.[2]

In the case of the business sector, it is not only possible but also inevitable that one follows the UK national accounting definition of residency given that data on the business sector in Scotland lean so heavily on the UK corporate appropriation account. More serious is the fact that by pro-rating a consolidated account, one is forced to assume that inter-regional intra-business flows cancel, e.g. that non-traded income from English companies earned by Scottish companies is matched by non-traded income from Scottish companies earned by English ones. This assumption is a deficiency in the estimation process, but it is made inevitable both by the absence of data and by the horizontal integration of companies in the UK.

The definition of residency, or indeed any definition for the government sector raises conceptual as well as empirical questions, since unlike the household and business sector it does not really exist. Three definitions were considered; in the first, the government sector would be defined by actual receipts and expenditure. This, however, would put the government massively in deficit since nearly all government revenue would have to be treated as a transfer payment from England. In the second, the government sector would be defined as if Scotland were independent; however, this would leave unresolved Scotland's contribution to such centrally managed expenditure as servicing the national debt, or defence.

The third definition, and the one adopted here, is to define the government sector on a regional basis in such a way that consolidated revenues and expenditures for each region sum to the income and outlay account for public authorities in the UK without offending some broadly acceptable criteria of equity.[3] On this definition the question is not whether centrally managed funds should be allocated to the regions, but how.

On this third definition, government revenue will be mainly derived from taxes on residents and indirect taxes on flows of goods and services in Scotland. The major problem of imputation concerns expenditure, although even this side is dominated by real flows, i.e. public authorities expenditure on goods and services, subsidies and transfers to the personal sector. Any imputation must be consistent with the fact that the rest of expenditure measures flows at market prices, and these may not coincide with benefits, so that it would be wrong to impute a share of, say, defence to Scotland in terms of the supposed benefits derived from it.[4]

Any imputation must also be consistent with the definition of the revenue side. This can be thought of as a combination of national tax rates and regional values. Assuming the tax rates bear some relationship to expenditure, then the ideal contribution of a region to a nationally managed fund is its relative economic prosperity.[5] Thus, one possible basis for imputation is Scotland's share of national gross domestic product (GDP). This basis was, in fact, chosen and it seems better than population shares. A region may be numerous, but poor, so that population shares tend to estimate benefits rather than expenditures.

The year 1973 was chosen, because it is the most recent year for which the full range of statistics are available and because it is the base year of the input–output tables we are preparing for Scotland. Before turning to the sector accounts, a word of warning should be given; the data for Scotland are not yet sufficiently reliable to base economic policy upon the accounts estimated in this paper. I have pointed out the policy implications of the results on the assumption that the results are accurate, but that assumption is a privilege open to academics which more practical people must forego.

The personal sector

The accounts for the personal sector in the UK are a consolidation of those for households and individuals, private non-profit making bodies serving persons (PNB) and life assurance and superannuation funds. This consolidation is imposed upon the UK by the availability of data, although efforts are now being made to deconsolidate the accounts; for Scotland, however, the available data can only be used to form a households and individuals account; the accounts for the other two sub-sectors were then added in to achieve comparability with the UK.

Table 1 records the estimated incomings and outgoings for households and individuals. Incomings are dominated by income from employment which is the sum of wages and salaries in cash, income in kind, employers' contributions to national insurance and pension schemes, and pay in cash and kind of the armed

Table 1   *Household and individuals' appropriation account for Scotland 1973*

Incomings	£m.	Outgoings	£m.
Income from employment	3696.0	Expenditure on consumption	3797.2
Income from self-employment	599.0	Current transfers to private non-profit-making bodies	49.1
Rent, dividends and net interest	387.4	National insurance and other contributions	335.0
Current grants from public authorities	515.0	Taxes on income	686.8
Other current transfers	249.1	Other current transfers	304.3
		Savings before providing for depreciation, additions to tax reserves and stock appreciation	274.1
Total	5446.5	Total	5446.5

Forces. The quoted figure, as for income from self-employment, is published by the Scottish Office [1].

The total for income from employment is dominated by wages and salaries and the estimate for this is based on a sample of earnings of those whose national insurance cards are held by the Department of Health and Social Security in Scotland. The primary source for income from self-employment is the Inland Revenue's Survey of Personal Income [2] broken down by region. No adjustment to income from self-employment has been made for stock appreciation since it is not known how total Scottish stock appreciation is divided between the personal and corporate sectors.

The rent component of income from property is dominated by the imputed rent from owner-occupation. Both paid and imputed rent received by households were obtained from the Central Statistical Office regional tables on this component of factor income [3]. Dividends and gross interest receipts are reported in the unpublished Family Expenditure Survey (FES) data for Scotland on income components [4]; given the small size of the sample, however, it seemed safer to take the ratio of Scottish to UK receipts as estimated by FES and use this division as a basis for breaking down household receipts in the Blue Book.[6] Interest paid was estimated in the same way and deduction from interest receipts gave the entry rent, dividends and net interest. Use of FES data, albeit implicitly, ensures consistency with the correct definition of residency.

Current grants from public authorities were taken from the Scottish Abstract of Statistics [6]. Other current transfers are dominated by pensions and annuities other than those from public authorities; this entry is not necessary for the UK because life assurance and superannuation funds are perforce consolidated with households. For Scotland, there are data in both FES and the Survey of Personal Incomes, but the most reliable method is to take the FES ratio of Scottish to UK receipts and apply this to the Blue Book figure for pensions and other benefits paid by life assurance and superannuation funds. The balance for other current transfers was taken from FES with intra-household transfers ignored.

Outgoings are dominated by expenditure on consumption, for which the major sources are FES and the National Food Survey (NFS) although there is independent information on such things as rates, free coal, gas and domestic water. Use of different sources means one must be very careful to avoid double counting.

The major question with the sample surveys concerns the technique of grossing up. A convention has gradually developed by which Scottish to UK ratios are taken from the surveys and applied to detailed Blue Book data on consumption expenditure [7]. The problem is that the latter at a disaggregated level includes not only the expenditure of the non-household sub-sectors of the personal sector, but also expenditure by foreign residents. It seemed safer, therefore, to gross up by the Scottish population to achieve consistency with the income side. It is consoling that the alternative estimate of consumption [8] differs by only five per cent from that in Table 1. Allowing for the expenditure of foreigners, private non-profit making bodies and life assurance companies reduces the difference to one or two per cent.

The Scottish population, however, must be defined more closely before it can be used to gross up. There are two estimates presented in the official statistics [6], home and total population, and the latter differs from the former by the addition of Scots residents abroad and by the subtraction of non-residents in Scotland. (The difference is in fact represented by members of the armed forces and merchant navy, rather than a pure definition of residency consistent with the national accounts). The procedure adopted, therefore, was to gross up by total population since this includes expenditure by Scots abroad whose income has already been accounted for, but excludes expenditure by non-residents whose income has been excluded. At a disaggregated level, household population was used to gross up where the item of expenditure was known to be limited to households.

In the case of alcohol and tobacco it was considered necessary to allocate a portion of the Blue Book figure to Scotland because of the problem of under-reporting in the sample survey. The Blue Book figure, however, was first adjusted to conform to a definition of household expenditure.[8]

Current transfers to PNB were taken from FES; income tax payments were estimated by applying FES ratios to the Blue Book figure adjusted for taxes paid by life assurance companies. This must be considered more reliable than income tax payments recorded for Scotland in Inland Revenue Statistics which exclude surtax and Schedule C income tax. National insurance contributions were

Table 2   *Personal-sector savings in Scotland 1973*

	£m.
Incomings on appropriation account (consolidated)	5619.3
Outgoings on appropriation account (consolidated)	5095.6
Savings (before providing for depreciation additions to tax reserves and stock appreciation)	523.7
Personal disposable income	4557.4
Savings as a % of personal disposable income	11.5%
UK savings ratio	11.3%

supplied by the Scottish Office. Other current transfers were dominated by contributions to life assurance and superannuation funds and the same procedure was adopted as for the income side.

The balance on the outgoings side represents savings. It is not possible to compare this with the UK since the latter does not produce a household account. It was, therefore, necessary to produce a consolidated personal sector account for Scotland and this is shown in Table 2. The account for PNB's was obtained from the UK on the basis of population shares, while that for life assurance and superannuation funds was obtained using FES data on the ratio of Scottish to UK receipts from and payments to these funds.

From Table 2 we obtain not only the savings for the whole of the personal sector, but also the savings ratio assuming that personal disposable income represents the same share of total personal income as it does for the UK.[9] The savings ratio is marginally higher for Scotland, but more sophisticated analysis of the Scottish savings performance requires the preparation of a time series on savings and this is something which my colleagues and I hope to work on.

The government sector

The combined public authorities' current account for Scotland is presented in Table 3. It corresponds to the consolidation of an actual local authority account with a central government account whose incomings are mainly imputed. Since nearly all outgoings correspond to real flows, this side will be dealt with first.

Goods and services consist mainly of current expenditure on goods and services estimated by the Scottish Office [6]. This estimate makes no allowance for defence and overseas relations and these were imputed to Scotland on the basis of Scotland's share in National GDP for the reasons given above.

It has been suggested that since this account aims to measure flows, not benefits, expenditure on defence could be measured by real purchases in Scotland. However, many regions have no defence installations and since their tax yields (on the methodology of this paper[5]) include an element designed to cover defence expenditure, it seems more equitable to impute expenditure in terms of ability to pay.

Subsidies paid in Scotland and grants to domestic sectors were also taken from the table on Identifiable Public Expenditure in [6], but grants paid abroad

Table 3   *Combined public authorities current account for Scotland 1973*

Incomings	£m.	Outgoings	£m.
Taxes on income		Goods and services	1209.1
1 Paid by house-holds	686.6		
2 Paid by life funds etc.	6.3		
3 Paid by corporations	152.4		
Taxes on expen-diture	970.0	Subsidies	200.7
National insurance etc. contributions	358.0	Grants	
		1 To other sectors	656.8
		2 Abroad	30.6
Gross trading surpluses	17.6	Debt interest	
		1 Paid by local authorities	238.0
Rent	208.0	2 Imputed to central government	152.7
Interest dividends etc.		Savings before providing for depreciation	54.1
1 From public corporations	80.0		
2 Other	63.1		
Total	2542.0	Total	2542.0

were imputed using Scotland's share of national GDP. Debt interest paid by
local authorities is a real flow and includes an unknown amount which would be
received by the nominal Scottish central government. This element is included in
the incomings side (see below), but it too is impossible to identify. Both incomings
and outgoings, therefore, are swollen by a small but unknown amount which
would normally disappear on consolidation, but the savings for the sector remain
unaffected.

The incomings side begins with two entries which represent outgoings of the
personal sector: taxes paid by households and individuals, and life assurance and
superannuation funds. The third entry, taxes on income paid by the corporate
sector, is more difficult to estimate. The Inland Revenue collects data on corporation tax paid in Scotland,[10] but this is almost certainly biased downwards by
the fact that much business income is attributed to companies registered in
England, but operating at least in part in Scotland. It seemed safer, therefore, to
apply the ratio of UK corporate taxes to corporate gross trading profits and
surpluses to Scottish gross trading profits and surpluses. Although this procedure
is somewhat crude, errors in the estimates will affect only the distribution of
domestic savings between sectors and not the total.

The estimate of taxes on expenditure was supplied by [8] and is consistent
with the methodology outlined in the book on gross domestic expenditure [7].

National insurance etc. contributions are the sum of household contributions and national health and redundancy payments. Gross trading surpluses were limited to those for local authorities and derived from local financial returns for Scotland. Even for the UK, central government gross trading surpluses are negligible. Rent, consisting of household rent paid to local authorities and the imputed rent for all public authorities derived from owner-occupation, was taken from CSO data [3].

Interest and dividend receipts were all imputed, since the actual receipts of local authorities are netted out against their expenditure in their accounts [12]. The first imputation concerns receipts from public corporations; these receipts represent the return on share capital owned by the central government as a trustee for the whole population, so the most equitable basis for imputation is population shares. Other interest and dividends consist of two parts: the first concerns receipts from other sectors accruing to the central government, and the same basis of imputation was used. The second represents interest receipts from local authority debt held by the central government. This disappears on consolidation for the UK, but reappears when the Scottish account is broken out. The receipts of interest from holdings of local authority debt by the UK central government were therefore broken down using population as a basis for imputation, so that the figure includes a certain amount of income from Scottish local authorities which is also included on the outgoings side.

Deduction of outgoings from incomings gives savings before providing for depreciation; these are small, but positive. The savings ratio (savings as a percentage of current income) is markedly lower for Scotland than for the UK (2.1 per cent compared with 6.5 per cent), but this is to be expected in a region where incomes are depressed relative to the national average and government expenditure is strongly influenced by Keynesian ideas on eliminating unemployment. Indeed it would not have been surprising if government savings were negative.

The corporate sector

This sector consolidates the appropriation accounts for companies, public corporations and financial institutions. It was not even possible to form a separate account for the public corporations.

The major incoming, gross trading profits and surpluses (see Table 4), is estimated by the Scottish Office as part of their work on GDP in Scotland [6]. It is not, however, truly independent.[11] A small deduction was made for the estimate of gross trading surplus accruing to Government in Table 3.

Other non-traded income for the UK eliminates (on consolidation) payments to and from companies in the UK. When the Scottish account is deconsolidated, some of these payments reappear. As we have no data, we have to assume that what Scottish companies receive as non-traded income from companies in the rest of the UK is matched by what companies in the rest of the UK receive from

Table 4   *Corporate-sector appropriation account for Scotland 1973*

Incomings	£m.	Outgoings	£m.
Gross trading profits and surpluses	948.4	Dividends and interest	550.8
Rent	27.1	Profits due abroad, net of UK tax and taxes paid abroad	258.8
Other non-traded income	243.0	Current transfers to charities	3.8
Income from abroad	431.1	Taxes on income	152.4
		Savings before providing for depreciation, additions to dividend and tax reserves and stock appreciation	683.8
Total	1649.6	Total	1649.6

Scottish companies. In the manufacturing sector this is unlikely to be true, but payments to and from financial institutions are likely to dominate this item and for these institutions the assumption may be true.

Other non-traded income (i.e. after deduction of rent) is composed mainly of interest on government debt, and interest earned by financial institutions on loans to the non-corporate sector. Since financial institutions themselves are the main holders of government debt in the corporate sector, a method of pro-rating the Blue Book figure springs to mind in which the asset structure of financial companies in Scotland and the rest of the UK is examined.

Data are available from the Bank of England on the asset composition of financial institutions [13]. Many of these, e.g. American banks, operate in all regions, but some, e.g. the London clearing banks, are almost limited to one region. By summing the assets of the Scottish clearing banks and comparing them with the assets of the other regionally-located financial institutions, we obtain a measure of Scotland's share of other non-traded income assuming that the effect of non-regionally-located financial institutions is broadly neutral. This technique was used for only two components of bank assets, holdings of government debt and advances, since these contribute most to non-traded income and a weighted average was taken to give a pro-rating figure for Scotland of 7.2 per cent.

Income from abroad was pro-rated from the UK figure using the share of the Scottish to UK gross trading profits and surpluses. The share was calculated before deduction of stock appreciation since the latter is not available on a comparable basis for Scotland and the UK.

On the outgoings side it was assumed that dividends and interest, current transfers to charities, profits due abroad net of UK taxes and taxes paid abroad were all proportional to Scotland's share of UK profits. Taxes on income

Table 5   *Combined capital account for Scotland 1973*

Uses of funds	£m.	Sources of funds	£m.
Gross fixed capital formation		Personal savings	523.7
(i) Public sector	647.0		
(ii) Private sector	736.3		
		Government savings	54.1
Book value increase in stocks	354.3	Corporate savings	683.8
		Net borrowing from abroad	476.0
Total	1737.6	Total	1737.6

refer to taxes paid and are taken from the government account. Additions to dividend and tax reserves do not figure in this account, because savings need to be recorded for each sector on a comparable basis. If tax accruals were treated as a corporate sector outgoing, they would also have to appear as part of government income.[12]

The balance gives savings before providing for stock appreciation and additions to dividend and tax reserves. It is 7.2 per cent of the comparable UK total, a figure which is below the Scottish share of UK gross trading profits and surpluses. The major difference in the two accounts is the low Scottish corporate rent receipts compared with the UK.

Conclusions

The sum of sector savings gives domestic savings and these constitute sources of funds in the combined capital account for Scotland (Table 5). Uses of funds are represented by the increase in the book value of stocks and gross domestic fixed capital formation by the public and private sectors. The stock appreciation element of the book value increase was taken from the Scottish Economic Bulletin [1], while the estimates of the physical increase in stocks and fixed capital formation were taken from unpublished estimates previously cited [8].

The estimate of fixed capital formation in [8] excludes any investment in offshore North Sea oil. In 1973 North Sea oil activity was very low with zero output and some operating expenses (mainly wages and salaries) implying trading losses on the exploration and production side. While the wages and salaries appear in households' income from employment, the trading losses are virtually ignored because the Scottish Office breaks down UK gross trading profits by order level on the basis of order level employment ratios. Thus, there is an inconsistency in the treatment of oil activity with employment income included, traded income excluded and fixed capital formation excluded.

It will eventually be necessary to eliminate this inconsistency in the published accounts; to do so, however, will involve decisions about what part of North Sea

Table 6   *Comparison for Scotland and UK of sector contributions to gross capital formation 1973 (%)*

	Scotland	UK
Personal savings	30	32
Corporate savings	39	52
Government savings	3	9
Net borrowing from abroad	28	7
Total	100	100

activity represents Scottish territorial product, the resident status of the oil companies operating there and the tax take of the Scottish government sector. Such decisions are arbitrary and are best represented by a matrix of assumptions (see Appendix) from which the reader can make a choice. For 1973, the accounts can be put on a consistent basis by ignoring employment in petroleum and natural gas exploration and production, but this was so small (less than 800 employees) that it was not thought necessary.

As expected, net borrowing from abroad in 1973 was positive and this means the current account of the balance of payments was in deficit (see Table 5). Relative contributions of different sectors, including ROW, to gross capital formation are given in Table 6 and compared with the UK. In 1973 the UK as a whole was also a net borrower from abroad, but the percentage contributions for the two countries are very different.

Reference to a net borrowing requirement obscures the fact that capital flows are a two-way process. The balance of trade in goods and services can be estimated as the difference between GDP and gross domestic expenditure (GDE) [8]. This was negative for Scotland in 1973, i.e. there was a trade deficit of £724 million, but the net borrowing requirement — £476 million — was lower so that Scotland had a net positive balance in transfer and factor payments of £250 million. As most of this will be bank interest, which is earned on lending, it looks as if Scotland was a net borrower from abroad while its financial institutions were net lenders.[13]

Although this paradox is quite common, it invites the suggestion that the current account deficit could be reduced by requiring financial institutions to channel more of their funds to domestic sectors. This argument is false, since financial institutions cannot by their lending policy alter *per se* the level of domestic savings; with domestic savings of 10 and gross capital formation of 20 the *net* borrowing requirement will remain at 10 whether all the funds are recycled within Scotland or exported. However, the lending policy of financial institutions can radically affect the form of financing and by channelling domestic savings abroad, they increase the dependence of the private sector especially on private capital flows in general and direct foreign investment in particular.

The net borrowing requirement shown in Table 5 — 8.9 per cent of GDP compared with 2 per cent for the UK — is high. Indeed, it accounts for 53 per

Table 7   *Comparison of Scottish and UK combined capital accounts*
            1973 £m.

	(1) Scotland	(2) UK	(3) (1) as % age of (2)
Personal savings	523.7	5 727.2	9.1
Government savings	54.1	1 704.0	3.2
Corporate savings	683.8	9 365.0	7.3
Total domestic savings	1261.6	16 796.0	7.5
Private gross fixed capital formation	736.3	8 236.0	8.9
Public gross fixed capital formation	647.0	5 579.0	11.6
Total capital formation	1 737.6	17 999.0	9.6

Notes: Savings are before providing for stock appreciation and total capital formation includes the book value increase in stocks.

cent of the total UK net borrowing requirement in 1973 and compares with an average of 2.5 per cent of GDP for those OECD countries in deficit in 1973. It is, however, comparable with the net borrowing requirement of developing countries such as Greece.

If all parts of the Scottish economy had performed according to what one might expect on the basis of population shares, then the Scottish net borrowing requirement would have been 9 per cent of the UK figure. That it was not is due, as Table 7 shows, to the below average (in terms of population shares) level of domestic savings and above average level of investment. Table 7 also shows, however, that savings deviated more than investment from the levels predicted by population shares, that within domestic savings the main deviant was the government sector and that within capital formation it was the public sector.

The behaviour of the public sector, therefore, was the main determinant of Scotland's high net borrowing requirement in 1973 and it is the public sector whose behaviour is most likely to change if the status of a separate region should give way to independence. It is very difficult to predict which way the net borrowing requirement would move if Scotland did become independent and such an exercise is made largely illusory by the presence of North Sea oil, but it seems reasonable to assume that much public sector activity is concerned with ironing out differences between regions and that this stimulus to investment would disappear if the backward region became independent. This would tend to reduce the net borrowing requirement.

The debate on devolution now in progress in the UK is essentially political, but employs economic arguments most of which are unproven at best or false at worst. By focussing on the situation before the emergence of North Sea oil, this paper (it is hoped) can shed some light on the economic aspects of the devolution debate and the long-term viability of the Scottish economy. It cannot, however, determine whether Scotland would be better or worse off under independence since that depends on a host of unknowns such as the productivity of public sector investment which this paper has not considered.

In terms of this debate, the relevant conclusions to be drawn are that (1) the performance of the private sector, households and corporations, has not differed significantly from that of the UK, that (2) the pre-North-Sea-oil net borrowing requirement or current account deficit has been high by OECD standards, but not by that of developing countries, that (3) it has been mainly due to the savings and investment performance of the public sector and that (4) this is the part of the economy which is most likely to change should devolution occur.

Appendix: *Impact of North Sea oil on the Scottish balance of payments*

It was stated above that the net borrowing requirement for Scotland in 1973 was estimated without taking into account North Sea oil and gas activity. Had we done so, the net borrowing requirement would have risen to about £670 million with the additional foreign borrowing of £200 million needed to finance capital formation in the North Sea and the trading losses in exploration.[14]

The reasons for ignoring North Sea activity in 1973 were given above. It cannot, however, be ignored in any forecast of the BOP, but any estimate involves so many assumptions that it is best to present a mix of assumptions from which the reader can make a choice. This is done in Table 8, where the net borrowing/lending position of Scotland in 1980 is forecast on different assumptions. The net borrowing/lending implications of North Sea gas activity have been assumed neutral, i.e. uses and sources of funds being in balance, so that Table 8 is primarily concerned with the net effect of North Sea oil on the Scottish economy.

Had North Sea oil not existed, incomes, investment, domestic savings (and by implication net borrowing) might have been expected to expand in line between 1973 and 1980 in real terms. In column 1 this 'basic' real annual average growth rate has been set at 4 per cent to reflect the improved prospects for Scotland and the world economy up to 1980. Column 1 also assumes that the rate of investment in North Sea oil will be at its peak in 1980 rather than declining (to reflect slippage in production time-tables) and as a consequence that government revenue and oil company profits will be consistent with a daily production rate of 986 000 barrels, well below the expected peak.[15] Output has been valued at $12 per barrel and as this was the mid 1974 price, all values have been converted to 1974 prices.

Column 1 next assumes that 10 per cent of government revenue accrues to Scotland as a windfall, i.e. it contributes wholly to government savings and therefore sources of funds in the capital account. It also assumes that only 50 per cent of oil company profits contribute to savings, the remainder going as interest or dividend payments or profits remitted abroad. Finally column 1 assumes that all North Sea activity falls within Scottish territorial waters. The result is a massive balance of payments deficit with a net borrowing requirement equivalent to 15 per cent of GDP.

In column 2, therefore, the 'basic' growth rate is reduced to 2 per cent — more in line with past performance — but, although the absolute value of the net borrowing requirement declines, the proportion of GDP it represents remains the same.

Columns 1 and 2 are both pessimistic about the time needed to develop

Table 8 *Scottish net lending/borrowing in 1980 under the impact of North Sea oil*

	(1)	(2)	(3)	(4)	(5)	(6)	(7)
(A) 'Basic' growth rate	0.04	0.02	0.04	0.04	0.04	0.04	0.04
(B) North Sea oil investment	1200	1200	600	600	600	600	600
(C) Oil revenue	1688	1688	3000	3000	3000	3000	3000
(D) Share of (C) accruing to Scotland	0.1	0.1	0.1	0	0.25	0.1	0.1
(E) Oil company trading profits	1296	1296	2400	2400	2400	2400	2400
(F) Oil company savings share of (E)	0.5	0.5	0.5	0.5	0.5	0.3	0.3
(G) Scottish share of North Sea activity	1.0	1.0	1.0	1.0	1.0	1.0	0.5
Net borrowing + Net lending −	+1213.8	+1108.2	−69.4	+230.6	−519.4	+412.0	+230.3
Net borrowing/lending as percentage of GDP	+14.8	+15.5	−1.0	+3.0	−6.4	+5.0	+3.0

Rates of growth are annual averages in real terms (1974 prices). Values are in £m.

North Sea oil. By contrast, column 3 assumes that oil production will be at its peak by 1980 with Government revenue from oil running at £3000 million per year and the trading profits of oil companies set at £2400 million. By contrast, oil capital formation is assumed to drop to £600 million which is the expected level at which expenditure will settle (see Chaper 4 of [17]).

This combination of assumptions moves Scotland marginally into surplus and transforms her into a net lender. It presumes, however, that 10 per cent of oil revenues are earmarked for Scotland and, while this is in line with Scotland's shares of national population and GDP, it is still a matter of great debate. On present policies, Scotland would not receive any of these revenues and if this should happen — see column 4 — Scotland would revert to a net borrower. A revenue 'take' of 25 per cent, which some have argued is the amount needed for Scotland to revitalise her industrial base, would transform her back to a net lender of significant proportions.

The current account of the BOP, therefore, appears very sensitive to the share of oil revenues accruing to Scotland (if they do not accrue to Scotland, they would appear in the accounts as a transfer payment to the rest of the UK, i.e. a BOP debit). Even more delicate is the question of oil company savings; the presence of many foreign companies in the North Sea anxious to remit profits overseas and stockholders of all companies anxious to see the high economic rent of the North Sea reflected in dividends as well as the recurring need to fund the debt interest on borrowing from financial institutions suggest that a savings ratio of 50 per cent may be too high. If this ratio fell to 30 per cent, Scotland (see column 6) would have to borrow from abroad at a rate of 5 per cent of GDP, and the level of borrowing would be almost as high in real terms as the borrowing requirement in 1973 (see Table 5).

So far, it has been assumed that all North Sea oil activity falls in Scottish territorial waters. It is true that for jurisdictional purposes the divide between Scotland and England has been set along the parallel 55° 50' and that nearly all current oil developments are north of this line. However, there is no logical inconsistency in Scots law and territory occupying different spatial coordinates, so column 7 assumes that only 50 per cent of oil activity falls within Scotland. The result is merely to reduce the net borrowing requirement rather than change the sign.

Clearly, then, Scotland could become a net lender with very favourable assumptions about oil production, oil revenues and oil company savings. These assumptions are unlikely to operate together for a long period and this confirms the picture of Scotland in the long run as a net borrower. Whether this position will ultimately be revised depends on whether the inheritance from North Sea oil activity will be higher real rates of domestic savings which in turn depends on the growth in sector incomes. It is too early to say whether North Sea oil will induce a permanently higher rate of growth in the Scottish economy.

Notes

1   When deconsolidated, these transactions between producers constitute an input—output table.
2   This is not, however, true of income from self-employment where the income is allocated by place of assessment. As is stated in Inland Revenue Statistics [11], 'the incomes of the self-employed therefore are in general allocated to the region in which they carry on business'. We therefore have to assume that cross-border flows of self-employed income cancel out, but this is not an unreasonable assumption.

3   Such a definition may sound vague, but it is impossible to make it more precise without entering the realms of political philosophy. If equity, however, is to be satisfied, then it is a question of allocating flows in terms of the method most acceptable to an impartial observer and this I have tried to do.

4   This was an error in the Scottish Budget produced some years ago by the Treasury.

5   Let the national tax rate (τ) be divided into two: τ_1 which is set to yield revenue sufficient to cover regionally managed expenditure and τ_2 which is set to cover centrally managed expenditure. Revenue is thus given by τX where X is the tax base.

    Let $X = \Sigma x_i$ where each x_i represents the regional tax base; the regional tax contribution of the ith region to centrally managed expenditure is $\tau_2 x_i$ and its share of the total is therefore x_i/X for which GDP is surely a good proxy.

6   After adjusting the figure in Table 27 of the Blue Book [5] for rent receipts by households which have already been estimated.

7   The rationale of this technique is to be found in Chapter 4 of the work on Expenditure in Scotland by Begg, Lythe and Sorley [7].

8   This was done using estimates of consumption of these items by non-household members of the personal sector in [9] and estimates of non-resident expenditure in [10].

9   Personable disposable income, which is the denominator used in the UK savings ratio, is personal income less taxes on income, national insurance (etc.) contributions, transfers abroad (net) and taxes paid abroad. It cannot therefore be estimated directly for Scotland.

10   Although this information is collected under the auspices of [11], it is in fact only reported in [6].

11   See the notes on the method of preparing GDP in the summer 1976 issue of [1]. The Scottish Office figure also includes local authorities' gross trading surpluses which needed to be deducted.

12   For a useful discussion of this and other points in social accounting, see [14].

13   This suspicion is confirmed by figures published by the Building Societies Association showing that until and including 1973, deposits by Scots exceeded loans to Scots.

14   There are at least two ways of accounting for operations which incur current costs but no revenues (such as oil exploration): one is to treat the sum of costs as capital formation, while the other is to match them by a trading loss. It should be obvious that both treatments will increase the net borrowing requirement by the same amount.

15   The relationship between production, the value of output, government revenue and oil company profits is not mechanical. The relationship adopted here is broadly consistent with [15] and [16] and owes a great deal to Chapters 4 and 5 of [17].

References

[1] *Scottish Economic Bulletin,* Scottish Office, HMSO, Edinburgh (bi-annual).
[2] *Survey of Personal Incomes, 1972–73,* Board of Inland Revenue, HMSO, 1975.
[3] Unpublished data prepared by CSO (Central Statistical Office) and consistent with Rent Total published in [1].

[4] 'Family Expenditure Survey, Income of Households in the three year period 1972–4', Department of Employment, 1976 (unpublished).

[5] *National Income & Expenditure, 1964–74,* CSO, HMSO, 1975 (Blue Book).

[6] *Scottish Abstract of Statistics,* No. 5, 1975, Scottish Office, HMSO, 197

[7] H.M. Begg, C.M. Lythe and R. Sorley, *Expenditure in Scotland 1961–71* Scottish Academic Press, 1975.

[8] H.M. Begg, C.M. Lythe and M. Majmudar, 'Gross Domestic Expenditure for Scotland in 1973 and Forecasting Gross Domestic Expenditure to 1980', 1976 (unpublished).

[9] R. Maurice (ed.), *National Accounts Statistics: Sources and Methods,* CSO, HMSO, 1968.

[10] *Input–Output Tables for the UK,* CSO, HMSO (annual).

[11] *Inland Revenue Statistics,* Board of Inland Revenue, HMSO (annual).

[12] *Local Financial Returns: Scotland,* Scottish Office, HMSO (annual).

[13] *Quarterly Bulletin,* Bank of England, Economic Intelligence Department (quarterly)

[14] G. Stuvel, *Systems of Social Accounts,* Clarendon Press, 1965.

[15] A.G. Kemp, *Taxation and the Profitability of North Sea Oil,* Fraser of Allander Institute, Research Monograph No. 4, 1976.

[16] D.I. MacKay, *North Sea Oil Through Speculative Glasses,* Fraser of Allander Institute, Speculative Paper No. 4, 1975.

[17] D.I. MacKay and G.A. Mackay, *The Political Economy of North Sea Oil,* Martin Robertson, 1975.

10

MATERIALS, RESOURCES AND PRODUCTION: AN ENGINEER'S VIEW

H. J. PICK

Introduction

In Chapter 1 of her book *Structural Change in the American Economy,* Anne Carter (1970) writes as follows:

A distinguished group of economists presented contributions in the area of production functions at a 1964 conference on income and wealth. At that meeting, Evsey Domar pointed out that the papers contained not a single reference to inputs of materials.

This certainly is no small omission, for the development of new materials and new processes, and of machinery and plant for their manufacture and conversion into final products has been one of the major vehicles of productivity improvement and product innovation since the industrial revolution, as may be seen from Table 1. This, for example, shows the explosive rate of growth of the steel industry forming the basis of industry as we know it today. (In 1865 the UK produced half the iron and steel in the world, a reminder of the fact that changes in technology and investment in this area also play a major role in international patterns of industrial production, trade and power.) The table also shows the very fast rates of growth of aluminium, and the later and even more dramatic growth of plastics in the present century.

In her book Anne Carter goes on to say:

In studies ranging over many different levels of detail and representing different time periods and nations, it was tacitly accepted that modern analysis deals with only two factors of production: labor and capital. In the interests of reality, economists concede that more detail is desirable — that labor should be specified by types of skill and education, or by how much it has 'learned by doing'; that capital may be stratified by vintage; that perhaps the classical third factor, natural resources, should be introduced if and when there is information. However, it is very much in the current tradition to deal only in primary factors: the coal and ore and steel and chemicals and fibers and aluminium foil; sausage casings, wire products, wood pulp, electronic components, trucking, and business services that establishments furnish to each other are netted out. These remain enclosed in the economic black box that converts primary inputs into final output — value added to gross national product.

Anne Carter goes on to report details of a fascinating study aimed at making

Table 1   *Growth rate of major industrial materials from 1800 A.D.*

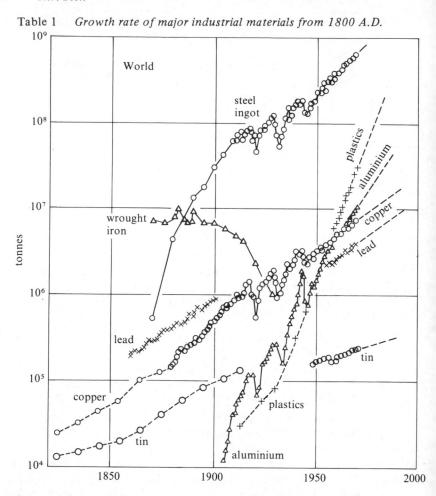

Source: Crowther (1974)

good some of these deficiencies, by bringing intermediate products in general and materials in particular into focus. She does so from the point of view of an economist. The present paper aims to describe materials and their conversion into intermediate and final products from the point of view of an engineer, in the hope that it may make some small contribution towards bridging the gap between economics and engineering.

Some aspects of the problem to be faced from this point of view in the context of the present discussion may be gained by a quotation from a 1976 NEDO monograph entitled *The U.K. and West German Manufacturing Industry 1954–72*, tl.e second paragraph of page x of which reads as follows:

One notable fact which emerges from these studies is that industrial structure (meaning throughout this monograph the sectoral distribution of output and factor inputs as well as the size structure of companies and plants) is very similar in the two countries. The similarity increased, in fact, throughout the period so that it was greater in 1972 than in the mid-1950s. This being the case, it is hardly surprising to discover that there was little difference in the countries' pattern of industrial growth. Patterns of demand that the two were trying to satisfy must have been very similar.

'Yet', the NEDO monograph goes on to say 'the difference in performance was considerable.'

Differences in performance must have been the consequence of differences other than those in industrial structure, and the NEDO report goes on to examine some of these.

But could it be that there is something fundamentally deficient in a concept of industrial structure which cannot account for differences in performance as great as those between the UK and Germany in the past twenty years?

The present paper does not attempt to answer this question but simply to describe some of the physical realities underlying industrial activity in the hope that this may prompt others to provide an answer.

In the past few decades there have been vast changes in the processes, plant and machinery available for economic production and in the technology and management environments required for their optimum operation.

In 'structural' terms their efficient exploitation will depend on the existence of specialist in-house or sub-contract plants able to invest in them on a sufficient scale to permit the employment of appropriate high-quality support services in the form of product, plant and tool design, etc., possibly on various levels of vertical and horizontal integration at the plant level which would not be detected by structural analysis at an aggregated level.

It would seem reasonable to pose the question whether differences in 'structure' which are significant from the point of view of performance are in fact discoverable at an aggregated level; or whether they are more likely to have something to do with features of the organisation of production and with capital structure which need to be described and analysed in engineering and management terms.

Materials conversion

There are now many materials and many manufacturing processes. Typical and economically still the most significant of these is steel, and a sequence for the progressive conversion of iron ore into final products is shown in Table 2. It consists of many processing stages and of many progressively changing forms of intermediate product, each requiring its own characteristic inputs of capital, labour, energy and of indirect materials.

Manufacturing as a whole may be considered as a series of parallel and inter-related sequences of conversion processes of this kind; involving the conversion of natural resources (the real primary inputs?) such as mineral ores and fuels, forests and oceans, and a range of materials from ferrous and non-ferrous metals to plastics, timber, cement and quarry products.

Table 2   *Sequence of processes and intermediate products involved in the manufacture of final products from steel.*

Mining and
benefication
|
Iron ore   £13
(plus coke, limestone and sinter)
|
Blast furnace
|
Pig iron   £58
(plus ferro alloys, scrap and fluxes)
|
Steel making processes
|
Molten steel
|
Teeming
|
Ingot   £90
|
Primary cogging mill
|
Bloom
|
Re-rolling
|
Billet   £110
|
Re-rolling
|
Hot rolled products   £140
(black bar, hot rolled strip)
|
Pickling
|
Cold roll or cold draw
|
Cold finished products   £180
|
Machining, pressing etc
|
Engineering components   £700
(car bodies, machine parts etc)
|
Assembly and finishing
|
Final products

Source: Pick (1970b)

Table 3   *The flow from natural resources to final products through the manufacturing industries*

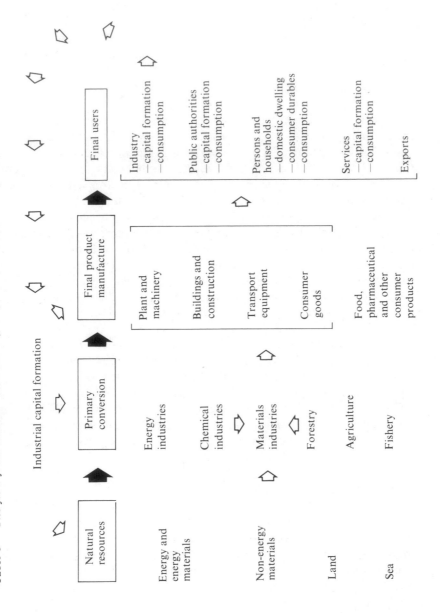

The summation of such flows is generalised in Table 3, prepared for the National Economic Development Office, which shows the progressive conversion of natural resources into the final uses, a summation of which constitutes the gross national product. The flows discussed in the present paper are indicated by hollow arrows, but these are interdependent with flows through other industries, a matter which will be discussed in a later part of the paper.

The objective from a national point of view is to maximise the output to final users in the right hand column with an optimum utilisation of available resources within the framework of current and foreseeable future physical and social constraints. Capital flows to industry have deliberately been marked as reverse flows as a reminder that, while the output of capital goods is commonly described as a final output, that part of it which is purchased by industry is from the short-term point of view in fact a consumption. Considered in this light capital formation is seen not to have any virtue in its own right, but only to be of benefit if more than adequate compensation is received in terms of future returns. Whether such returns are received in manufacturing industry will primarily depend on the quality of the engineering and marketing judgements made in firms. The greater the engineering and marketing foresight and the level of plant maintenance and improvement, the less will be the need to replace plant in a given period; the less will be the consumption of capital goods.

It is now proposed to discuss the role of materials in this overall pattern of flows, to consider their origin and destination and their part in the UK's balance of payments, finally to show how 'physical structure' materials relate to other resources such as energy and capital and to regional employment.

The role of physical structure materials and of energy materials in relation to USA GNP and population is shown in Table 4, taken from the 1973 'Final Report of the (USA) National Commission on Materials Policy'. The use of both classes of materials shows a progressive rise with GNP, but to a decreasing extent with time, because of increasing efficiency in their production and use, and as less materials-intensive service industries become a progressively increasing proportion of GNP.

The importance of materials production as an indicator of shifts in industrial power may be seen by reference to Table 5, which shows the growth of crude steel production in various parts of the world in the period 1950 to 1973. The overall effect of post-war industrial growth on a world-wide scale on steel production is shown in Table 6 and is indicative of the kind of curve which has prompted the 'Limits to Growth' controversy.

It is now proposed to consider where materials come from. In this respect there has been a very large change in postwar years, a period in which the USA has ceased to become a net exporter of materials to an extent which now makes it dependent on imports for an average of 15 per cent of its materials. In the UK too there has been progressive change in some materials, notably in iron ore, for which it has in the past relied on domestic ores, imports of which have increased from 33 per cent of consumption in 1946 to 82 per cent in 1974.[1]

Table 4   *Raw materials in the United States economy 1900–69*

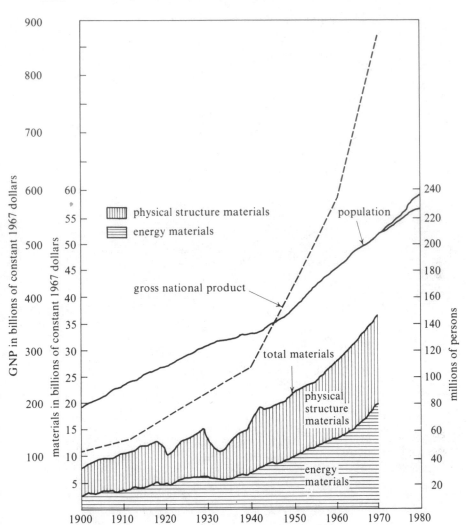

Source: Final Report of US Commission on Materials Policy, 1972

Because the UK relies on overseas imports of raw and other materials, these play an important role in its balance of payments, a fact which is well known. But the exact manner of the relation between materials and international trade requires detailed examination before reaching conclusions about its significance for the economy. The reason is that, while materials do indeed account for a significant proportion of UK imports, some 20 per cent in 1974, the UK also exports large volumes of processed materials, and these accounted for some 14 per cent of UK exports in 1974. Materials are also an essential ingredient for the

Table 5   *World crude steel production 1950–73 (1973 figures estimated)*

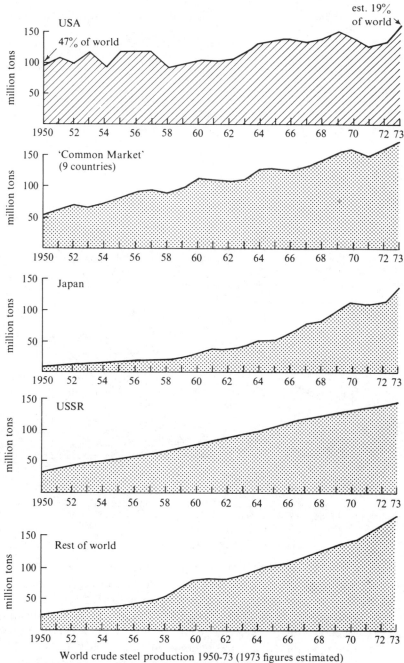

World crude steel production 1950-73 (1973 figures estimated)

Source: Proceedings of Conference on *Requirements for Fulfilling a National Materials Policy*

Table 6   *World crude steel production 1870–1968*

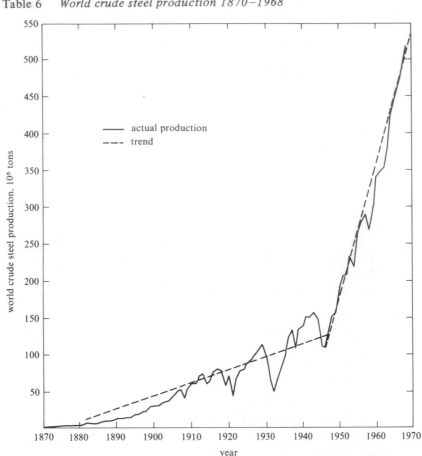

Source: Layton (1964) 'Economics and Management', *Journal of the Iron and Steel Institute*, June, p. 713

UK's exports of machinery and transport equipment, which accounted for 37 per cent of UK exports in 1974.

The importance of considering both imports and exports of materials may, for example, be seen by reference to the case of ferrous metals. While there is a deficit in this class of materials resulting from the import of ores, this is more than compensated for by the export of worked ferrous metals, so that there is an overall trade surplus for ferrous metals as a whole. Indeed there is a large international trade in steel; and the important factor from the point of view of the balance of trade here is not to conserve imports, but to be a successful competitor in this international market. There is also a positive balance for worked non-ferrous metals, although there is an overall deficit in this class of materials resulting from the large import bill for ores and ingots. For plastics too the UK

Table 7   *UK trade in materials compared with trade in other commodities and materials-containing machinery 1972*

£ million

	Imports	Exports	Balance
Engineering materials			
Total	1509	1066	− 443
Iron and steel	362	393	+ 31
Non-ferrous metals	622	360	− 262
Plastics	143	176	+ 33
Crude rubber	47	28	− 19
Wood, lumber, cork	253		− 253
Miscellaneous building materials	34	61	+ 27
Miscellaneous minerals	48	49	+ 1
Other materials			
Total	600	204	− 396
Textile fibres	213	108	− 105
Paper pulp etc.	172		− 172
Others	215	96	− 119
Chemicals (excluding plastics)	508	785	+ 277
Fuels	1242	239	−1003
Machinery and transport equipment			
Total	2238	4014	+1776
Non-electrical machinery	1040	2054	+1014
Electrical machinery and appliances	528	662	+ 134
Transport equipment	670	1298	+ 628
Other manufactured commodities			
Total	2471	2497	+ 26
Manufactures of leather and furs	47	67	+ 20
Manufactures of rubber	42	96	+ 54
Manufactures of wood and cork	142	11	− 131
Manufactures of paper and paperboard	311	102	− 209
Textile yarn, fabrics and articles	370	445	+ 75
Non-metallic mineral manufactures n.e.s.	531	560	+ 29
Manufactures of metal n.e.s.	136	290	+ 154
Other	892	926	+ 34
Food and beverages	2471	660	−1696
Total imports	11138	9746	−1392

n.e.s. = not elsewhere specified
Source: Annual Abstract of Statistics

has a positive trade balance, albeit not one with as great a surplus as would be desired.

An overall picture of the role of materials in UK trade may be seen from Table 7 which shows that over half the negative trade balance in engineering-type materials is the result of imports of wood etc., and that paper pulp etc., accounts for the largest single item of trade deficit among the other materials.

It follows that the major role of materials and of the materials industries from the point of view of the balance of trade is to underpin UK export trade, directly through the export of processed materials and indirectly through the

Table 8   *Destination of materials by category of final demand*

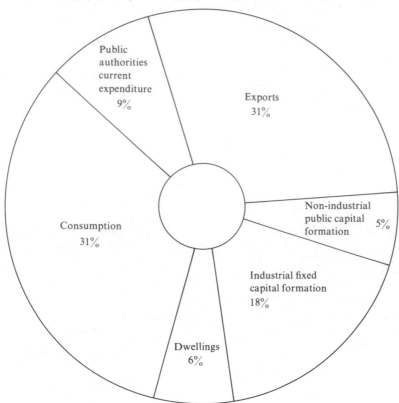

Source: P. Becker, PhD Thesis, University of Aston, 1976

export of engineering products. The large gearing obtained in the latter respect may be seen from the fact that the total import content (including materials and all other inputs) of the engineering and allied products which constitute the major exports of the UK manufacturing industries is in the range of 12 to 18 per cent.

The role of materials in this context is also emphasised by the chart in Table 8, which gives the destination of the output of the materials industries by various categories of final demand, as calculated from input–output tables by P. Becker at the University of Aston. Roughly one third each of the output of the UK materials industries has its destination in exports and in personal consumption, with approximately a further one third divided between the various forms of capital formation.

The part of GNP deriving from manufacture involves the conversion of raw materials into final products for domestic use and for export and it is now proposed to consider the resources consumed in the conversion process.

Table 9   *World aluminium production 1963*
Value added and value of output at various processing stages

Process	Product (Price)	Tons (millions)	Increase in value (millions)	Value in dollars (millions)
Mining	Bauxite ($ 8/ton)	30	240	240
Ore refining	Alumina ($ 75/ton)	12	660	900
Aluminium smelting and refining	Primary aluminium ingot ($ 450/ton)	6	1800	2700
Fabricating and casting	Wrought semis and castings ($ 1000/ton)	6	3300	6000

The build-up of value in the progressive conversion of Bauxite to wrought semi-finished aluminium products.

Source: Pick (1970b)

An approximate impression of resources consumed in conversion may be obtained by assuming that prices are approximately equal to costs (price = cost + profits). And for the case of steel it is seen from Table 2 that the original iron ore accounts for only a small proportion of the cost of final engineering components, the remaining price build-up being the result of the flow of other resources — capital, manpower, energy and indirect materials etc.

A similar pattern emerges from Table 9, which shows the progressive increase in 'value'[2] during various stages of the processing of aluminium in 1963, the value of the original as-mined bauxite again accounting for a small proportion of the cost of wrought semi-finished aluminium products. A similar pattern emerges for other materials, for plastics for example, and this accounts for the fact that the 300 per cent increase in the price of crude oil in 1973 only led to an increase of the order of 30 to 40 per cent in the price of many plastics products.

The picture of manufacturing which emerges from the above description is one of a sequence of process stages, with a range of resources flowing into each of the stages. This is symbolised in Table 10, which also indicates that there are transport, warehousing and other costs between process stages, and that industrial structure and geographical location will therefore play a part in manufacturing costs and efficiency.

What are the resources required for materials conversion? First capital; and Table 11 shows that approximately 40 per cent of the total stock of UK capital was in the materials producing industries and a similar proportion of the plant and machinery, a fact which should be noted in the context of the commonly advocated panacea of substitution as a possible response to supply constraints, or to other changes in economic circumstances. Substitution of materials can only take place by reinvestment in physical capital on a corresponding scale; sometimes, because new materials create new problems in design, production and use, also the creation of a new technology and education base. The time scale required for effective substitution on a large scale will obviously also be large.

Table 10   *Symbolic representation of physical inputs into manufacturing processes*

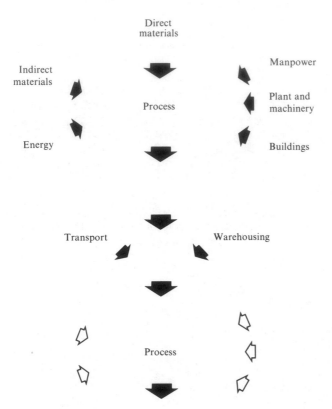

Energy plays an important role in materials processing and the relative energy inputs to various UK industries are shown in Table 12. This shows that the materials-producing industries are far greater users of energy than the engineering industries, and one consequence of this fact is that the indirect uses of energy by engineering firms through their purchases of materials is far greater than their direct purchases. This matter has been quantified, using input—output analysis, in work done at the University of Aston (Pick and Becker, 1975a) and the results are shown in Table 13. An interesting consequence of such an analysis is that resort to the obvious may not prove the correct course of action in the face of a supply constraint. An engineering firm wishing to contribute to a national objective of energy conservation can probably do so more effectively by considering the design of its products so as to minimise the use of materials rather than by attention to the energy consumed on its own premises.

Table 11   *Comparison of capital stock in the UK materials-producing and the materials-using industries 1974, at replacement cost*

(The total capital stock in UK manufacturing in 1974 was as follows:

Plant	32050	
Vehicles	1320	
Buildings	14027	
Total	47397)	

	Plant and machinery	Vehicles	Buildings	Total
Materials-producing industries	£ 7367 m. (41%)	£197 m. (21%)	£3088 m. (40%)	£10 652 m. (40%)
Materials-using industries	£10 741 m. (59%)	4737 m. (79%)	£4717 m. (60%)	£16 195 m. (60%)
Total	£18 108 m. (100%)	£934 m. (100%)	£7805 m. (100%)	£26 847 m. (100%)

Table 12   *Distribution of all direct energy purchases in heat-equivalent units by materials-producing and engineering-type industries in 1968*

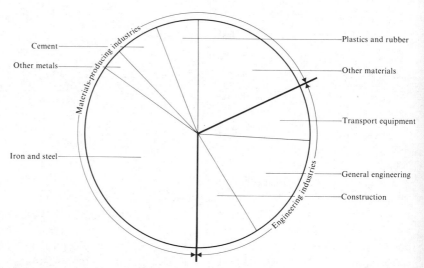

Source: Pick and Becker, 1975a

In parenthesis it may be noted that any serious attempt to save energy on a national scale cannot be effected by consideration of energy consumption in automobile manufacture, which in the USA is, according to Hirst (1972), only a small fraction of the total energy consumed on the road, and is indeed smaller than the energy used in petroleum refining itself.

Table 13   *UK direct and indirect purchase of all energy by the engineering-type industries in 1968*

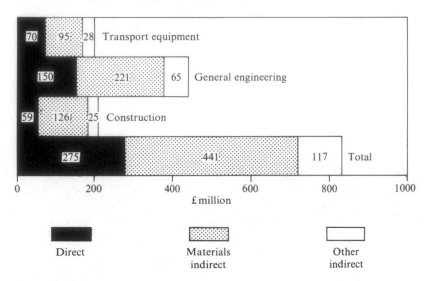

Source: Pick and Becker, 1975a

The final point which it is intended to discuss is the relation between materials and regional employment. Input—output analysis can be used to estimate both direct and indirect employment in various materials industries both on a national and on a regional basis. For the UK such a computation has been carried out by Becker at the University of Aston and some of his results are reproduced in Tables 14, 15 and 16. Any substitution of materials for one another or any differentials in the growth of various materials industries relative to each other will therefore have a differential effect on regional employment.

Input—output analysis can also be used to assess the resource intensities of any material and to assess the effect of absolute and relative changes in its use on resources. A systematic way of doing so has been developed by Becker, and two 'isoquants' showing the notional effect of the substitution of steel for aluminium on imports and on capital stock are shown in Table 17. No precision is claimed for these results, particularly for those on capital stock, but the curves are included to illustrate that input—output analysis, and no doubt other econometric techniques, can in principle be used to predict the effects of potential changes in technology on industry and on the economy generally; provided there is effective collaboration between engineers and economists.

Perhaps more attention should in future be devoted to this kind of Technology Assessment.

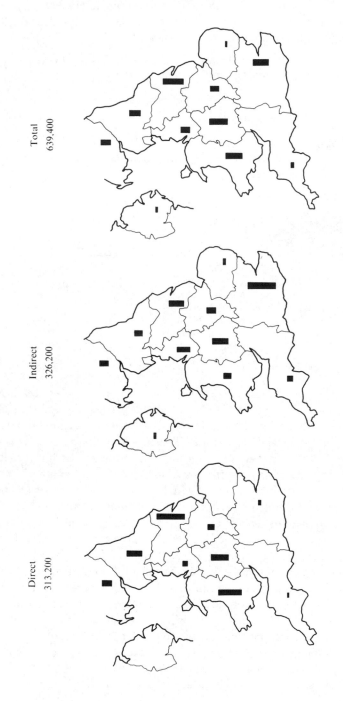

Table 14   *Regional distribution of employment in steel manufacturing, 1968*

Total
639,400

Indirect
326,200

Direct
313,200

Source: P. Becker, PhD Thesis, University of Aston, 1976

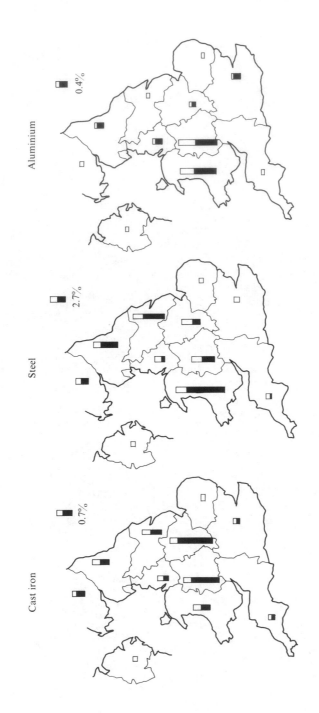

Table 15 *Regional intensity of employment in materials manufacturing. Direct (black bar) plus indirect (white bar) employment in materials manufacturing as percent of total regional employment, 1968. The percent labelled on each diagram is the average for the UK, and acts as a scale*

Cast iron   Steel   Aluminium

0.7%   2.7%   0.4%

Source: P. Becker, PhD Thesis, University of Aston, 1976

Table 16   *Regional intensity of employment in materials manufacturing. Direct (black bar) plus indirect (white bar) employment in materials manufacturing as percent of total regional employment, 1968. The percent labelled on each diagram is the average for the UK, and acts as a scale.*

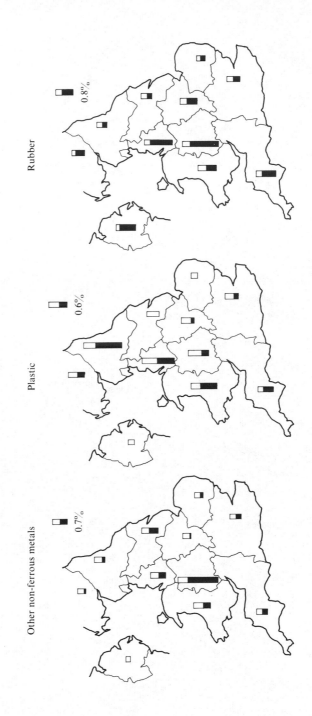

Other non-ferrous metals

0.7%

Plastic

0.6%

Rubber

0.8%

Source: P. Becker, PhD Thesis, University of Aston, 1976

Table 17   *Resource isoquant curves for substitution of steel by aluminium in engineering and construction industries. Effect on imports and capital stock. Each curve passes through combinations of π_a (cost of aluminium required to replace £1 of steel) and 100 k (percent of steel substituted for) with equal Δg (changed resource requirement)*

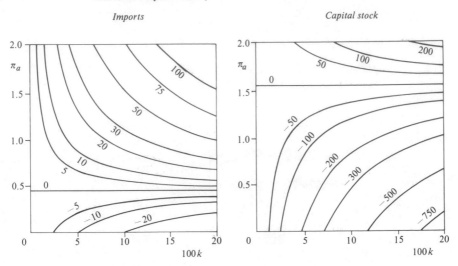

Source: P. Becker, PhD Thesis, University of Aston, 1976

It is proposed to conclude with a simple illustration of the importance and widespread effect of even mundane engineering decisions.

Table 18 shows three possible ways of manufacturing a steel shaft with the dimensions illustrated at the top of the diagram. If such a shaft, which has a finished volume of 8 cubic centimetres, were machined from solid, 18 cubic centimetres of bar material would be required to start with, 10 cubic centimetres being degraded to swarf. Simple changes in design and/or manufacturing method of the kind illustrated in Table 18(*b*) will reduce the initial material requirement to 9 cubic centimetres. The implementation of design improvements of this kind on a national scale would effectively imply a halving of the steel capacity required for a given level of engineering output; also a corresponding saving in energy and other inputs required in steel making. Widespread percentage savings of this order may not be practical. But much smaller savings could have important effects; particularly as many stages are often involved in the conversion of natural resources into final products (as for example in Table 2), each of which may involve some waste of material. Table 19 shows the cumulative effect of wastage at each of ten process stages. To produce one ton final output, if each process stage requires an input weight of 1.1 tons for each 1 ton of output, implies an input requirement of 2.6 tons to the first stage.

Table 18   *The effect of design and manufacturing method on the input weight required to produce a component having a volume of 8 cubic inches*

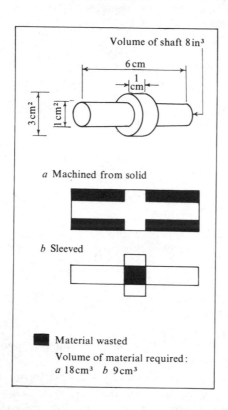

a Machined from solid

b Sleeved

■ Material wasted

Volume of material required:
a 18cm³   b 9cm³

A reduction in the ratio of input weight to output weight at each stage from 1.1 to 1.05 would reduce the initial input requirement from 2.6 to 1.6 tons. The actual yield achieved in industrial processes depends on engineering, management and investment decisions, and it is a summation of these which determines whether a nation produces a reasonable output from its resource base.

Notes

1   It may here be worth noting that the commonly expressed view that the international problem of raw materials supply primarily involves the developing countries is not borne out by the facts, except for the case of mineral fuels. In 1973 the developing countries only accounted for 5.1 billion dollars worth of the export trade in ores and minerals out of a total of 13.9 billion. The non-communist industrialised countries on the other hand accounted for 7.1 billion and the Communist countries for 1.7 billion. The total of all world exports in that year was 559 billion of which

the non-communist industrialised countries accounted for 392 billion
(Edward R. Fried, *Science*, 20 February 1976, p. 641).

2 The concept of 'value added' as used by the economist is a puzzling one to
   the engineer, who, at present levels of profit would tend to describe the
   items usually included in 'value added' as his manufacturing costs. Would
   it be more accurate to talk about 'costs added' or 'resources consumed'
   rather than about 'value added'?

Table 19   *Weight of material input required per ton of final output in a
             10 stage process sequence with a ratio of (input weight)/
             (output weight) = a; for a = 1.05 and 1.1*

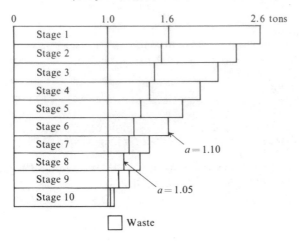

Source: Becker and Pick (1975b)

References

Previous relevant publications by the author and by P. Becker on which the
present paper is based and to which reference may be made for details of sources
and methods:

Pick H. J. (1968a), 'Materials and Processes in Component Production — The
    Interrelation Between the Requirements of Fabrication Service and Cost',
    in *Avoidance of Failures in Fabrication and Service*, Iliffe, London.

    (1968b), 'The Role of Materials in Engineering and in the Economy', *Metals
    and Materials*, 1968, vol. 2, pp. 263–79, 293.

    (1970a), 'The Challenge of the New Materials Technology', *Metals and
    Materials*, vol. 4, pp. 145–51.

    (1970b), 'Some Economic Consequences of Technical Decisions', *Materials
    Science and Engineering*, vol. 10, pp. 301–23.

    (1973), 'The Relation Between Materials and Manufacturing Systems', in
    G. H. Gudnason and E. N. Corlett, (ed.), *Development of Production
    Systems and the Need for Further Research*, 2nd International Conference
    on Production Research, Copenhagen, Taylor and Francis, London.

Pick H. J., and Becker P. (1975a), 'Direct and Indirect Uses of Energy and
    Materials in Engineering and Construction', *Applied Energy*, vol. 1, no. 1.

(1975b), 'Resource Implications of Materials Waste in Engineering Manufacturing', *Resources Policy,* vol. 1, no. 3.
Becker P. (1976a), *Materials, Engineering and the Economy: An Input–Output Study of Technical Decisions in the U.K.,* PhD thesis, University of Aston, Birmingham, England.
(1976b), 'The Economic Role of Engineering Materials in the U.K.', *Resources Policy* vol. 2, no. 3.
(1976c), James Watt Memorial Lecture, University of Aston.

Other references

Carter A. P., *Structural Change in the American Economy,* Harvard University Press, 1970.
Crowther J., 'Substitution – for Communal or Sectional Benefit', Proceedings Harwell Conference on 'Conservation of Materials', 1974, p. 263.
Hirst E., 'How Much Overall Energy Does the Automobile Require?', *Automotive Engineering,* July 1972.
NEDO, *The Plastics Industry and its Prospects,* 1972
NEDO, *The U.K. and West German Manufacturing Industry 1954–72* (ed. M. Panić), 1976.
USA Department of Commerce, *1963 Census of Manufactures.*
USA Congress, *1972 Final Report of the National Commission on Materials Policy,* Chairman: J. Boyd.
USA Congress, Office of Technology Assessment (1974), Proceedings Hennicker Conference, *Requirements for Fulfilling a National Materials Policy.*

11

UNEMPLOYMENT IN BRITAIN: AN INTERPRETATION OF THE LAST TWENTY-FIVE YEARS

J. TAYLOR

The underlying trend in Britain's unemployment rate has continued to drift upwards during the past 25 years. A higher and higher unemployment rate has been associated with each successive major slump, with the result that unemployment in the current recession (1975–76) will be nearly three times as great as occurred during the recessions of the 1950s and early 1960s (see Figure 1).

What has gone wrong? Can we deduce from this increasingly poor performance that attempts to control the economy have become less and less successful? It is easy to blame the policy makers (and their advisers) for the long-run deterioration of Britain's unemployment rate, but such casual condemnation is too glib. This paper investigates the possibility that something fundamental has happened to the unemployment rate with the result that the target rates of unemployment set during the 1950s and early 1960s are now out of reach. Not all economists, indeed, agree with this view. Blackaby [1976], for example, argues that the target rate of unemployment has been too high in recent years and he consequently recommends policy makers to return to the target of 1½ per cent set during the 1950s and early 1960s.

In this paper, the movements in the unemployment rate during the period 1951–75 are analysed with a view to discovering whether the long-run upward trend in unemployment is simply a consequence of the economy being run at a lower pressure of demand or whether the upward trend is the result of 'other factors'. Isolating and identifying these 'other factors', if they exist, is clearly crucial if an efficient target unemployment rate is to be set.

The upward drift in unemployment

The UK unemployment rate is plotted in Figure 1 alongside three other indicators of labour market pressures — the vacancy rate, the Wharton index of spare capacity and the CBI index of capacity utilisation.[1] It is immediately apparent from casual inspection of the data that the unemployment rate has behaved remarkably differently, in one important respect, to the other three variables:

I am indebted to the Nuffield Foundation for their financial support and to the DHSS for guidance on the available data. I am also grateful to John Cope, Harvey Armstrong, John R. King, Geof Smith and to my colleagues at the University of Lancaster for many helpful discussions.

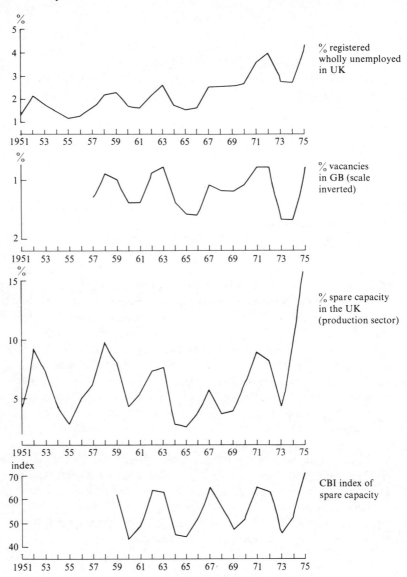

Figure 1.   Unemployment and three indicators of the pressure of demand

there is a distinct upward trend in the unemployment rate, implying that unemployment shifted against the other variables during the study period. This is most clearly seen in Figure 2, which shows three distinct relationships between unemployment and the spare capacity index, one for each of the three periods 1951–61, 1962–66 and 1967–75. It is this upward drift in the unemployment rate that is the main focus of attention in this paper.

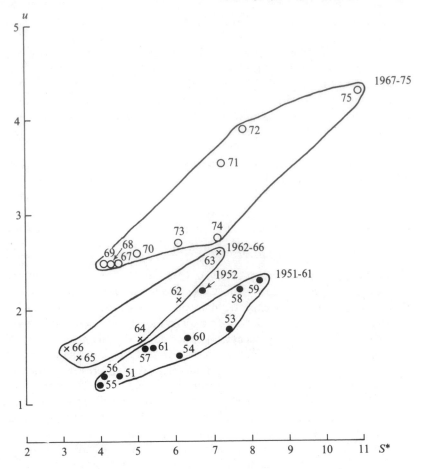

Figure 2.   The upward drift in unemployment

u = % registered unemployed (UK)
$S^* = \frac{1}{2}S_t + \frac{1}{3}S_{t-1} + \frac{1}{6}S_{t-2}$ (t = year)
S = % spare capacity (Wharton index)

Note
Unemployment was unusually high in 1952 due to the serious recession in
the textile industry.

A theoretical framework and some hypotheses

Until quite recently, economists were generally of the opinion that post-war
movements in the unemployment rate in Britain were the result almost entirely
of fluctuations in *aggregate* product demand. During the last few years, however,
attention has been focused on the possibility that movements in unemployment

have been caused by factors other than changes in aggregate product demand. Increasing support is being given to the view that the 'equilibrium unemployment rate' has increased substantially. This means either that the underlying trend in unemployment has risen because of an increase in the mis-matching between the demand and supply for labour, thus resulting in more structural unemployment; or alternatively, that the upward trend in unemployment may have resulted from a change in the job search behaviour of unemployed workers. The latter may have become 'more fussy' in accepting job offers (Reder [1969]) thus causing an increase in the time spent unearthing an acceptable job.

This suggests that Britain's unemployment rate has increased for one (or more) of three reasons: (i) because of a fall in aggregate demand; (ii) because of an increase in the structural mis-matching between the demand and supply for labour; or (iii) because unemployed workers now deliberately spend more time in searching the market for a job. Each explanation is now examined in turn:

A fall in aggregate demand

Fluctuations in aggregate product demand are transmitted to the labour market through the demand for labour. More specifically, the demand for labour depends directly upon the expected demand for goods and services, which suggests that any model purporting to explain movements in unemployment must allow for the effect of changes in expected product demand.

It could be argued that the trend increase in the unemployment rate during the last decade is the consequence of a persistently lower pressure of demand than during the first two post-war decades.[2] Although the spare capacity index denies this hypothesis, it is conceivable that the way in which the spare capacity index is constructed (i.e. joining the assumed full capacity output peaks by linear segments) could have resulted in the serious underestimation of productive potential during the last decade (and therefore the serious underestimation of spare capacity). It cannot be denied that this is indeed a possibility, though in view of the available evidence from other indicators of the pressure of demand, such as vacancies and the CBI index (see Figure 1) it seems most unlikely that this has occurred. Moreover, the fitting of linear segments to the output peaks is constrained by the rule that the trend fitted to the output peaks must follow the underlying output trend. In other words, the spare capacity index is designed to correlate closely with the corresponding measure of deviations from the underlying output trend (Taylor and McKendrick [1975]).

It is worth noting that the implication of the argument that spare capacity has been seriously underestimated since the mid 1960s is that the underlying growth in the productive capacity of the economy has been considerably higher than is reflected in the underlying trend of real output. Figure 3 shows two capacity ceilings: Q^* is the capacity ceiling calculated from the spare capacity index given in Figure 1, and $\bar{Q}$ is the capacity ceiling that would have existed if the relationship between the unemployment rate and spare capacity had remained stable throughout the study period (i.e. for the 1951–61 relationship

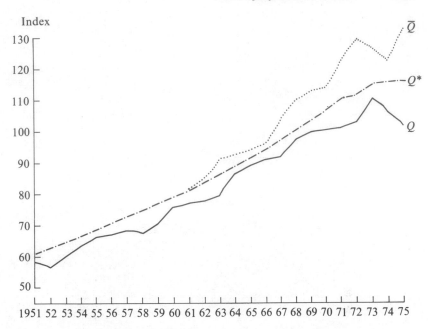

Figure 3.   The index of industrial production and two estimates of capacity output

Q = index of industrial production.

Q^* = estimated capacity output $\left(Q^* = \dfrac{Q}{100 - S}\right)$, S = estimated spare capacity.

$\bar{Q}$ = estimated capacity output assuming the 1951–61 relationship between u and S^* in Figure 2 held throughout the study period

i.e. $\bar{Q} = \dfrac{Q}{100 - \bar{S}}$ where $\bar{S} = S$, 1951–61

$\qquad\qquad\qquad\qquad$ = estimated from u and the 1951–61 regression of u and S, 1962–75

shown in Figure 2 to hold during 1962–75). For the purpose of this paper, and in the continued absence of evidence to the contrary, it is therefore taken as *given* that the pressure of demand has not been seriously underestimated during the past decade compared to earlier years.

An increase in the structural mis-matching between the demand and supply for workers

Structural unemployment occurs if changes in consumption patterns and production techniques take place too quickly. Such changes lead to differential growth rates in the demand for labour between different occupations, industries and different geographical locations; and the supply of labour may not respond quickly enough to the changing pattern of labour demand, with the result that the extent of mis-matching between labour demand and labour supply gets

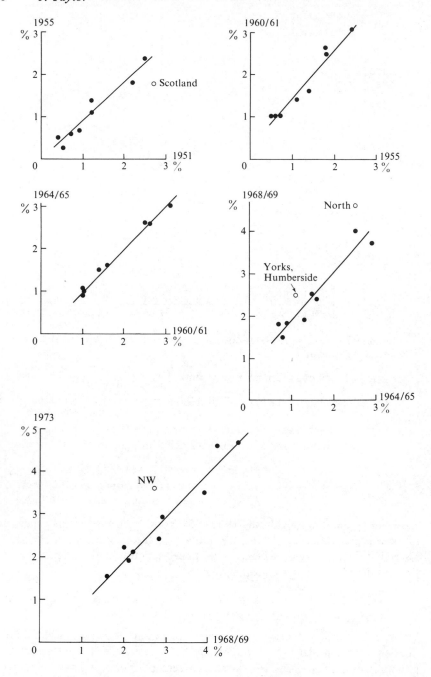

Figure 4.   The regional distribution of unemployment in Britain:
changes over time

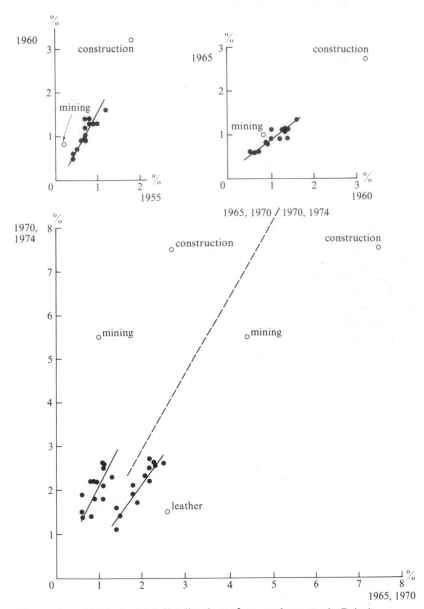

Figure 5.   The industrial distribution of unemployment in Britain: changes over time

worse. The mis-matching arises either because of frictions to the geographical movement of labour (resulting in greater disparities in unemployment), or because of the occupational immobility of labour (resulting in greater industrial/ occupational disparities in unemployment), or more often because of a combination of both.

The process of structural change is a continuing one and structural unemployment is a continuous feature of a changing economy. But the question we seek to answer now is whether structural unemployment has increased in Britain during the study period, particularly during the 1960s (when the shifts in unemployment were most apparent). If structural unemployment had increased, we would expect this to be reflected in a change in either the regional or industrial patterns of unemployment, or both.[3] An examination of the regional pattern of unemployment at successive peaks in the business cycle indicates a high degree of stability during the study period. Figure 4 shows very little change in the regional distribution of unemployment from one cyclical peak to the next. Further investigation reveals that this is true for both male and female unemployment rates. The only significant exception to this generally stable pattern of regional unemployment rates is that Yorkshire and Humberside and the North experienced an upward shift in their unemployment rates relative to other regions between 1965 and 1970. But the overall stability of the regional unemployment patterns suggests that the upward drift in unemployment cannot be explained by structural changes.

The result is not so clear cut when we look at the industrial pattern of unemployment and how it has changed over time. Figure 5 shows that the industrial pattern of unemployment was far less stable than the regional pattern. Nevertheless, only the mining industry exhibited a severe change in its relative position in the industrial unemployment league.

Even if the pattern of industrial unemployment had changed markedly during the period, however, we could not have concluded categorically that changing consumption or production techniques were responsible. The composition and characteristics (e.g. sex, age, skill, etc.) of workers differs considerably between industries and it is conceivable that factors affecting the unemployment rate from the supply side of the labour market could disturb the industrial pattern of unemployment. The point of this qualification will become apparent in the next section.

On the evidence available,[4] it cannot be argued that changes in consumption patterns or in production techniques have caused any substantial increase in structural unemployment — apart from isolated instances — during the study period. (This does not deny, of course, the existence of serious structural problems in particular regions of Britain.) Nevertheless, it could still be argued that there have been major changes occurring throughout British industry which would cause unemployment to increase across the board (i.e. in all industries and in all regions). One possibility (mentioned by Metcalf and Richardson [1972] but subsequently dismissed by them) is that the increasing rate of wage inflation in the late 1960s and again in the 1970s caused employers to switch into labour-saving capital equipment. The ratio of the price of labour to the price of capital,[5] however, fluctuated around a long-run downward trend during the study period. Clearly, the high labour content in the production of capital goods precludes any significant shifts in the price of labour relative to the price of capital. Furthermore, there are no discernible shifts in the capital/labour ratio, which proceeded along a smooth exponential trend.[6]

The unemployed have deliberately lengthened the duration of their search for a job

Unemployed workers search the market for a job in order to acquire more information about available jobs. They search in order to 'produce' job offers (Alchian [1970]). But for how long will an unemployed worker search? Unemployed workers will not necessarily accept the first job offer that comes along. They may prefer to turn down the offer in the hope of producing a better offer by continuing their search (Holt and David [1966]). Theoretically, the search process can be regarded as an investment in human capital (Mortensen [1970]). Turning down a job offer involves further search, and therefore further costs in the form of earnings foregone (plus any additional costs), and the searcher will consequently decide how long to search by attempting to maximise the rate of return on these costs. In essence, the theory argues that the search will continue whilst the present value of expected benefits from searching outweighs the expected costs. There is no point in prolonging the search if the expected costs of doing so outweigh the expected benefits. We can therefore expect a longer period of search if either search costs fall or if the expected benefits from searching increase.

The worker's expectations about forthcoming job offers, which determine the expected benefits of search, will be strongly influenced by the pressure of demand in the labour market. More, and better, job offers will be forthcoming during periods of high demand, thus raising the expected benefits of search. This will have the effect of inducing more voluntary quits and prolonging the duration of job search (Corry and Laidler [1967]). But even though job search is likely to intensify during periods of high demand, we know from experience that this positive effect on unemployment will be swamped by the negative effect of a high pressure of labour demand.

Fluctuations in the pressure of demand, however, can only account for *fluctuations* in job search activity. More pertinent to an explanation of the upward drift in Britain's unemployment rate is the possibility that continuously falling search costs, due to increasing unemployment benefits, have had a positive effect on the duration of job search. More exactly, higher unemployment benefits *relative to income foregone* have reduced job search costs substantially during the study period, leading some researchers to argue that this is a major reason for the upward trend in Britain's unemployment rate (Gujarati [1972], Maki and Spindler [1975]).

Whichever way the figures are presented, there can be no doubt that the costs of job search for most unemployed workers were greater at the beginning of the study period than they were at the end. Two sets of hypothetical calculations can be used to demonstrate this fact. First, the Department of Health and Social Security has calculated the ratio of standard weekly unemployment benefit (plus the earnings related supplement where appropriate) to net average weekly earnings for a typical male manual worker. Six ratios are calculated for the years 1948–74, ranging from a single man to a married man with four children. Figure 6 shows the ratio for a married man with two children, the main features being the upward trend in the standard rate/net earnings ratio between 1960 and 1967 and the sudden upward shift in the total benefit/net earnings ratio in 1966 due to the appearance of the earnings related supplement.

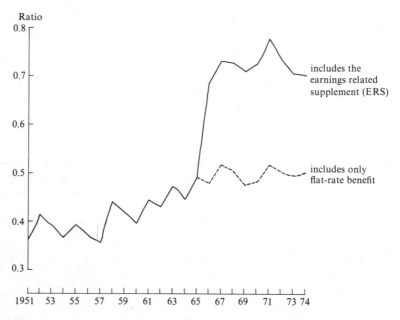

Figure 6.   Ratio of unemployment benefit to net earnings (for a male manual worker on average earnings and with two children)

Note

Net earnings = average weekly earnings (male manual workers) in October each year plus family allowances less tax and national insurance contributions.

Unemployment benefit = flat-rate benefit plus the ERS (October each year).

Source: *Social Statistics* (1973 and 1974), DHSS.

There are two disadvantages with these data as they stand. First, the ratio of unemployment benefit to net earnings ignores the fact that tax payments fall as earned income falls. (Note that unemployment benefit is not taxable.) Second, the ratio of unemployment benefit to net earnings ignores the fact that many wives work. Since the activity rate of married women in the work force doubled during the study period (i.e. from 22 per cent in 1951 to 42 per cent in 1971), we should consider the effect of unemployment on net household income.

The implication of extending the calculations to cover the entire household is that employment decisions are made within the context of the entire household. Net household income has therefore been calculated for a man on average earnings under different family and employment circumstances (see Table 1).

Table 1   *Net household annual income under different employment and family circumstances*

Employment status of husband and wife	Net household annual income for households in which husband is unemployed as a percentage of net income for households in which husband is employed for full year			
	1951/52	1961/62	1971/72	1974/75
Case 1: married man, 2 children				
Husband unemployed 26 weeks, wife = housewife	68	73	96	95
Husband unemployed 26 weeks, wife at work full year	78	80	94	92
Case 2: married man, 0 children				
Husband unemployed 26 weeks, wife = housewife	68	73	91	88
Husband unemployed 26 weeks, wife at work full year	78	78	90	88
Case 3: single man				
Unemployed 26 weeks	64	67	83	79

See appendix 1 for more details.

The annual financial costs of unemployment for a typical household, but under different circumstances, are discernible from Table 1. Net annual income for a household in which the husband is unemployed is expressed as a ratio of net annual income for a household in which the husband works the full year. This is done for four tax years: 1951/52, 1961/62, 1971/72 and 1974/75. It should be noted that the 1971/72 and 1974/75 calculations include the earnings related supplement (ERS). The picture emerging from the calculations is unambiguous: the costs of searching for a job, measured in terms of the loss of income relative to the income that would have been earned assuming no unemployment, have fallen considerably during the study period, particularly since the introduction of the ERS. In 1951, for example, a family with two children in which the wife was working and the husband was unemployed for six months (both assumed to be manual workers and on average weekly earnings) would have had a joint net household income equal to 78 per cent of the joint income they would have had if the husband had not been unemployed. By 1971, this percentage had risen to 94 per cent. Similar increases occurred for single men, but to a smaller extent.

It is clear from Figure 6 and Table 1 that the costs of job search have fallen substantially during the study period, particularly since the introduction of the ERS. But this reduction in the costs of job search is not universal: the calculations presented in Table 1 apply only to men. We should also consider the costs of unemployment to females. For a number of reasons, the costs of job search (measured in terms of income foregone) will be greater, on average, for women than for men. About three quarters of married women workers are not eligible for unemployment benefit.[7] Hence we see the well-known phenomenon of married women disappearing from the registered workforce during recessions.[8] Those women actually covered for unemployment under the national insurance scheme are treated in the same way as single men irrespective of their marital status. But they differ from single men in an important respect: they earn less. As a consequence, a larger proportion of women receive only the flat-rate benefit (i.e. 36 per cent for women compared to 24 per cent for men in 1968 and 24 per cent compared to 16 per cent in 1974).[9] The reason for this is simply that women earn only half as much as men (on average) and a smaller proportion therefore qualify for the earnings related supplement.

Hence, given that search costs have fallen more on average for men than for women, we would expect the duration of job search to have increased more for men than for women (other things being equal). In terms of the relationship between unemployment and spare capacity (as in Figure 2), we would expect to see a greater upward drift in the male unemployment rate than in the female unemployment rate. Figure 7 shows that this has been the case. Indeed, the upward drift was confined entirely to men. There is no evidence of a corresponding upward drift for women. This is perhaps surprising, since even though far fewer women experienced a fall in search costs, and even though the fall was considerably less for women than for men, we would still have expected to see an upward drift. Indeed, unemployment data for the Census years of 1961 and 1971 indicate that the unemployment rate for single women has risen relative to that of married women.[10] This drift is reflected in the upward trend in the ratio of unemployed single women to unemployed married women (Figure 8), particularly after 1966. Further disaggregation of the unemployment/spare capacity relationship is required before firm conclusions can be reached about the upward drift. It would be particularly interesting to know to what extent the upward drift differed between different types of worker.

Although males have, on average, a greater financial incentive to register their unemployment than females, this may not be the only reason for the widening gap between male and female unemployment rates. First, it may be argued that employers have found it increasingly more attractive (economically) to employ women rather than men. The fact that the relative wage of females to males (for full-time manual workers) remained virtually static during the 1960s discounts such an explanation (assuming relative productivity rates also remained unchanged). Second, and more plausibly, the upward drift may have been concealed for females because of the phenomenon of unregistered unemployment, which is likely to have become more important as married female workers have become a larger proportion of the female workforce. Estimates of unregistered female unemployment for the study period, however, do not lend support to this explanation (see Appendix 3). Adding unregistered unemployment to registered unemployment simply leads to an increase in the slope of the unemployment/spare capacity relationship (Figure 9), as indeed we would expect from the discouraged-worker hypothesis. There is no evidence of an upward drift.

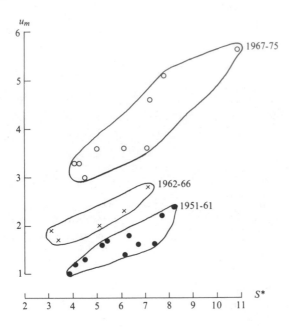

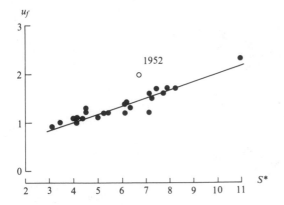

Figure 7.   The upward drift in unemployment: males (u_m) and females (u_f)

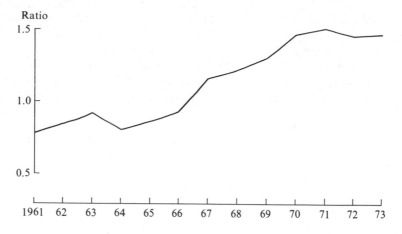

Figure 8.   Ratio of single to married women unemployed

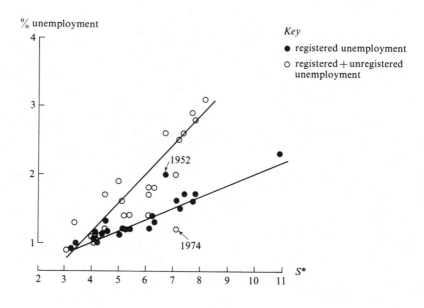

Figure 9.   The upward drift in unemployment: registered and
unregistered females

Key
· registered unemployment
∘ registered + unregistered
  unemployment

An empirical analysis of unemployment in the UK 1951–75

Finally, we turn to the estimation of the effect of higher unemployment benefits on the UK unemployment rate. As our previous analysis of the regional pattern of unemployment and changes in this pattern did not produce any evidence that structural unemployment has increased during the study period, the following statistical analysis of the UK unemployment rate proceeds on the assumption that two factors *only* account for most of the movements in Britain's unemployment rate:

(i) changes in the expected demand for goods and services, and

(ii) the significant fall in job search costs.

The object of the exercise is to investigate the relative contribution of these two factors to the unemployment rate.

The influence of aggregate product demand on the unemployment rate derives directly from the fact that employers determine their labour requirements according to their expectations about the future demand for their product. In so far as these expectations are based upon recent trends in the pressure of demand, we can use a distributed lag of the index of spare capacity as our measure of expected product demand. But in addition to this, there may be sudden changes in business confidence which override expectations based on recent trends in the pressure of demand. The July 1966 deflationary measures, the 1974 miners' strike and the concurrent oil crisis are the most obvious examples during the last decade. Such sudden changes in business confidence may have a marked effect in the short run on the demand for labour, causing temporary 'shake outs' (or perhaps encouraging employers to play a waiting game if they had otherwise intended to take on more labour).[11] The index of business confidence constructed by the Confederation of British Industry (CBI) from its quarterly investigation is used to qualify the index of spare capacity as a measure of expected product demand.

On the supply side of the labour market, it was previously argued that the marked reduction in the costs of job search due to increases in the ratio of unemployment benefit to net earnings could have caused a rise in unemployment by inducing a lengthening of the period of job search. Indeed, one of the main purposes of increasing the benefit/earnings ratio by adding an earnings related supplement (in 1966) was to encourage unemployed workers to search the market more thoroughly before accepting a job offer, part of the reasoning behind this being that there would be long-term gains to the economy resulting from a more efficient matching of workers to jobs. Earlier work on quantifying the effect of rising unemployment benefits on unemployment (Maki and Spindler [1975]) used the ratio shown in Figure 6. But since it would be useful to quantify the separate effect of the earnings related supplement, two variables are used in this analysis to measure the effect of benefits, i.e. the flat rate benefit/earnings ratio and the ERS/earnings ratio.

The results of the time-series regression analysis are presented in Table 2.

Since the business confidence index was available only from 1958, two sets of regressions were run, one for the whole period with the confidence index excluded and the other for the shorter period (1959—75) with the confidence index included. Before we discuss the results, a potentially serious problem needs to be recognised: it is by no means certain that the two benefit/earnings ratios simply reflect the influence of reduced job search costs on unemployment. In the first place, the flat-rate benefit/earnings ratio follows an upward time trend and could thus be acting as a proxy for any other 'missing' explanatory variables which are also on an upward time trend. Second, and perhaps more importantly, the ERS/earnings ratio closely resembles a shift dummy since it has a value of zero from 1951 to 1966 and suddenly shifts upwards in 1967,[12] fluctuating very little from 1967 until the end of the period. Thus it could be acting, like its partner, as a proxy for any other missing explanatory variable which suddenly appeared at the same time as the earnings related supplement.

One possibility is that higher overheads due to the introduction of the redundancy payments and industrial training schemes in the mid 1960s caused employers to dis-hoard labour to reduce their overheads. But the dis-hoarding explanation can account for only a once-and-for-all shake out of labour, not for the permanent upward drift in unemployment which we have observed. Alternatively, redundancy pay could be used by those made redundant to finance a longer period of unemployment. Another possibility is that the appearance of the Selective Employment Tax (SET) in 1967 was responsible. But if this was the case, we would have expected an upward shift in the unemployment rate of the service sector relative to that in the production sector (since SET was imposed only on service industries). Since no such shift in this ratio occurred, we must conclude that SET is unlikely to have been responsible for the shift.

The regression results presented in Table 2 broadly confirm our expectations.[13] All three unemployment rates (total, males and females) are sensitive to changes in the pressure of demand and to changes in business confidence, though the female unemployment rate is less sensitive than the male rate. The lower coefficients on the spare capacity and business confidence variables in the female unemployment rate equation (equation 6) are explained by the appearance of unregistered unemployment during recessions.

On the supply side, the results support the contention that increases in the flat rate/earnings ratio and the introduction of the ERS in 1966 both had an effect on unemployment. The results suggest that the flat-rate benefit contributed an additional 0.3 of a percentage point to the unemployment rate during the 1950s and the early 1960s, and a further 0.1 of a percentage point in the late 1960s (according to the estimated coefficient on FRB_{-1} in equation 5). The introduction of the ERS in 1966 apparently had a substantial effect, causing an upward shift in the unemployment rate by about 0.7 of a percentage point between 1966 and 1967. The effect of both the FRB and the ERS is (as predicted) even greater when males are considered alone.

Time-series analysis suggests that the ERS had a considerable effect on unemployment immediately after its introduction. This contradicts the findings of Mackay and Reid [1972], who argue that the rise of unemployment benefits had only a weak effect on male unemployment. This discrepancy between the two results can, however, be explained: Mackay and Reid derive their estimate from cross-section data. The fact that variations in unemployment benefit between redundant males have not resulted in any substantial inter-individual variation in the duration of their unemployment does not necessarily imply that a change in benefits *over time* would not have an effect on the duration of each individual's unemployment duration. We are seeing the familiar discrepancy between time-series and cross-section results: a 'flatter' relationship is observed in the cross-section analysis. It should also be noted that the sample used by Mackay and Reid contained only males made redundant by the engineering sector in the Midlands. Generalising from their results would therefore be dangerous.

Table 2   *Time series regression analysis of unemployment in the UK, 1951–75*

Equation number	Dependent variable	Constant term	S^*	BC_{-1}	FRB_{-1}	ERS_{-1}	$\bar{R}^2$	DW
1951–75								
1	u	−1.42 (2.58)	0.23 (9.51)		4.23 (3.37)	3.59 (5.65)	0.93	1.71
2	u_m	−2.73 (3.15)	0.29 (7.45)		7.03 (3.56)	6.13 (6.14)	0.93	1.52
3	u_f	0.38 (4.75)	0.16 (12.55)				0.88	1.67
1959–75								
4	u	−1.09 (1.00)	0.22 (7.83)	−0.005 (2.10)	3.75 (1.61)	3.42 (4.69)	0.93	1.54
5	u_m	−2.20 (1.41)	0.29 (6.96)	−0.007 (2.16)	6.15 (1.85)	5.80 (5.57)	0.94	1.32
6	u_f	0.46 (6.43)	0.15 (12.97)	−0.004 (4.30)			0.94	1.95

(   ) = t-ratios. Note: 'female equation' was run from 1953 since 1952 was untypical (see Figure 4).

Definition of variables

u, u_m, u_f, = rate of unemployment (total, males, females) in the UK.
S^* = index of spare capacity in the UK production sector (see text).
BC = index of business confidence. Source: CBI surveys.
FRB = flat rate unemployment benefit ÷ average net earnings. Source DHSS, *Social Security Statistics 1974*.

The relative contribution of each of the explanatory variables to changes in the UK unemployment rate can best be seen by considering the years during

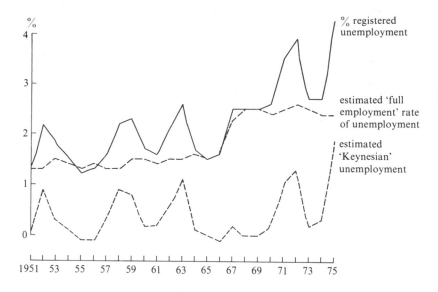

Figure 10.   The estimated 'full-employment' rate of unemployment and 'Keynesian' unemployment in the UK 1951–75

Note

The 'full-employment' rate of unemployment was calculated from equation 4 in Table 2 by assuming that S^* was at its full employment level (arbitrarily set at $S^* = 4\%$) throughout the study period. BO_{-1} was set at its average value for the study period and UB_{-1} and ERS_{-1} assumed their actual values.

which the changes in unemployment were large (see Table 3). To take an example, between 1966 and 1967 (the year of the supposed 'shake out' of labour) the unemployment rate increased from 1.6 per cent to 2.5 per cent, about 60 per cent of this increase being 'explained' by the introduction of ERS and the remaining 40 per cent by the fall in expected demand. By contrast, the rise of unemployment from 2.6 per cent to 3.5 per cent in 1970–71 and the rise from 2.7 per cent to 4.3 per cent in 1974–75 were both explained entirely by a fall in expected demand. It is particularly worth noting that the rise in unemployment between 1974 and 1975 was as much a result of the seriously depressed state of confidence in British industry (due to the miners' strike, the oil crisis and two General Elections) as it was a result of the low level of demand. Only in 1976 are we seeing the full effects of the depressed state of aggregate demand during the past two years.

A useful feature of the unemployment regressions is that they can be used to estimate the 'full-employment' rate of unemployment. Once this has been done, 'Keynesian' unemployment is obtained as a residual by subtracting the estimated

Table 3 *Actual and predicted change in unemployment*

	Actual change Δu	Predicted change Δu^*	Error $\Delta u^* - \Delta u$	Estimated contribution of each variable to actual change			
				S^*	BC_{-1}	FRB_{-1}	ERS_{-1}
Total unemployment (u)							
1959–60	−0.6	−0.6	0.0	−0.4	−0.2	−0.1	0
1964–65	−0.9	−0.5	0.4	−0.4	−0.2	0.2	0
1966–67	0.9	1.0	0.1	0.3	0.1	−0.1	0.7
1970–71	0.9	0.6	−0.3	0.5	0	0	0
1972–73	−0.8	−0.7	0.1	−0.4	−0.2	0	−0.1
1974–75	1.6	1.2	−0.4	0.8	0.4	0	0
(1975–76)		(0.9)		(0.9)	(0)	(0)	(0)
Male unemployment (u_m)							
1959–60	−0.6	−0.9	−0.3	−0.5	−0.2	−0.1	0
1963–64	−0.6	−0.6	0.0	−0.6	−0.3	0.3	0
1966–1967	1.1	1.6	0.5	0.4	0.1	−0.1	1.2
1970–71	1.0	0.8	−0.2	0.6	0	0	0.1
1972–73	−1.5	−1.0	0.5	−0.5	−0.3	−0.1	−0.2
1974–75	2.0	1.7	−0.3	1.1	0.6	0.1	−0.1
(1975–76)		(1.2)		(1.2)	(0)	(0)	(0)

Predicted change obtained from equations 4 and 5 (Table 2) by predicting annual rates and subtracting ($\Delta u^* = u_t^* - u_{t-1}^*$). To obtain the relative contribution of each explanatory variable to Δu the estimated coefficient on each explanatory variable was multiplied by the variable in question and the changes were then calculated as above. Errors due to rounding.

full-employment rate from the actual unemployment rate. Both these rates are shown in Figure 10 (together with an explanation of how the full-employment rate was estimated). The picture is clear. The full-employment rate of unemployment rose very slowly during the period 1951–66 from around 1.3 per cent to around 1.6 per cent. It then took an upward leap in 1967 rising to a peak of 2.6 per cent in 1971 and finally fell towards 2.4 per cent in 1975. As far as 'Keynesian' unemployment is concerned, only one feature really stands out: the recessions of 1972 and 1975 were both more severe than any previous recession during the study period. The 1975–76 recession, for instance, was twice as severe as the 1958 recession.

Conclusions and policy implications

Two explanations of the annual changes that have occurred to Britain's unemployment rate during the last 25 years have been offered in this paper. Short-run fluctuations in the unemployment rate are explained by corresponding fluctuations in expected product demand. This is the familiar Keynesian explanation.

In addition to these short-run fluctuations in expected demand, however, the underlying trend in the unemployment rate drifted upwards during the first half of the 1960s and then suddenly shifted upwards to a new higher level between 1966 and 1967. This paper has argued that a plausible explanation for these two phenomena is the fall in search costs for unemployed workers due to higher unemployment benefits. The main piece of evidence is the disparate behaviour of male and female unemployment rates during the study period. Using the unemployment benefit/earnings ratio as a measure of search costs, it is clear that these costs have varied substantially between individuals. This paper has suggested that this may be the reason for the widening gap between male and female unemployment rates and between the unemployment rates of single and married women.

It is important to note that this paper does not argue that unemployment has drifted upwards because of an increased preference for unemployment as opposed to work. There can be no doubt, for instance, that the vast majority of redundant workers would have preferred to stay in their old jobs rather than join the ranks of the unemployed. This paper simply argues that unemployed workers are likely to spend more time searching for a job in 1975 than they did in 1951 (allowing for differences in the demand for labour), the reason being the considerable fall in search costs during the study period. The increase in the unemployment benefits/earnings ratio, particularly the introduction of the ERS, has permitted the unemployed to search the market more carefully. To use Mackay's and Reid's [1972] phrase, 'job snatching' has been deliberately discouraged.

The main policy implication of this paper is that the 'full employment' rate of unemployment rose by about one percentage point (from $1\frac{1}{2}$ per cent to $2\frac{1}{2}$ per cent) between the 1950s and the first half of the 1970s. This does not imply, however, that $2\frac{1}{2}$ per cent should be accepted as a policy target (given that nothing is done to change the 'full-employment' rate of unemployment), since a $2\frac{1}{2}$ per cent unemployment rate could well require a pressure of demand which is 'too high' in terms of its inflationary consequences. It would be more sensible to expand the economy more and more gradually as the $2\frac{1}{2}$ per cent full-employment limit is approached.

But all this assumes that the full-employment rate of unemployment will remain unchanged. This is entirely uncertain. There can be no guarantee that it will remain stable. According to the research reported in this paper, the duration of job search will remain at its present level (allowing for the effect of fluctuations in aggregate demand and for possible structural changes) unless the costs of search rise noticeably. This would require earnings to rise faster than unemployment benefits during the next few years. If this is regarded as undesirable either for equity reasons or on the grounds that the increased duration of search has resulted in long-run net benefits for both the worker and the employer (in so far as it raises labour productivity by improving the matching of workers to jobs), then we must simply accept the permanently higher unemployment rate as an intended consequence of the higher benefits. Perhaps more research on the benefits of job search to the economy is required.

Appendix 1   Data used in assessment of Personal Income Tax for Table 1

	to nearest £			
	1951/52	1961/62	1971/72	1974/75
Annual gross earnings: men (includes family allowance)	445	818	1655	2576
women	236	403	822	1405
Earned income relief	$\frac{1}{5}$	$\frac{2}{9}$	$\frac{2}{9}$	
Personal allowance: married men	190	240	465	865
single person	110	140	325	625
Wife's earned income relief	110	140	325	625
Child allowance: under 11	70	100	155	240
11 to 16	70	125	180	275
Tax rates	50 at 0.15p 200 at 0.255p SR = 0.455p	60 at 0.0875p 150 at 0.2125p 150 at 0.3125p SR = 0.3875p	SR = 0.3875p	SR = 0.33p
Reduction per child			42	52
National insurance + graduated contributions:* men	13	41	88	155
women	2	6	8	10

*No tax relief on national insurance contributions after 5 April 1965.
Sources of data:
British Labour Statistics, Historical Abstract (table 41) and 1973 Yearbook (table 26).
D. of E. *Gazette,* December 1975 (table 123).
DHSS, *Social Security Statistics 1974* (tables 40.01, 40.04).
Inland Revenue, Annual Reports, Cmnd 3508 (table 23), 5804 (table 30).

Appendix 2   Unemployment benefit

	to nearest £			
Duration of unemployment	1951	1961	1971*	1974*
Case 1: married man,† 2 children Unemployed 26 weeks	77	166	510	688
Case 2: married man,† 0 children Unemployed 26 weeks	55	120	414	520
Case 3: single man Unemployed 26 weeks	34	75	318	410

*Includes the ERS (6 weeks of ERS for 8 weeks unemployment; 24 weeks ERS for 26 weeks unemployment). See *Social Security Statistics 1974,* table 46.05 for more details, especially note (6).
†Wife = housewife.

Appendix 3   Unregistered unemployment

There are two methods of estimating unregistered unemployment. Method 1 is to regress workers who have opted out of the national insurance scheme (*T)* on a pressure of demand variable and a trend term (to allow for the time trend in *OPT*). A 'full-employment' value of the pressure of demand is then fed into the estimated regression equation to obtain estimates of the 'full-employment' opted-out workforce (*OPT**). *OPT** − *OPT* is the estimate of unregistered unemployed. The other method is to fit linear segments to *OPT* to obtain an estimate of *OPT**. Whichever method is used, the estimates have to be deflated before being added to the registered unemployed since the unregistered unemployed are mainly part-time workers. A factor of 0.5 was therefore applied to the estimates to convert them into full time equivalents. Joshi Heather kindly permitted me to use her *OPT* data. See 'Cyclical Variations in the Employment of Opted-Out Married Women and Pensioners, G.B. 1961−74', Economic Adviser's Office, DHSS (mimeo).

Notes

1 These indicators of the pressure of demand are discussed elsewhere (Taylor and McKendrick [1975]). See Klein [1960] and Phillips [1963] for theoretical discussions of spare capacity and see Klein and Preston [1967], Taylor, Winter and Pearce [1970], Briscoe, O'Brien and Smyth [1970] and Hilton and Dolphin [1970] for empirical work which supports the use of the Wharton trend-through-peaks procedure (despite its limitations as a measure of the pressure of demand).

2 It should be noted that in so far as changes in the structure of industry may have resulted in a relative expansion of the more cyclically sensitive industries, the average level of spare capacity would have increased. But this would be fully reflected in the spare capacity index since it is a weighted average of 16 separate industry indices.

3 See the Department of Employment *Gazette*, 'Trends in the composition of the unemployed', March 1973.

4 See Bowers *et al.* [1970], [1972], for a more detailed analysis of the structural aspects of unemployment in the UK.

5 Capital costs were approximated in various ways, using alternative discount rates. No marked shifts in the ratio of labour costs to capital costs seem to have occurred during the study period.

6 For the UK manufacturing sector, $\ln(\ln(K/L))$ fluctuates around a linear time trend.

7 The percentages of males, single women and married women who opted-out of the national insurance scheme were, respectively, 1.3%, 8.4%, and 73.2% in 1962 (and 1.4%, 10.7% and 74.7% in 1973). See *Social Security Statistics 1974*, DHSS, table 40.12, p. 200.

8 See Taylor [1966], [1968] and [1970].

9 See *Social Security Statistics 1974, op. cit.,* table 1.32, p. 22. The 1973 Department of Employment sample survey of the unemployed indicated that the ratio of unemployment benefit to expected earnings was 0.42 for men and 0.30 for women. See the D. of E. *Gazette,* March 1974.

10 The unemployment rates in 1961 and 1971 were as follows: 1.3% and 3.8% for men, 0.9% and 1.8% for single women, and 1.2% and 0.7% for married women.

11 As suggested in Taylor [1972], [1974].

12   All the explanatory variables are lagged one period, with the exception of
      the spare capacity index which is formed from a simple distributed lag
      (see Table 2).
13   To test for the stability of the relationships, the regressions were run for
      the period 1951–66. The estimated regression coefficients changed very
      little (apart from that on S^* in the u_m equation which fell to 0.19 from
      0.29).

References

Alchian, A.A., 'Information Costs, Pricing and Resource Unemployment' in E.S.
     Phelps (ed.), *Microeconomic Foundations of Employment and Inflation
     Theory* (Macmillan, 1970).
Blackaby, F.T., 'The Target Rate of Unemployment' in G.D.N. Worswick
     (ed.), *The Concept and Measurement of Involuntary Unemployment*
     (George Allen and Unwin, 1976).
Bowers, J.K., Cheshire, P.C. and Webb, A.E., 'The Change in the Relationship
     between Unemployment and Earnings Increases: A Review of Some
     Possible Explanations', *NIER*, 1970.
Bowers, J.K., Cheshire, P.C., Webb, A.E. and Weeden, R., 'Some Aspects of
     Unemployment and the Labour Market, 1966–71', *NIER*, 1972.
Briscoe, G., O'Brien, P. and Smyth, D.J., 'The Measurement of Capacity
     Utilisation in the United Kingdom', *Manchester School*, 1970.
Corry, B. and Laidler, D., 'The Phillips Relation: A Theoretical Explanation',
     Economica, 1967.
Gujarati, D., 'The Behaviour of Unemployment and Unfilled Vacancies: Great
     Britain 1958–71', *Economic Journal*, 1972.
Hilton, K. and Dolphin, H., 'Capital and Capacity Utilisation in the UK: Their
     Measurement and Reconciliation', *Oxford Bulletin*, 1970.
Holt, C.C. and David, M.H., 'The Concept of Job Vacancies in a Dynamic Theory
     of the Labour Market', in *The Measurement and Interpretation of Job
     Vacancies*, NBER, 1966.
Klein, L.R., 'Some Theoretical Issues in the Measurement of Capacity',
     Econometrica, 1960.
Klein, L.R. and Preston, R.S., 'Some New Results in the Measurement of
     Capacity Utilisation', *American Economic Review*, 1967.
Mackay, D.I. and Reid, G.L., 'Redundancy, Unemployment and Manpower
     Policy', *Economic Journal*, 1972.
Maki, D.R. and Spindler, Z.A., 'The Effect of Unemployment Compensation on
     the Rate of Unemployment in Great Britain', *Oxford Economic Papers*,
     1975.
Metcalfe, D. and Richardson, R., 'The Nature and Measurement of Unemploy-
     ment in the UK', *Three Banks Review*, 1972.
Mortensen, D.T., 'Job Search, the Duration of Unemployment and the Phillips
     Curve', *American Economic Review*, 1970.
Phillips, A. 'An Appraisal of Measures of Capacity', *Papers and Proceedings of
     the American Economic Association*, 1963.
Reder, M.W., 'The Theory of Frictional Unemployment', *Economica*, 1969.
Taylor, J., 'Estimating Labour Reserves: A Study of the Furness Sub-Region',
     Manchester School, 1966.
     'A Regional Analysis of Hidden Unemployment in G.B., 1951–66', *Applied
     Economics*, 1971.
     'The Behaviour of Unemployment and Unfilled Vacancies: Great Britain,

1958–71. An Alternative View', *Economic Journal,* 1972.

Unemployment and Wage Inflation (Longman, 1974).

Taylor, J. and McKendrick, S., 'How Should we Measure the Pressure of Demand', *Lloyds Bank Review,* January 1975.

Taylor, J., Winter, D. and Pearce, D., 'A 19 Industry Quarterly Series of Capacity Utilisation in the UK, 1948–68', *Oxford Bulletin,* 1970.

12

INDUSTRY AND TECHNICAL PROGRESS

C. F. CARTER

At the Belfast meeting of the British Association in 1952, it was decided to appoint a committee 'to study the problems of speeding up in industry the application of the results of scientific research'. After a period of preliminary work, the committee was reconstituted in 1954 with the Royal Society of Arts and the Nuffield Foundation as joint sponsors with the BA, and with the title of the 'Science and Industry Committee'; and, endowed from various sources with what then seemed the princely sum of £20 000, it set to work. I was its Chairman and Professor B.R. Williams, now Vice-Chancellor of the University of Sydney, was Secretary: and we were joint authors of three reports, published as books by the Oxford University Press. These were *Industry and Technical Progress* (1957), *Investment in Innovation* (1958), and *Science in Industry* (1959).

In writing these books we were trying to solve a problem, which we defined in the following terms:

First, in the present situation of the U.K., increases in production are closely dependent on the application of scientific and technical knowledge. Second, a high rate of increase of production is desirable not only for its own sake, but also to give relief from the overstrain which has affected the British economy since the war. Third, the special position of Britain in international trade makes it dangerous for the country to fall behind the technical progress of its competitors. The cost of technical stagnation would not simply be stagnation in the standard of living: it would be a falling back, a mounting up of economic and political problems which would become worse the longer they were neglected. The United Kingdom's position has, and will continue to have, something of the nightmare quality of running up a descending escalator.[1]

Twenty years have passed since these words were written, and the nightmare continues. Though the British standard of living has risen substantially, much greater rises have been recorded in most other developed countries: so that Britain is now numbered among the poorer nations of Western Europe. The design, technical sophistication, quality or durability of British products have too often proved inadequate. Social, economic and political problems have multiplied, to a degree which endangers the stability of a society long renowned for its stable equanimity.

In 1956 we certainly hoped for better than this, though we recognised that there were problems deep in the structure of the British economy and social system which would be difficult to solve. Were we wrong to identify as a main issue that a country like Britain must seek an improvement in its economic situation by making a better and more scientific use of its brains? Or, did we, rightly identifying the problem, fail to find the true hindrances to its solution? Or was our analysis broadly correct, but ineffective because we, and other contributors to the discussion, failed in persuading people to take the necessary action? Or are we to suppose that the British brain, even when applied, is ineffective compared with (say) the German, the Japanese or the French?

These are not questions which I can hope to answer in a single paper: and indeed they are of such importance, and are so obviously related to the British Association's concern with the interface between science and public affairs, that I venture to suggest that the Council of the BA might renew its interest of twenty years ago. The identification of the application of science as *a* main influence on economic success can, in my view, hardly be wrong, even though we might now wish to join as a second main influence the achievement of a motivation to work hard. Therefore it remains important to identify and to remove the hindrances to the application of science, and I believe that the BA could still play a part in this. What I propose to do here is to suggest a few ideas, stimulated by a rereading of what Bruce Williams and I wrote, and by my subsequent experiences. One problem which economists have never properly solved is that of dealing, clearly and accurately, with the factor of production labour. It is not enough to enumerate broad categories of workers: the factor consists of actual occasions or periods of application of specific skills or qualities, and these applications are exceedingly varied. I fear that Professor Williams and I may have contributed to the unthinking enthusiasm of the period for expanding the total number of scientists, technologists and technicians, without any sufficient analysis of just what they would do. To be fair to ourselves, we did in fact discuss particular shortages and particular uses[2] but our policy proposals were too vague. Twenty years on, facilities in higher and further education for science and technology have been expanded far beyond the capacity of the schools to provide candidates willing and able to take the courses: despite this, a greatly increased flow of scientists, technologists and technicians has become available to the economy: and the movements of salaries offer no general evidence of excess demand. Does this mean that part of the hindrance to the application of science in industry has been removed, or was the problem misconceived?

It will help, I think, if the use made of scientists and technologists is considered under the following heads:

1   First-rate creative ability in formulating major ideas based on research, in the conduct of development, and in design.
2   Scientists and technologists for more routine or minor research, development and design, and for assisting the top-flight creative minds.
3   Scientists and technologists for the oversight of production, for marketing and for other functions not research and development.

4 Technicians for the support of all the above.
5 The diffused understanding and appreciation of science in society (and particularly in government and the civil service and among non-scientific managers).

It is evident that a great contribution to our economic problems could be made if there was a fuller availability or better use of first-class creative minds. This is a somewhat mysterious subject, for high creative ability is difficult to define, and both its origin and the precise way in which it is used are obscure. I did a little exploration in my presidential address to this Section in 1961,[3] and I regret that others have not taken the matter further. Since 1961, three things have happened which render it rather less likely that first-rate creative minds will be fully developed, rightly distributed or retained. First, the school system has become much more preoccupied with improving opportunities for those of low ability than with giving special treatment to the gifted. Second, the whole educational system has acquired some additional degree of ideological bias against productive industry, whose effects are reinforced by the greater security offered by many non-industrial occupations, and the high pay thought to be available in a prodigal public sector. But, third, though this pay differential certainly exists in some areas and is unfavourable to the attraction of high ability to industry, it is also true that taxation policy (and, more recently, incomes policy) have made it more difficult to use exceptional rewards to attract high ability to places where it is needed, and more likely that some of it will be lost to other countries.

For this group, therefore, I recommend the adoption of what is said to be the policy of the Soviet Union: that is, an unashamedly elitist education for the highest level of ability (not, of course, socially elitist, but providing special educational resources): vigorous efforts to lead public opinion − and, particularly, opinion in the educational world − to an understanding of the importance of industrial excellence: and a readiness to regard high rewards for top levels of ability not as an occasion for envy and control but as an appreciation of an essential contribution. It is anomalous that we reward pop stars more highly than Nobel prize winners, who are a very scarce resource indeed: the difference in treatment is a consequence of our institutional and social structure, rather than a straight result of market forces. Since the contribution of creative minds often arises from their ability to use the interaction of different disciplines, it would be well if the education offered to this special group gave opportunities for that interaction, rather than being completely specialised.

There is no substitute for the taking of special measures to develop and retain the best. No multiplication of the number of scientists of inferior or narrower ability will make good inadequacy at the highest levels. But lesser abilities can do simpler or more routine things, and provide support and assistance to creative genius. I see no reason to believe that the present supply of qualified scientists and technologists is inadequate, at this more humble level, for research, development and design: if there were a continuing shortage, I would expect it to show itself in an upward pressure on salaries, even in our regulated world.

Professor Williams and I, however, drew attention to the inadequate involvement of qualified manpower in functions other than research and development, and particularly in the control of production.[4] On reflection, I think we were only partly right. There are some sorts of production, perhaps only a few, which as they grow in scale and technical complexity will require the use of more fully trained scientists and technologists 'on the shop floor': the atomic energy industry is a possible example. There are other sorts of production in which it is a consequence of technical advance that the monitoring of the production and the treatment of breakdowns require fewer highly trained men. Thus, an advanced electronic telephone exchange is programmed to identify and bring to attention its own faults, and repairs which in an earlier technology required a lot of craft skill may involve, not a higher skill, but simply the ability to plug in a standard replacement unit. This means that the number of staff needed to 'keep things going' will fall considerably, though very high levels of expertise will be needed at the design stage.

The balance between these two tendencies requires investigation, but I would think it reasonable to expect that the propensity to 'design out' production and maintenance problems is a growing one. In some industries (such as steel) there may be an interim stage in which relatively highly qualified people monitor the process on banks of instruments, having displaced craftsmen who used to do the job in a cruder way. But, even there, the line of advance is surely towards instruments which set in motion their own corrective actions, and record progress automatically. I therefore doubt whether it is true that, in the later stages of the application of science to industry, 'a much larger number (of scientists and technologists) . . . is needed, in the control of production processes – a stage reached by the U.S.A.'[5] American use of PhDs in production departments, though obviously having some advantages, may be predominantly a waste of their training. *Some* additional manpower, qualified at a rather high level, will be needed because of the increasing complexity of design; but the presumption of the economic necessity of having a vast army of scientists and technologists now seems to me mistaken.

A better case can be made for having a very large increase in the number of technicians. An enlargement of development and design will need them; and in the production process the complexity of machines and instruments will increasingly need technician rather than craft training. Many countries, however, seem to find it easier to expand the number of graduates than to expand the number of sub-graduate technicians. Again, this is not entirely wasted, since an apparent over-training may provide a flexibility in changing circumstances which a more narrowly trained person would not possess. However, in many industries there are institutional reasons (recruitment ages, career structures, etc.) why the graduate and technician streams are separate and difficult to mix. Although, with increasing numbers, graduates are percolating down into jobs previously regarded as appropriate to technicians, this transfer is imperfect, and some significant technician shortages are likely to persist.

Thus far, my argument has favoured attention to quality, rather than number, of graduates; and a continued priority for the training of sub-graduate technicians. (Why does Britain continually lose the opportunity to provide two-year Junior Colleges?) These are the scientific professionals, but there remains the need for a much higher level of scientific understanding among non-professionals. As we said in *Science in Industry:* 'There can be few people in positions of high responsibility in the United Kingdom who have not had to study the plays of Shakespeare; but there are no doubt many who could scarcely distinguish the law of Ohm from that of Boyle.'[6] We argued for a higher level of 'scientific literacy', to help to remove impediments to communication and to provide a greater flexibility in the labour force.

Some progress has no doubt been made, and the British Association and the media have contributed to it. But there are still too many who accept, and on occasion boast about, their almost total ignorance of science, mathematics and technical subjects. Professor Williams and I drew attention to the early age at which decisions about specialisation are made at school.[7] More students now study mixtures of science and arts or social science subjects; but the question which is still too little discussed is why important choices of subjects need to be made in secondary education at all. Would it not be better if the main subjects were compulsorily studied by all students up to the age of 18? No crucial decisions would then be taken on inadequate information at an early age: every student would have a developed literacy and numeracy, and some understanding of science: every student would have the flexibility in developing a career which comes from the mastery of a broad range of subjects.

You can at once imagine the objections: some students just 'cannot do' mathematics and science: a broad curriculum would give inadequate time to bring each subject to a proper level. The first objection ignores the considerable flexibility of reasonably intelligent minds when facing a compulsory task which yields a desirable outcome. I would not make music compulsory for the tone-deaf: but I have not heard convincing evidence that there exists a genetically determined mathematics-deafness. (Mathematics and science, after all, are capable of being taught either as abstract or as concrete and 'practical' subjects: I suspect that most students could learn in one way or the other.) It is worth remembering that a very large part of the population can successfully master a highly skilled craft, namely the safe driving of a car. The intelligent and the stupid, the manually dexterous and the ham-fisted, the technically adept and the technically ignorant — all manage it, because they want or need to drive. I suspect that, similarly, a much wider range of boys and girls could achieve scientific and mathematical skills if they needed them. As for the demands for time by the subject specialists, do we really think that in the final outcome our present system gives us an advantage over the countries which have a broad secondary curriculum? Do we believe that the amount of work which we expect from teenagers (and their teachers) is optimal? Perhaps they could study more subjects, and still arrive at the same standard.

I must apologise for this detour into the affairs of Section L (Education), especially as my line of argument cuts across those interminable discussions about the future of A-levels. Let me now turn to another matter, namely the influence of government on scientific progressiveness. Professor Williams and I did not consider that government control or 'red tape' was a serious inhibiting factor, and we suggested that the net effect of government action must be favourable to the speedy application of science, because the government provides so much of the educational and research system as a free good.[8] In the last twenty years, government intervention in the economy has greatly increased, much of it having the public intention of making possible the employment of improved methods. I would today wish to see a reassessment of its influence, since I think it possible that it is harmful. In doing this, I would forget the argument that the State pays for education, since this is true in all countries, and in any case the cost of education is reflected in local and national taxation. It remains a valid point that government provides, as a service available to all, some research which individual firms might have to do for themselves (and might then tend to keep to themselves). To set in the balance against this favourable factor, however, are three substantial adverse influences on progressiveness:

1   The major supportive interventions of government have been to obstruct and reverse the natural action of economic forces to gain a political or social advantage, usually the protection of existing workers. It is conceivable that the massive injection of State funds into a company which would otherwise be bankrupt might achieve a technical breakthrough, so that a new, well-equipped, progressive enterprise can operate with high productivity and notable success in conquering world markets. The difficulty is to think of well-established examples where this has happened: and it is easy to think of several where it has not. This is not surprising, because the effect of State support on both workers and managers is to make it possible to avoid unpleasant but necessary decisions. Some kinds of State help involve such strong political pressures to keep things as they are that the attainment of a viable progressiveness is almost inconceivable. I can, for instance, imagine no worse way of solving the problems of shipbuilding than by nationalisation, *unless* indeed the Secretary of State for Industry is prepared to be a ruthless dictator and totally abolish the industry in several of its established centres.

2   For the average firm, the weight, complication and variability of government interventions have created a climate of opinion unfavourable to investment and innovation. It can be argued that the opinion is not justified − that Britain is not the most highly taxed nation, that government interferences in other countries (for instance, the United States and Canada) are also onerous. But the opinions of decision makers matter, even if unjustified. Those opinions relate not just to taxation but to price

controls, income controls, planning controls, pressures relating to social responsibility, safety regulations, the high cost of redundancies, the increasing complexity of relations with trade unions, restrictions on monopolies, the impact of financial investigations: and above all to uncertainty, and especially the uncertainty as to whether the government will in the end run away from the unpleasant decisions needed to control inflation. (Few business men now believe that they can prosper from the consequences of high inflation.) It is of course true that some of the interventions of government are necessary to prevent other evils which would inhibit investment. It is the feeling that governments rather *like* interfering, and (despite the manifest inefficiency of some of their means of doing so) will interfere *more* than is necessary, which industry finds so discouraging.

3 A particular aspect of this discouragement is the belief that governments will give priority to their own purposes – crudely, to the winning of votes: that this inevitably leads to an enlargement of public sector spending, particularly for welfare, more rapid than the economy can sustain: and that this in turn leads either to unduly high levels of taxation or to deficit finance which complicates monetary control and increases the danger of inflation. Furthermore, government tends to provide a degree of employment protection for its own servants which private industry cannot match (the Crombie code is an example), to pay high salaries (the principle of comparability being more readily biased one way than the other), and to offer fringe benefits such as inflation-proofed pensions. This leads to a maldistribution of ability, and also to a greater caution in industrial decisions because the best decision is seen as one which makes nobody redundant.

As economists, you may be unhappy about many of these lines of thinking: for it may still be true that *if* industry invested heavily in innovation, it would create such an active and expanding economy that many of the problems of inflexibility would be less worrying. Redundancy, for instance, is much less of a problem if there are five vacancies for every man unemployed. But, of course, gloom in decision makers is an extremely important economic fact. The situation, as I mention above, needs reassessment, but I believe that it might be found that the present relations of government and industry are unfavourable to technical progressiveness.

Apart from the 'climate of opinion', there is another inhibiting factor which deserves attention. Innovation means, very often, the construction of new factories, the laying out of a new plant rather than piecemeal substitutions for or improvements of individual machines. There is evidence from several countries of a long-run tendency for the costs of this construction to increase much faster than the general price level. This is related to the secular tendency for all building and construction costs to rise faster than other costs, and is also related to the costs created by social and environmental controls. The introduction of major innovations is thus made more difficult, and indeed the joint effects of high construction costs and high rates of interest must have led to the abandonment of many schemes. It is somewhat mysterious that the relative price movement should exist — after all, there have been many innovations in methods of construction: it needs investigation.

We have heard recently many appeals to industry to invest, and accusations from the left wing that capitalists have 'gone on strike' and are refusing to do things which the country needs. Our book *Investment in Innovation* discussed the very real complexities of investment decisions. Apart from the effects of real changes in profitability, and of general shifts in the climate of opinion, are they being made as well as they should be?

This is another area for enquiry, and I offer only my personal impressions. I would guess that it would be found that British managers are not as good at making decisions about innovatory investment as they should be, for these reasons:

1   *Insularity*   Too much effort is used in reinventing things, or in producing private British systems which are no better than those being developed in other countries (and are probably designed in a way which makes them unsuitable for export). It should be remembered that the *essential* part of a country's research and development is the ability to keep in touch with and understand the discoveries being made in the rest of the world, and to adapt them to local circumstances. One could have a highly successful economy without having any significant discoveries of one's own; this is indeed obvious, for small countries cannot possibly afford to be active in more than a tiny part of the possible areas of research and development, and must necessarily depend on the international flow of ideas and licensed knowledge. Instead of pretending that we are self-sufficient, we would do well to concentrate research, development and design in areas which are given insufficient attention in all countries, in those in which there are impediments to the international flow, and in a few in which we can build on acknowledged success. Many more of our scientists and technologists should be travelling the world and unashamedly copying or adapting the best practice they find.

2   *Sloppy analysis*   Keynes attributed many business decisions to 'animal spirits' rather than a precise calculation of returns and probabilities; but this cannot be taken as a recommendation to be followed. It has to be admitted, of course, that an *ex post* examination of an innovatory investment will very often show that the assumptions behind it were wrong. No amount of forethought will remove the uncertainties of business, and an effort to 'get everything right in advance' may only lead to such a delay, and such a tangle of considerations, that the investment never gets off the ground: the Channel Tunnel project is an example. It is an essential characteristic of a good business man that, when appropriate, he is willing to take a timely decision on partial information, rather than miss an opportunity by waiting for a greater certainty.

So there are plenty of excuses for being wrong. What should not be excused, however, is the decision which is made in a sloppy or ill-argued way, ignoring information which is readily to hand and obviously relevant. Although a full assessment requires new case-studies, I have the impression that sloppy analysis is much too common in British industry, and also in government: and, if this is so, it raises questions about the recruitment and education of our managers, and the penalties which they pay for inadequate performance.

3 *Misdirected effort* Very great disparities continue to exist in the scale of research and development effort, and the interest in innovation, in different industries. These disparities are, of course, in large part technically determined; everyone would expect the aircraft, atomic energy or telecommunications businesses to require more research, and to give rise to more frequent innovations, than (say) textiles, food processing, or the collection and distribution of letters. But the differences are also in part the product of conventional ideas and of past history. We drew attention to a need for positive action to bring good minds to bear on the problems of backwardness:

> We suggest that backwardness is self-perpetuating, both in firms and industries; the backward firm, even if it can be made to desire technical progress, is ill placed to command the resources (and in particular the human ability) necessary to begin that progress. It will take much ingenuity by industry and government to break up the crust of habit and to divert lively and able minds from the places where change is most likely to those where it is most needed.[9]

Nothing like enough has been done to concentrate those efforts which are controlled and influenced by government on the areas of backwardness, or to offer differential inducements to stimulate backward firms. In particular, it is a pity that Britain has not learnt more from its own success in agriculture. British agriculture is, by world standards, technically progressive; and, though this is assisted by certain features of its structure, the industry provides an example of the rapid spread of new ideas to numerous and independent-minded producers — a structure which in other industries is often used as an excuse for backwardness. The specially protected status of agriculture may provide a partial explanation, but I think one should look also at the effect, over the years, of patient and effective advisory services. A similar continuous effort might be of great value in other industries with a large number of small producers. The influence of government should be constantly exercised against the assumption that some industries are exciting and scientifically progressive, while others have to be left to decay in self-perpetuating backwardness. It may be that some of the most interesting opportunities await a fresh look at some of the industries which everyone assumes will never greatly change, and British managers may be biased in their investment because of a conventional attitude to these opportunities. Perhaps the most important of all our conclusions of twenty years ago was that summarised in the following passage:

Technical progressiveness is related to the general quality of the firm; and attention to other aspects of its general quality — for instance, to management efficiency or to salesmanship and market research — helps to create the conditions for technical progress. In other words, the use of science is not an optional extra to be attached to the firm, but an expression of the whole attitude of the firm.[10]

In a preceding chapter we had enumerated a whole series of these interrelated aspects of general quality, which were established by our case-studies as tending to be present in technically progressive, and absent in technically backward, firms. These covered all parts of the firm's activity, from the initial survey of potential ideas through research and development (if present) to production and marketing, and also the communication between and interrelation of these parts, and the strategic decisions about future activities. One possibility to be considered, therefore, is that the effective use of British scientific and technological skills is being inhibited by crucial weaknesses in other areas of management responsibility. It is possible, also, that new weaknesses have appeared since the 1950s; for instance, shop-floor resistance to innovation was then identified as no more than an occasional factor present in both progressive and unprogressive firms, but it is conceivable that it may now have a stronger influence because of the increased power of the unions and the difficulties attached to making workers redundant.

It would be putting our conclusions too strongly to say that technical progress requires simultaneous excellence in each main area of a firm's activity: plainly this would set an impossibly high standard. But there are plenty of examples of the frustration of potential strength in science and technology by particularly serious weaknesses in other areas. Sloppy and insular investment decisions have already been mentioned: another leading trouble area is marketing. There are still too many business men who think of marketing as 'salesmanship', that is the art of selling a predetermined product by persuasion. Therefore too many British products are not close enough to what the purchasers, at home or abroad, really want or will continue to want: they do not embody an exact and imaginative appreciation of what will satisfy people in the various markets. Industrial machinery and equipment is often well made in traditional designs, but fails to embody refinements of accuracy and control which customers will increasingly demand. Durable goods bought by consumers have too many faults, and arrangements for servicing to ensure reliability are not adequate: a part of the considerable demand for imported cars, for instance, certainly arises from the search for reliability at a moderate price. Many of these marketing failures are related to the fault of insularity: producers have simply failed to observe the quality and design provided by foreign competitors, and have not analysed the reasons why the foreign products are in demand.

You may say that these are criticisms founded on selective examples, and that all countries may expect to show such examples. That is true: but the special problem of the British economy is shown if one tries to list the industries which are undeniably well up with world competition, with products well suited to the real desires of their markets. The list is short: much too short for an economy as exposed as ours. Somehow British industry must be persuaded to do its market research better, and, until it does, some of its technical potential will be frustrated.

Another continuing area of difficulty is the relationship between a firm's research and development (assuming it to be large enough to have those functions) and its production. There never was much point in isolating a group of boffins in a country house, leaving them to pursue their scientific hunches without a consciousness of the special problems of production and the costs and profits which it will involve. Indeed, since there will in any case be cultural differences between research and production staff, particular trouble needs to be taken to bring them together and to integrate their work. Yet there are still examples of research establishments whose projects will not bear economic scrutiny, and which as a consequence are wasting scientific talent which could be put to better use elsewhere. (I am not, of course, saying that all scientists should do applied research: but if one is *intending* research to be applied, let it be effective.)

What lies behind these and other examples of failures to achieve the 'general quality' which allows science and technology to flourish and be effective can only be an inadequate standard of management. In twenty years nearly all the more senior management of firms will have changed: those now in positions of senior responsibility represent the management development practices of the recent past, but of course will have come into industry in the 1960s or earlier, and therefore may show up the recruitment failures of that earlier period. The latter observation, however, yields no comfort, for there is not much evidence that careers in business management (outside a few prestige areas such as the merchant banks) have grown in popularity with people of high ability. In other words, the management material of the 1990s may not be intrinsically much better than what we have now.

On the other hand, there have been great increases in the quantity of management education. There are still criticisms of its content, and doubts about the quality of many of the teachers: but overseas comparisons suggest that we have not done badly. The effects of better education for managers are delayed, so perhaps one can entertain the hope that the 'general quality' of firms will now improve.

I am, however, not sure if this will happen. It seems to me that what British managers often lack is a disciplined mind. Let me give an example of what I mean. As an arbitrator, I have seen over many years a sample of the presentations of the employers' case made by firms both great and small. I am frankly appalled by the low quality of many of these presentations (often much worse than the case made by the union side), and I do not think that the quality is improving. It is not simply that employers get into a muddle about labour relations — any of us may do that — but that senior managers seem incapable of presenting a logical case and hammering their points home with relevant evidence. A similar disappointment in management quality used to trouble me when I had to observe cases in the Restrictive Practices Court. The word which best describes the trouble is 'sloppiness'; it is a readiness to accept the second best in thinking out a problem, a laziness of the mind.

This will not be put right by attending some of the courses in general management, however interesting or thought-provoking they may be. One needs something like the combined effect of the rigidly disciplined French school system and the *hautes écoles:* or the tremendous pressures of competition which bring out the best at the top levels of US management. I suspect one would get better managers from the intensive study of a narrow but difficult management technique than from more general courses: for the trained and disciplined mind can move outwards into new areas — as, for instance, so many accountants have done. However it is done, it is important that British industry should set very high and rigorous standards for managers, and show its dissatisfaction with the second best.

The problem with which we began twenty years ago is still with us. There is no easy way out by saying that Britain is choosing a less affluent society with a sounder sense of values. Economic success is not the highest good in life, but no country can continue with such a record of economic failure and decline without a profound loss of confidence and most serious social and political consequences. Too much of what I have said today relies on partial impressions; there is need for a continuing programme of study, to enable us to judge where Britain is having success in conquering its problems and what are the key points at which further action is needed. The effective use of science and technology is, above all, about the motivation, selection, education and deployment of human beings, and about the opportunities and disadvantages set for them by the social and industrial structure and the climate of opinion within which they operate. There are issues here on which the British Association, working at the interface between science and the public, could have a great and valuable influence.

Notes

1   C.F. Carter and B.R. Williams, *Industry and Technical Progress* (Oxford University Press, 1957), p. 2.
2   See especially C.F. Carter and B.R. Williams, *Science in Industry* (Oxford University Press, 1959), ch. 11.
3   C.F. Carter, 'The Economic Use of Brains', *Economic Journal,* March, 1962.
4   *ITP,* p. 191.
5   *ibid.*
6   *SI,* p. 127.
7   *ITP,* p. 92.
8   *ITP,* p. 174.
9   *ITP,* pp. 191–2.
10   *ITP,* p. 190.

13

ENERGY POLICY FORMULATION

P. LESLEY COOK

The concept of the energy industry sector stems from the low elasticity of demand for energy and the high elasticity of substitution between the four main fuels. As coal, electricity and gas are nationalised and oil increasingly under state ownership and subject to control, there are four decision areas and in each there is the power to plan.

The case for an energy policy lies in the inadequacy of the market mechanism.

First, within the energy sector the long-term elasticities of substitution are so high that for each industry it is the policies pursued by the others which mainly determine demand. Hence the smooth working of the market mechanism depends upon anticipation of the actions of others.

Second, there are important externalities from the energy sector as a whole. Decisions made in the fuel sector affect other parts of the economy, but the externalities would be neglected if decisions were made in response to the market.

These two general points suggest the need for centralised policy making but, in this form, do not explain why the problem of policy formulation is difficult. There is clear public demand for 'energy policy', but, when one asks the question *'What should energy policy look like?'* the answer is not obvious. Should it be a firm set of forecasts? Should it be a set of rules? Or what?

Prior to the oil crisis of 1973 energy policy was a matter for the expert (technologist, statistician, economist, econometrician), and experts were, in the 1960s fashion, expected to produce the answer.

Our perception of the problem and the public confidence in experts – or, more kindly, the public's understanding of the role of the experts – is now radically changed. This is reflected in the widespread debate on pollution, depletion, the interests of future generations, the safety of nuclear power and oil policies. The National Energy Conference held on 22 June 1976 in the Church Hall, Westminster would have been inconceivable even in 1972. It was not, I think, a total success but, as the President suggested, we have to learn to discuss major economic issues in the public forum.

There are a number of features which now make energy policy peculiarly difficult – I will take them under 4 heads – although they are strongly inter-connected.

1   The impact of energy policy on the economy is greater.
2   Present decisions affect very long periods into the future.
3   There is great uncertainty.
4   There are no longer clear objectives. The problem is no longer one of optimisation; it is one of decision making under uncertainty.

1 *The impact of energy policy on the economy* is potentially much greater because of the four-fold increase in oil prices and the possibility of substantial further increases.

Substantial changes in the quantity of oil traded now have substantial effects on the UK terms of trade, which – in turn – cause major adjustments in the economy which are difficult to achieve rapidly. The UK, unlike West Germany or Japan, has been unable to increase exports and we have to anticipate that a rapid change to importing large quantities of oil in the 1990s would cause the same problem.

The Cambridge Energy Group see the possibility of a net change in oil imports of 100m. tons (equal to present consumption) in the 1990s. This would involve greater adjustment than that required after 1973.

2 *The impact of energy policy on the future* has increased with the recognition that fossil fuel resources are finite. North Sea reserves are variously predicted to last, if not conserved, for 25–40 years and world output is likely to begin to fall by 2000. The prospect of depletion gives rise to the possibility that real income in the future might be lower and therefore it is more important to consider the future.

Whereas in 1967 a basic 8-year time horizon was used, we now have to think in terms of a whole time path over at least 50 years, rather than a single planning date close enough for fairly accurate forecasts to be made.

The need to consider a whole time path and not planning dates also stems from the fact that depletion gives rise to turning points and not steady growth. The supplies from both the North Sea and world oil fields will rise and then fall and this will be associated with turning points in the relative prices of other fuels. The demand for coal may well fall before rising again. The proving of fast reactors is likely to cause the price of uranium to stabilise and perhaps fall in the short term. The whole problem is now very much more complex and sensitive than it was when the assumption of a perfectly elastic supply of oil 'at competitive prices' (1967 *Fuel Policy*) was virtually unchallenged and rather gradual rates of change were envisaged.

3 *Much is now seen to be uncertain*

(*a*) Will the world price of oil rise by 50 per cent, 100 per cent or 200 per cent by 1995 and what will it be by 2020? Will it rise steadily or in sudden jumps? Uncertainty about price flows partly from uncertainty about demand elasticities. Very little is known about price elasticities and old energy coefficients are now of little value.

(*b*) The uncertainties about nuclear power have had much publicity. There are fears about safety, fears about the dangers of plutonium and doubts about the eventual feasibility of fusion.

These uncertainties are compounded by the high long-term elasticity of substitution between the fuels which means that the current value of oil depends upon nuclear prospects, the current price of uranium depends upon both oil prospects and fast reactor prospects and the future of coal depends upon both. Coal, oil and uranium are all depletable resources and present scarcity values depend upon future values. Finally, we do not know how far the demand for the four major fuels will be moderated by the development of solar, wind, wave and geothermal power. (In principle this problem can be taken as an aspect of the problem of forecasting the demand for the major fuels.)

We have, in the past, assumed that income per head would grow and that future generations would be substantially richer. Even this is not certain since we cannot be so sure that technical advances will offset the rising cost of depletable resources and, for the UK, we do not know how far after c. 1990 the terms of trade will deteriorate. This depends partly on energy policy itself.

Since we are uncertain about future standards of living we can say very little about the marginal utility of income in the future as compared with the present. Future income is of greater value the poorer one expects to be in the future. This assessment is critical for depletion policy, where a real choice between now and later is presented.

4 *The problem is now one of risk taking under conditions of uncertainty rather than a problem of optimisation* — and the stakes are high. It is no longer enough 'to have regard to security of supplies'. There are now major choices between more and less risky strategies, and subjective assessments of the possible outcomes must be made. The risk problem, which was subsidiary when oil was cheap and expected to remain cheap, is now central.

A major effect of this change is that it is no longer possible to specify objectives of energy policy in any precise way — even if technologists and econometricians could draw up a great pay-off matrix with the probabilities, the politicians could not specify the risks they were willing to take. Would they minimax, minimise regret, maximax or go for the highest MEV? Energy problems now demand this type of decision.

Carl Kaysen once startled an audience in Cambridge, and me, by declaring that the computer could not replace the business man because the business man does not know what he is doing. The aphorism is relevant . . .

The point is that when a decision is made in the face of uncertainty, the decision maker can seldom distinguish between his assessment of the probabilities and his valuation of the possible outcomes. Uncertainty is now a major feature of the energy policy problem.

These four general features of the energy problem have implications for policy formulation.

The long-term horizons, and the related uncertainties, partly explain the inadequacy of the market mechanism. The actions of others cannot be anticipated and the externalities are too important.

The uncertainty makes the suggestion that industries should operate according to marginal pricing and investment rules an unrealistic option with little content. Marginal analysis and optimisation are of little use without firm information — in particular, marginal costs are very uncertain.

Equally, the uncertainty and the need for flexibility rules out full central planning in quantitative terms.

The four major fuel industries are very large, complex, organisations. They are not selling homogeneous products into homogeneous markets, they are dealing with complex and changing markets, differentiated products and changing technology; and, as a result, a high order of management, capable of making complex technological and commercial decisions is required. The industries cannot be 'run from Whitehall'. What is needed is a middle way between centralisation and devolution — that balance is both hard to find and hard to maintain.

The industries themselves want guide-lines but resent 'interference'. The distinction is fine, but the institutional and managerial balance is an important ingredient of the problem of policy formulation.

The problems are formidable and increased by the frightening number of people who wish to have a finger in the pie:

The central government
The sponsoring ministry
The politicians (Select Committees)
The managements of the main fuel industries
The major industries which supply the fuel sector (e.g. heavy electrical
    industry and the Atomic Energy Authority)
The consumer
The Confederation of British Industry
The Trades Union Congress
The trade unions of the fuel industries
The conservationists and environmentalists

Now to proposals:

The first is that energy policy formulation should be divided into three distinct phases and different bodies should be responsible for each. The concept of 'an Energy Policy' as a single comprehensive set of proposals is too simple. The problem must be broken down because there are so many decisions to be taken by so many interested parties. A simple grand design would be much too inflexible and detailed: technical and professional planning must be an almost continuous process.

The second proposal, which follows from the first, is that the decisions should be taken sequentially — starting at the long-term. The three categories I propose are:

1 *Long-term strategy* This should comprise the broad guide-lines for the major decisions which affect the distant future — say up to 2040. The date is a matter of choice; but acceptance of the need for a long-term strategy is acceptance of the view that the interests of future generations matter — and this is in clear conflict with a discount rate of 10 per cent in real terms.

2 *Medium-term strategy* This should be formulated in the light of the long-term strategy and should be a more detailed strategic plan for the next 20 years — up to c. 1997. This is a period long enough to make investment appraisals of all but the very durable investment, e.g. coal mines. Although it would not cover basic oil depletion strategy, it would be long enough for appraisal of the investment for exploitation of oil and gas and the settling of more precise quantities from the North Sea. It is also a period long enough for bringing about significant switches between fuels by price and marketing policies. The medium-term strategy should give the longer term guide-lines for the corporate plans and investment programmes of the individual industries — which is where detailed policies are implemented.

3 *Short-term policies* These, in a quite strict Marshallian sense, should be formulated whenever disequilibrium gives rise to problems of adjustment which indicate special measures. This would normally be when unforeseen problems develop, but might also be the result of a need to make other difficult or rapid adjustments. The 1967 *Fuel Policy* was very largely concerned with the problems of the coal industry and it is this type of difficulty which would call for a short-term policy document — which is, essentially, what the 1967 White Paper was.

I stress the point that the decision making should start with the long-term strategy and work back through the medium-term strategy to the corporate plans of the industries; short-term policies should be superimposed as required. This has the advantages that the long term would be considered seriously and not pre-empted by short-term and medium-term pressures. (Without a strategy there is a great danger that there will be divergent views which only become apparent when the Ministry seeks to understand the implications of the invest-ment plans of the industries.) The disadvantages of the system would, of course, be severe if short-term crises were so major and so frequent that the responses to short-term pressures destroyed the long-term strategy (or if events repeatedly showed it to be ill-founded). Sequential planning does not eliminate conflict, but the existence of strategies reduces the power of short-term pressures. Revisions of long-term and medium-term strategies might, of course, have to be uncomfortably frequent and they might then lose credibility.

The formulation is designed to offer the managements of the industries guide-lines within which to work but to leave a very high degree of freedom as to the exact way in which they should try to meet the uncertainties. It is they who must develop investment plans which give a measure of short-term flexibility, must evolve marketing policies which anticipate changes in demand and they must take responsibility for these actions.

I now want to look more closely at long-term strategy. The first stage is to understand the possible time-paths into the future and the relevance and magnitude of the major uncertainties. This has, particularly in the last two years, led to the analysis of scenarios. The creation and analysis of scenarios is a difficult art rather than a science. The size and complexity of the problem makes it impossible to model it all, major simplifications have to be made and even then only very few of the possibilities can be examined; rates of change are not constant and there are clear turning points and the number of variables is enormous; 32 variables come from only 2 values for each of 5 variables. The possibilities and the interrelationships must be examined but this work does not produce a policy. Choices have to be made.

The second major problem is that of agreeing on the main value judgements. This is essentially a political matter but not one which can be put to the electorate in any direct way. The problem of agreement on value judgements has, I think, been neglected − attention has focused on the necessary job of trying to reduce uncertainty (this is largely the business of the professional) and the fact that energy policy is also a matter of real choice depending on value judgements has been somewhat obscured. Evaluation of the chances of nuclear accident is one sort of problem; the valuation of cheaper electricity and the valuation of the costs of death and destruction is quite another.

Similarly the valuations of future against present units of income is a matter of taste − the selfishness or altruism of the present older generations is crucial in the matter of depletion policy.

As argued earlier, it is impossible for people to distinguish clearly between their estimates of the risk and their valuations of different outcomes. Those who give little value to marginal income 40 years hence *may* have high time preferences, or they may be optimistic about technical progress − they can't really say which.

Similarly, those who dismiss nuclear danger and advocate the rapid development of fast reactors *may* think the probability of accidents is low or they may have a strong wish for high living standards and be rather impervious to disaster − a short life and a merry one!

It is because much of the debate is really a matter of conflicting value judgements that energy policy leads to a good deal of frustration. It also explains the large number of people who feel capable of taking part in the decision making.

I have stressed the element of real choice based on value judgements. I cannot therefore propose a correct strategy, only my preferred strategy − and this I press.

My strategy indicates the *type* of policy statement which should be produced and the areas of debate. I cannot distinguish clearly between the valuations of possible outcomes and the assessments of probabilities − but I can state some of my prejudices:

(*a*) I have a high aversion to reductions in future real income and think the chances of very large and sudden rises in the cost of oil are high, and the ability of the UK economy to pay rather miserably low.

(*b*) I have considerable concern for future generations

(*c*) I have sufficient concern for the dangers of nuclear energy to wish to proceed relatively slowly and I have not clear confidence that there will be abundant nuclear energy.

A long-term strategy based on these assessments would be:

(*a*) Future prices of all fuels should reflect high scarcity values until uranium efficient reactors are proved both economic and safe. (High fuel prices in the UK would *ceteris paribus* be associated with reductions in other taxes.) This conservationist policy should be associated with clear advertising to alert people to the strong possibility of higher future energy costs. I do not think that this can be left to the industries. As we see at present, the commercial people are there to sell!

(*b*) There should be control of depletion of North Sea oil and gas. Not only should we ensure that North Sea oil production falls slowly so as to avoid a major turn-round in the balance of payments and a rapid deterioration in the terms of trade, but also we should retain oil capacity for well into the twenty-first century in order to mitigate any world oil crises. This policy must, in view of the uncertainty and instability of oil prices, be expressed in terms of quantities. I suggest that we should retain enough oil reserves to meet 25–30 per cent of present demand in the period 2010–40. The pattern with reserves of c. 3500m. tons might be:

1980–90	100m. tons per annum
1990–2000	75m. tons per annum
2000–20	50m. tons per annum
2020–40	30m. tons per annum

Imports would increase steadily after c. 1990 and perhaps sooner. The severity of the control over depletion would be dependent upon increases in proved reserves. Although I see this policy of retaining capacity to meet 25–30 per cent of demand in 2010–40 largely as insurance, it might – if world prices rose rapidly – prove to be good speculative stock holding.

(*c*) Major investment in significant new coal capacity should be postponed. Reserves should not be lost by early pit closure but coal should be regarded primarily as a reserve fuel to be used when oil output falls and world fossil fuel prices rise – this would certainly happen if really extensive use of nuclear proved unacceptable. After falling through the 1980s, planned coal capacity should begin to rise in the 1990s in anticipation of demand due to (i) the high price of imported oil; (ii) the demand from the gas industry as North Sea gas output falls; and (iii) the possibility of slow development of fast reactors (hence high uranium prices).

(*d*) The electricity industry should plan on the basis of high cost fossil fuel and high cost uranium until the mid 1990s. Fast reactors, or perhaps thorium reactors, could well be proved by then and this would give freedom from the fear of uranium scarcity and permit the massive use of electricity. The demand for electricity would increase rapidly if prices were expected to be relatively low and it would replace gas and oil in many uses. Marketing policy is important as premature growth in demand would be expensive and disruptive since the possible rate of construction is limited.

(*e*) The gas industry is faced with the opposite problem. Gas, rather than electricity, should be used over the next 20 years but after that the future is uncertain. The industry must plan in the light of the possibility that gas will lose markets to electricity but at the same time gain markets from oil with gas made from coal. There is a high premium on flexibility.

This energy strategy should be debated against other strategies. For example, very high aversion to nuclear risk (or great pessimism about the safety of nuclear reactors and the handling of plutonium) is associated with the expectation of very high world oil prices. These views indicate a policy of slow North Sea depletion and very strong measures to control demand.

A strategy based on low concern for future generations and confidence in technology would be very different. These views indicate a policy of rapid North Sea depletion (at a rate which minimises the cost of exploitation), energetic preparation to build large numbers of nuclear plants (including fast breeders), and little or no development of coal capacity until well after 2000. The short-sighted optimist has few immediate problems.

The differences between strategies based on different value judgements and broad assessments are very great; although each strategy is imprecise, the differences are large enough for the broad statements of policy to be very valuable. The long-term strategy should, after extensive public debate, Green Papers, etc., be published by the government as the first and major step in energy policy.

A long-term strategy of this type does not, however, provide a sufficient policy framework for the corporate plans and investment decisions of the individual industries. This is the role of the medium-term strategy – the 20 year strategy. A major standing committee reviewing progress and producing regular strategic documents is required to formulate medium-term strategy. This is a more professional and technical matter. Technical, managerial and commercial judgements are a crucial input and decisions must be based on quite detailed estimates of quantities and costs. Here the managements of the industries, as well as the government, are of a major importance. Trade union and consumer representation may also be included.

Strategic planning over 20 years still cannot be precise. All that can be done is to ensure that the industries know enough of the overall strategy and the major features of the strategies of the other industries to give them as good a framework as possible against which to develop their individual programmes.

I do not have time to offer a medium-term strategy but, within the long-term strategy which I have outlined, the main features could be:

(i) Settling in quantitative terms (with margins) the oil depletion pattern in the light of the long-term strategy and current reserve estimates.

(ii) Settling the extent of investment in new coal capacity for the early 1990s when new capacity might well be required. The lead times in coal are very long — 10 to 15 years — and numerous major projects can be undertaken simultaneously.

(iii) Settling the extent to which the electricity industry should go ahead with a major thermal nuclear programme rather than attempt to limit demand in the period between the early 1980s (when existing capacity is fully taken up) and the mid 1990s when uranium efficient reactors may be proven.

These are fearfully difficult questions but they should not be allowed to dominate discussions of long-term strategy and they should not determine long-term strategy.

They must be settled and they should not be settled either by the individual industries, as in the 1974 Coal Enquiry, or within the context of the Ministry approval of the Corporate Strategic and Investment Plans of the individual industries.

My object was to find a middle way between centralisation and devolution. Central strategies confined to the long- and medium-term, with responsibility for actual programmes devolved upon the industries, offer — despite the difficulties — the best solution.

The Ministry would then have guide-lines, albeit rather fuzzy ones, against which to monitor the individual industries. They would be monitoring for compatibility with this agreed and published strategy. The industries, in their turn, would know both the energy strategy and the general form of the governments' long-term policy measures.

The main thrust of my argument is that the energy problem is so exceedingly difficult that we must learn to live with broad strategic agreements because neither detailed plans nor the establishment of objectives and economic rules can do the job. We live in a sophisticated and difficult world in which there are real choices to be made in conditions of great uncertainty.

14

ADAM SMITH AND MARKET CAPITALISM

D. A. REISMAN

In an era when doctrinaire acceptance or dogmatic rejection so often replace sincere discussion and reasoned argument, the haunted intellectuality of Adam Smith appears as out of place as Gulliver among the Lilliputians; and yet the real importance of Adam Smith is in truth to be found rather in the questions he asked than in the answers he provided. Smith was not unique in associating market capitalism with individual freedom. He was unique, however, in developing a guarded and careful institutionalist approach to market equilibration, anthropocentric rather than reiocentric and dynamic rather than static in nature; in formulating his model in terms of structure, system and interdependence to such an extent that his contribution cannot but be situated firmly in the general equilibrium tradition that runs from Quesnay to Leontief; and in stressing that price sensitivity is not the only kind of sensitivity that obtains even in the free market place.

It will be the task of this paper to demonstrate that Adam Smith's greatest relevance to thinkers two centuries after the publication of *The Wealth of Nations* lies rather in his method than in his model. We shall proceed as follows: In the first section we will examine Smith's theory of free markets; in the second and third sections we will look more closely at the supply and demand curves respectively; and in the final section we will summarise what we regard as Adam Smith's chief contribution to the discussion of market capitalism.

The case for the market

Adam Smith believed in the beneficial effects of competition, the profit-motive and the free market mechanism, and recommended that matters of business be delegated to businessmen, whose self-interest has the unintended outcome of benefiting the community. In the marketplace, he noted, 'every individual is continually exerting himself to find out the most advantageous employment for

All works cited are by Adam Smith
WN = *The Wealth of Nations*
LJ = *Lectures on Justice, Police, Revenue and Arms*
MS = *The Theory of Moral Sentiments*
EW = *The Early Writings of Adam Smith*
'ED' = 'An Early Draft of Part of the Wealth of Nations'
LR = *Lectures on Rhetoric and Belles Lettres*
Full references and further reading are given on pp. 222–3

whatever capital he can command. It is his own advantage, indeed, and not that of the society which he has in view. But the study of his own advantage naturally, or rather necessarily leads him to prefer that employment which is most advantageous to the society' (*WN* I p. 475). It is as if the businessman were led by an invisible hand to promote group interests while only seeking to further his own, a distinction between manifest and latent functions which optimistically suggests that private vices might turn out to be public virtues. After all, while 'the brewer and the baker serve us not from benevolence, but from self love' (*LJ* p. 169), at least they do serve us and advance our material welfare, and this points to the following general rule: 'The natural effort of every individual to better his own condition, when suffered to exert itself with freedom and security, is so powerful a principle, that it is alone, and without any assistance, not only capable of carrying on the society to wealth and prosperity, but of surmounting a hundred impertinent obstructions with which the folly of human laws too often incumbers its operations' (*WN* II pp. 49–50).

The fact is that matter has a momentum of its own 'altogether different from that which the legislature might choose to impress upon it' (*MS* p. 343); and for this reason idealistic 'men of system' (*MS* p. 342), who like all other confused and misguided fanatics are exposed to 'innumerable delusions' (*WN* II p. 208) in their attempt to lead nature rather than follow her, are doomed to failure. Smith recorded that he had 'never known much good done by those who affected to trade for the public good' (*WN* I p. 478) and recommended the dissolution of interventionist and restrictive institutions, thereby allowing matter to find its own level and nature's laws to be observed in both senses of the word. Smith's example of the 'natural price' (defined as 'the central price, to which the prices of all commodities are continually gravitating' (*WN* I p. 63)) illustrates his admiration for 'the superior genius and sagacity of Sir Isaac Newton' ('The History of Astronomy' p. 100 in *EW*) and reminds us that he regarded trade secrets, collusive arrangements, settlement laws, primogeniture, entails, monopolies granted by charter and statutes of apprenticeship as undesireable impediments to the law of gravity applied to social phenomena.

Once human frustration of natural momentum has been terminated, 'the obvious and simple system of natural liberty establishes itself of its own accord' (*WN* II p. 208), and this development is to be welcomed. For one thing, natural liberty is so pleasing from an aesthetic point of view that utility may indeed be an unintended outcome of the pursuit of beauty: after all, 'fitness' and 'happy contrivance' are beautiful in themselves, and it is only human nature that 'the exact adjustment of the means for attaining any conveniency or pleasure should frequently be more regarded than that very conveniency or pleasure' (*MS* p. 258). Moreover, natural liberty is optimally suited to the attainment of the end for which the beautiful and well-oiled machine of human society was designed, as surely the promotion of human happiness as the end for which the watch is intended is 'the pointing of the hour' (*MS* p. 126).

Just as the perfection of the watch makes us praise the watchmaker, so the smooth functioning of natural liberty increases our respect for Divine benevolence and design. The hand of the Creator is visible at the level of means (witness the key role of instinct, as crucial for economic as for population growth (*MS* p. 110)) and also at the level of ends. Smith believed that God's will is to be derived empirically from God's works, often manifested in man's practice, and drew the conclusion that God was opposed to asceticism and the mortification of the flesh: 'The happiness of mankind, as well as of all other rational creatures, seems to have been the original purpose intended by the Author of Nature when he brought them into existence' (*MS* p. 235), a fact to which all 'the works of Nature' (*MS* p. 235) testify. Clearly, Smith's plea for the 'obvious and simple system of natural liberty' (in place of 'preference' and 'restraint' (*WN* II p. 208)) was also a defence of the 'Superintendent of the Universe' against the challenge of the 'man of system'; and his stress on induction from experience (in place of dependence on 'the abstruse syllogisms of a quibbling dialectic' (*MS* p. 203)) was also an invitation to trust in God.

If God's goal is human happiness, then there is much to be said for the sensitivity of the market mechanism, as a simple example will demonstrate. Suppose, starting from a position of market equilibrium, that there is a shift outward in the demand curve for a commodity, caused either by a sudden emergency (as where 'a public mourning raises the price of black cloth' (*WN* I p. 67)) or simply a rise in income (in 'wealth and wanton luxury' (*WN* I p. 64)). Competition among would-be consumers of the good drives up prices and profits and stimulates capitalists to transfer their capital from lower-return employments (allowing for non-pecuniary considerations and assuming perfect knowledge of alternative opportunities) (*WN* I pp. 62–3). New entry and increased competition among would-be sellers lead in turn to a fall in the price of the good and thus increased consumption, since purchasers act as if they face a downward-sloping demand curve (*WN* II p. 401). Indeed, the percentage rise in quantity demanded may actually exceed the percentage fall in price (the reason that coal-proprietors 'find it more for their interest to sell a great quantity at a price somewhat above the lowest, than a small quantity at the highest' (*WN* I p. 186)). Whatever the situation high profits induce more new entrants and encourage more competition until ultimately 'perfect liberty' leads to the establishment of an 'ordinary rate of profit', the lowest with which a mobile and profit-oriented investor 'can content himself without being a loser' (*WN* I p. 161). At that point a new market equilibrium will be established, market signals having brought about a new 'natural balance of industry, or a disposition in the people to apply to each species of work precisely in proportion to the demand for that work' ('ED' p. 346).

In summary, the 'higgling and bargaining of the market' ensures a 'rough equality' (*WN* I p. 36) of value in exchange and an allocation of resources so efficient and so sensitive that it must serve as a shining example to schemers who design wasteful interventionist measures such as the Navigation Laws (*WN* II pp. 114–16). There is, all in all, a strong case for nature and market compared with politician and plan.

Supply

Adam Smith believed that 'the uniform, constant, and uninterrupted effort of every man to better his condition [is] the principle from which public and national, as well as private opulence is originally derived' (*WN* I p. 364). What he did not make entirely clear, however, is whence springs that self-love which so powerfully promotes the welfare of the community.

The source might be human nature. Smith argued that men are made of 'coarse clay' (*MS* p. 230) and have a 'base and selfish disposition' (*WN* I p. 371), and stated categorically that the desire to better our condition 'comes with us from the womb, and never leaves us till we go into the grave' (*WN* I pp. 362–3). A psychological explanation of pecuniary self-love as intrinsic to human nature, however, much understates Smith's conviction that social survival is as important to a sensitive man as physical survival. Man has, Smith believed, 'an original desire to please, and an original aversion to offend his brethren' (*MS* p. 170), and it is this drive which makes him both a scientist (since observation of habitual associations and the multiplied reactions of our fellow men is the key to social standards of propriety) and a conformist (since our peers love the norm, and 'the chief part of human happiness arises from the consciousness of being beloved' (*MS* p. 56)). Evidently pecuniary self-love is not to be seen in isolation but is instead to be derived from love of fellowship and 'sympathy' (the coincidence of sentiments).

This does not, of course, imply that an individual ought to neglect his material interests. On the contrary, since virtue consists in balance, some 'prudence' appears eminently proper when combined with some 'benevolence' and some 'justice': 'Regard to our own private happiness and interest . . . appear upon many occasions very laudable principles of action' (*MS* p. 445). The point is simply that self-interest must be constrained by self-control to a degree pre-scribed by society if we are to escape the proper 'hatred or contempt' (*MS* p. 204) of our fellows. Thus a money-grubbing wheeler-dealer might become rich, but he would also be condemned for putting excess before moderation and made to feel rejected, an outsider, a hideous specimen (since aesthetic pleasure is related to 'whatever we have been used to' (*MS* p. 289) in a par-ticular breed as seen in a particular social looking-glass). And even if others were unaware of his failing, the Don Juan of the business world would still himself suffer from a guilty conscience and spoiled identity (becoming as he would 'the object of his own hatred and abhorrence' (*MS* p. 121–2)). The fact is that men desire 'not only praise, but praise-worthiness, or to be that thing which, though it should be praised by nobody, is, however, the natural and proper object of praise' (*MS* p. 166), at least at a particular time and in a particular place.

Basically, the self-interested businessman, should he want sympathy for his passion, has no choice but to 'flatten . . . the sharpness of its natural tone, in order to reduce it to harmony and concord with the emotions of those who are about him' (*MS* p. 23). His primary objective is neither riches (although utility may be an unintended outcome of propriety) nor applause (since the real spectator is often biased or misinformed), but to win the entire approbation of the impartial spectator (who knows the whole truth about the individual's motivations and society's standards of right and wrong) by prospering with propriety. The businessman tries to see himself as others see him and to act the part others expect of him, for he knows that mankind tends to respect those who approach the mean type of conduct associated with each calling and to censure deviation: 'We expect in each rank and profession a degree of those manners which, experience has taught us, belonged to it . . . A man, we say, should look like his trade and profession' (*MS* p. 292). *What is* acquires the force of *what ought to be* as norms are internalised: 'Our continual observations upon the conduct of others insensibly lead us to form to ourselves certain general rules concerning what is fit and proper either to be done or to be avoided' (*MS* p. 224).

A businessman acts as a businessman habitually does in a given society lest he render himself 'the proper object of the contempt and indignation' (*MS* p. 194) of the collectivity. Curiously, however, the behaviour-patterns to which he conforms are also uniquely appropriate to one in his station; for 'the objects with which men in the different professions and states of life are conversant being very different, and habituating them to very different passions, naturally form in them very different characters and manners' (*MS* p. 292). We have here a case of existence, not essence; of man in situation rather than the cult of the individual; of economic determinism rather than the unfolding of innate gifts. We have here a case where society takes a malleable lump of wax and moulds it into the shape that the group not only by tradition is used to seeing but also needs; a case of coordination not through the price-mechanism but through the work-function, since a man's character is more the result than the cause of the way in which he earns a living. None of us is likely to have a useless or improper essence precisely because what we *are* seems to arrive *post festum*.

Consider some examples. Indolence and extravagance are both natural and proper in a nobleman (whose mind seldom faces any challenge save possibly 'to figure at a ball' or 'to succeed in an intrigue of gallantry' (*MS* p. 78) and whose revenue renews itself year after year without any effort on his part (*WN* I p.468)); abstract contemplation and severe gravity in a clergyman (whose mind is continually focused on the 'awful futurity' (*MS* p. 294) facing man); dissolution in a soldier (whose pay is unrelated to effort (*WN* I pp. 492–3) and who is in any case never far from death (*MS* pp. 294–5)); 'hardness of character' (*WN* II p. 431) in a customs-inspector. The work-function also renders the factory-operative 'stupid and ignorant'(*WN* II p. 303) due to overconcentration on a single repetitive operation and the absence of intellectual challenge (*WN* II p. 304).

The general rule is this: 'The understandings of the greater part of men are necessarily formed by their ordinary employments' (*WN* II p. 302). Applied to the businessman, this rule helps to explain that industry and trade naturally form in him habits of 'order, oeconomy and attention' (*WN* I p. 433) and 'probity and prudence' (*MS* p. 77) (but unfortunately also vices such as 'mean rapacity' (*WN* I p. 519) and 'avarice and ambition' (*WN* II p. 232), perhaps to be expected in an insecure social-climber whose income and position depend on nothing but 'the labour of his body and the activity of his mind' (*MS* p. 77)). Such a man has no time for political responsibilities; is cold but correct in personal relationships; avoids excessive risks. He is able to evaluate new investments carefully; and 'if he enters into any new projects or enterprises, they are likely to be well concerted and well prepared' (*MS* p. 315). Businessmen are honest and 'faithful to their word' (*LJ* p. 253), since at all times 'a dealer is afraid of losing his character' (*LJ* p. 253). They seek out 'new divisions of labour and new improvements of art' (*WN* II p. 272) in order to squeeze 'as great a quantity of work as possible' (*WN* I p. 292) from a given quantity of input, for they know that they can 'justle' existing competitors out of a trade 'by no other means but by dealing upon more reasonable terms' (*WN* I p. 375).

In short, the conditions of the business life 'breed and form' (*WN* II p. 103) habits of frugality, industry and self-sacrifice, as these are the preconditions for adaptation to the particular environment. A man does not become a business-man because he is frugal and honest but is made frugal and honest by his job, since a merchant indulging excessively in 'liberality, frankness, and good fellow-ship' (*WN* II p. 188) would soon be ruined and thus no longer a merchant at all. Clearly, if citizens of a mercantile commonwealth typically are to be recognised by their 'narrowness, meanness, and selfish disposition' (*WN* II p. 188), they are not to blame: such conduct, as we have seen, has 'a propriety independent of custom' (*MS* p. 293).

Since work makes men, it is understandable that Smith viewed the classes associated with the State with great reservation. Competition among politicians is likely to mould an 'insidious and crafty animal' (*WN* I p. 490), forced to intrigue and scheme by a frantic and factious environment where ambition is likely to get out of hand (*WN* II pp. 137–8). And the bureaucrat is apathetic and inefficient because of lack of challenge and incentive. On the Crown lands revenue is low in large measure because of bad management, the 'abusive management' of 'idle and profligate bailiffs' (*WN* II p. 357), the 'negligent, expensive, and oppressive management' of 'factors and agents' (*WN* II p. 347). There is little incentive to maximise revenues in which one has no share (*WN* II p. 241), and Smith made clear that bureaucrats are not at fault for acting as their situation naturally directs: his censure was directed toward 'the situation in which they are placed', not 'the character of those who have acted in it' (*WN* II p. 158). At the same time, a healthier situation should be created, not least by selling off the Crown lands to industrious farmers whose private interest in productivity corresponds to that of the nation.

As it happens, however, bureaucracy is not purely a problem of the public sector. In the private sector the South Sea Company, for example, like the East India Company, had suffered from 'the loss occasioned by the negligence, profusion, and malversation of the servants of the company' (*WN* II p. 269).

The problem arose because it had an 'immense capital divided among an immense number of proprietors' (*WN* II p. 267), few of them able to understand the Company's business, all of them willing simply to 'receive contentedly such half yearly or yearly dividend, as the directors think proper to make to them' (*WN* II p. 264). The owners did not exercise the necessary 'vigilance and attention' to prevent 'wasting', 'embezzling', 'disorderly conduct' (*WN* II pp. 276–8), 'folly' and 'depredations' (*WN* II p. 268) on the part of their managers, and it was only natural that those managers chose to turn a sick situation to their own advantage: 'The directors of such companies . . . being the managers rather of other people's money than of their own, it cannot well be expected, that they should watch over it with the same anxious vigilance with which the partners in a private copartnery frequently watch over their own' (*WN* II p. 264).

Business requires 'such an unremitting exertion of vigilance and attention, as cannot long be expected from the directors of a joint stock company' (*WN* II p. 278). Here free trade is the answer, for Smith believed such companies (having no genuine economies of scale and considerable diseconomies due to the indifference of managers) only survived because of monopolies artificially created by charter. Free trade means the reversal of the managerial revolution and the replacement of salaried bureaucrats by wide-awake entrepreneurs, a process from which the nation as a whole cannot but gain.

With hindsight, it is clear that Smith underestimated the future of the corporation. He did note that some industries (iron-works (*WN* I p. 295), coal-mines (*WN* I p. 295), the silk industry (*WN* I p. 494), the capital goods industry (*WN* II p. 159)) were fixed-capital intensive and expensive to enter; but apparently he regarded industrial economies of scale (together with the cost of large-scale enterprise, probably beyond the purse of the owner-operator) as the exception rather than the rule and tended to apply the model of the small-scale corn merchant to industry as well as to trade. Then, too, he also believed that, while the business of invention and innovation was clearly passing from the worker to a new class of specialists (a 'very few people' ('ED' p. 344) whose trade it is 'not to do any thing, but to observe every thing' (*WN* I p. 14)), the brains of this technostructure could nonetheless be bought in without making research and development a fixed cost to the firm.

Naturally, Smith would have wanted to rethink the role of the State in a world of economies of scale (if only because a smaller number of firms can more easily indulge in 'a conspiracy against the public' (*WN* I p. 144) to raise prices in the absence of social regulation of restrictive practices) and corporate bureaucracies similar in goals and structure to the civil service. After all, he was not hostile to the State on principle, and noted that in some foreign republics State enterprise had proved a success: witness the fact that the government of Berne did a flourishing trade in loans to other states (*WN* II p. 344) and the government of Hamburg ran a public pawn-shop, wine-cellar, apothecary and bank (*WN* II pp. 342, 344). The problem was not simply government in general, but the British government in particular; for whereas the administrators of Venice and Amsterdam had proven themselves 'orderly, vigilant, and parsimonious' (*WN* II

p. 342), the British government had typically demonstrated 'slothful and negligent profusion' (*WN* II p. 342). Historically speaking, England had 'never been blessed with a very parsimonious government' (*WN* I p. 367), but had been saddled with leaders showing more of the idleness and indolence (*WN* I p. 358), the dissolution of manners (*MS* p. 46), the wastefulness (*WN* I p. 468) of the landed classes than the parsimony and industry of the merchant. Moreover, the British government had come under the influence of vested interests offering biased advice: clearly it was not a nation of shopkeepers but 'a nation whose government is influenced by shopkeepers' (*WN* II p. 129) that had instituted the Mercantile system at the expense of their countrymen (thereby proving yet again that greedy peddlars 'neither are, nor ought to be, the rulers of mankind' (*WN* I p. 519)). In Britain, weak leaders misinformed about trade had in the past been all too often swayed by 'the passionate confidence of interested falsehood' (*WN* I p. 522) to 'warp the positive laws of the country from what natural justice would prescribe' (*MS* p. 502); and even the political balance of powers (represented by the fact that the House of Commons had been absolute in money bills since 1688 (*LJ* pp. 44–5)), while desirable in itself, would not make State regulation an adequate substitute for the market and the law of gravity.

Even for a country such as Britain, however, Smith did envisage a role for State intervention, not just in ensuring defence and justice but in providing public works where social benefits exceeded private benefits (say, in aiding the education industry to teach the masses 'the elementary parts of geometry and mechanics', so useful to productivity in any 'common trade' (*WN* II p. 306) if still not an antidote to the occupational hazard of 'mental mutilation' (*WN* II p. 308)). He also recommended that the State use its powers of discriminatory taxation for gentle social engineering, albeit via the market: hence he advised *ad valorem* taxation rather than taxes on bulk (since precious commodities are often light (*WN* II p. 250)) and a highway toll levied most heavily on luxury carriages (to penalise 'the indolence and vanity of the rich' (*WN* II p. 246)). And he advocated nationalisation of the postal system (*WN* II p. 246).

Perhaps in a more parsimonious and balanced commonwealth Smith would have proposed a greater role for the State in economic affairs. It is only fair to note, however, that the foreign republics he singled out for praise were not only characterised by a good balance of power between hereditary and mercantile classes, but also by a total lack of popular participation. Smith feared the 'thoughtless extravagance' (*WN* II p. 342) of democracies; believed that a man with a mutilated mind is likely to be deceived by 'quacks and imposters' (*MS* p. 367) (although the mob had of course been able to play an intelligent part in the primitive democracies of hunting societies anterior to the division of labour (*WN* II pp. 233–4; *LJ* p. 262)); and was convinced that the *canaille* prefer paternalistic to representative government in any case (*LJ* p. 54). Such elitism was common currency in the eighteenth century. It is unlikely to be common currency today.

Demand

Adam Smith was in no doubt that economics is about scarcity and stressed the need to provide 'a plentiful revenue or subsistence for the people' (*WN* I p. 449). He announced that 'the riches of a country consist in the plenty and cheapness of provisions' (*LJ* p. 130) and made a growing supply of goods and services (along with provision of revenue for the State) one of the twin goals he proposed for political economy (*WN* I p. 449).

Smith also believed that the problem of scarcity was on the way to being solved. He noted that nowadays economic activity is often oriented towards satisfying 'many insignificant demands, which we by no means stand in need of' (*LJ* pp. 159–60), and implied that even the lower classes now participate in the affluent society (since wages are clearly above subsistence) (*WN* I pp. 82–3). This does not, of course, mean that such luxuries ought not to be consumed. While Smith noted that the 'great wants of mankind' (for food, clothing and housing) (*WN* I p. 180) are so modest that they can be satisfied 'by unassisted labour of the individual' (*LJ* p. 158) even without the division of labour, he hardly adopted a puritanical attitude towards cultural needs over and above 'the gratification of the bodily appetites' ('The Imitative Arts' p. 148 in *EW*). On the contrary, he stressed that consumer preferences are not random but laid down by society, and that men thus have a positive duty to observe the customary proprieties: 'When we say that a man is worth fifty or a hundred pounds a-year . . . we mean commonly to ascertain what is or *ought to be* his way of living, or the quantity and quality of the necessaries and conveniencies of life in which he can *with propriety* indulge himself' (*WN* I p. 307. Italics mine).

Obedience to social norms concerning the habitual association of subject and symbol substantially restricts the freedom of choice. In the case of dress, for example, custom has in England rendered leather shoes a necessity for both sexes and all classes (although not in Scotland or France) (*WN* II p. 400), and an Englishman afraid of mockery and anxious to win 'the entire approbation of the impartial spectator' (*MS* p. 314) would also be well advised to wear a linen shirt (*WN* II p. 405); for truly 'a man would be ridiculous who should appear in public with a suit of clothes quite different from those which are commonly worn, though the new dress should in itself be ever so graceful or convenient' (*MS* p. 284). Clearly 'grace' and 'convenience' are inadequate to explain choice without reference to 'the peculiar manners and customs of the people' (*WN* I p. 132). In such a world, social facts are to be explained by other social facts and individuals are seen to behave in a manner both predictable and aesthetically pleasing out of a love of social survival: obviously no sensitive man wants to be as ridiculous, as out of place, as a sow in a drawing-room or Gulliver among the Lilliputians (*LR* pp. 40–1).

Smith was thus concerned with relative rather than absolute deprivation, for he identified commodities largely as socially-prescribed status symbols. He recorded that 'with the greater part of rich people, the chief enjoyment of riches consists in the parade of riches' (*WN* I p. 192); and implied that it is the desire for increased conspicuous consumption that causes a man to sacrifice still more of 'his ease, his liberty, and his happiness' (*WN* I p. 37) in order to obtain still more command over commodities (for a poor man simply cannot afford to buy the expensive status symbols of a higher social station).

Smith recognised that people want goods. He was not, however, convinced that people need them. Students schooled in the textbook theory of consumer sovereignty will be shocked by his arrogant dismissal of many effectively-demanded commodities as 'trifling' (*WN* I p. 368), 'frivolous' (*MS* p. 259), 'contemptible' (*MS* p. 263), 'childish' (*WN* I p. 437), by his intolerance towards 'trinkets and baubles' (*WN* I p. 439), by his cavalier rejection of the verdict of the market whenever it offended his philosophical sensibilities. Students trained in the inductivist approach to total demand will be astonished by his stoic apathy and his refusal to identify increased commodity consumption with increased human happiness: 'Happiness and misery . . . reside altogether in the mind' (*WN* II p. 308), he argued, and observed that 'the beggar, who suns himself by the side of the highway, possesses that security which kings are fighting for' (*MS* p. 265). This suggests that, since there is little difference between one permanent situation and another, the obvious solution to the problem of scarcity is not to increase supply but to reduce demand. After all, for most men work is unpleasant (even Oxford dons face an upward-sloping supply curve for labour (*WN* II p. 284), and this would not be the case if their duties were as enjoyable as, say, hunting and fishing (*WN* I p. 113)); and it hardly seems worthwhile to sacrifice one's energy, one's tranquillity, one's peace of mind, if at the end of the day one can but fall back exhausted on the blissful banks of a mirage.

Clearly, since he believed that for most men 'consumption is the sole end and purpose of all production' (*WN* II p. 179) and since he also believed that consumption is without any doubt a 'deception' (*MS* p. 263), it follows that Smith could have recommended repose rather than change. He chose not to do so, however, for two reasons: first, because he recognised as a scientist that the philosopher cannot turn the acquisitive society on its head simply by propounding his own opinions while ignoring the momentum inherent in matter; and, second, because he in fact welcomed the social dynamism that industry put in motion. After all, by producing commodities men produce institutions as well; and Smith, a believer in social progress, was convinced that the latent function of the 'deception' of commodity-utility was likely to be major social change which the philosopher could contemplate with the utmost pleasure. He hoped, in other words, via the free market mechanism, to harness the stallion of economic determinism to the plough of social reform. Seldom has so massive an attempt at social engineering been more skilfully presented or more carefully concealed, as will be evident from an example of the way in which Smith believed demand-led growth could act as the motor of social progress: the resounding defeat of the Roman Catholic Church.

In the Middle Ages the Church, like any other great landowner, maintained private armies out of its agricultural surplus, and it deployed them according to 'one uniform plan' (*WN* II p. 322) as order by 'one man' (*WN* II p. 319). The concentrated monopolistic monolithic multinational power of the Church made it 'the most formidable combination that ever was formed against the authority and security of civil government, as well as against the liberty, reason, and happiness of mankind' (*WN* II p. 325). Fortunately, the market is the enemy of the Pope. To begin with, the introduction of an exchange economy (emanating in the first instance from the mercantile ports (*WN* I pp. 427–8)) meant that clerics, like secular landowners, began to use the surplus for their own 'vanity, luxury, and expence' (*WN* II p. 326) rather than waste it on retainers and charity. This weakened their military might and also alienated the masses who, 'provoked and disgusted' (*WN* II p. 326), were ready to be plucked by even 'the most ignorant enthusiast' (*WN* II p. 331). Then too, not only did the market pave the way for Reformation by undermining the power and prestige of the clergy, but it provided a model for the future. Smith proposed that there should not in a country be one Church but 'two or three hundred, or perhaps . . . as many thousand small sects' (*WN* II p. 314), all competing for customers. In a situation of perfect competition such sects are bound to gravitate towards a natural price, 'that pure and rational religion' which wise men have always and everywhere 'wished to see established' (*WN* II p. 315); whereas oligopolists, in confessional markets with a small number of large corporations, are likely to employ 'all the terrors of religion' (*WN* II p. 319) and the 'grossest delusions' (*WN* II p. 325) in order to consolidate and expand business (as the examples of France (*MS* p. 253) and Ireland (*WN* II p. 483) indicate). Finally, market capitalism is responsible for 'order and good government' (*WN* I p. 433) and economic growth; and both security and freedom from want are essential if men are to be set free from 'pusillanimous superstition' ('The History of Astronomy' p. 49 in *EW*) and directed towards experiment, observation and induction of God's will from the study of God's works.

Such institutional change, however desirable, is not obtained without a cost, since demand-led growth implies a double veil of tears. Men sacrifice themselves first at the stage of production and then at the stage of consumption, and never grasp that the economic weapon is only the motor of progress so long as they do not see that it is powered by a 'deception'. Manipulation via demand-led growth is more powerful than manipulation by advertising and more successful than manipulation by politicians, precisely because it is the most hidden of the hidden persuaders.

Conclusion

Adam Smith's relevance to the modern reader is to be found more in his method than in his model, and specifically in the following features of his approach.

First, a stress on the momentum inherent in matter (which in the economic sphere could be respected by a system of free enterprise, perfect competition, political *laissez-faire* and market pricing based on conditions of supply and demand) and a warning that it is virtually impossible save by induction from unfettered experience for man to derive knowledge about mechanistic forces, natural laws and positions of equilibrium.

Second, a belief that economy, society and polity ought to be studied together as mutually determinant within the framework of a large-scale interdisciplinary systemic whole; a conviction that even Economic Man must be seen as a social animal; a sociologist's awareness of conventions, status-groups, classes (as in his more corporatist than individualist attitudes to consumer behaviour and character patterns).

Third, a theory of social causality based on a marriage between the assumption of sensitivity (that men record group standards of propriety and then conform to these norms so as to deserve approbation in the process of human interaction) and the postulate of malleability (that human nature is basically wax or clay, to be moulded by the invisible hand of economic determinism).

Fourth, a normative as well as a positive dimension imposed by the simple fact that a vote for the market is also a vote for massive social change in a world where reality is not static but dynamic and the observer is compelled to regard the present as but a moment in history; and thus a philosophical orientation imposed by the need to choose between two social matrices.

Fifth, a recognition of overdevelopment as well as of underdevelopment, and a hint that the price of progress can be measured in units such as the mental mutilation of the factory operative, the spread of commodity hedonism, the triumph of utility over sensitivity and propriety, the universality of a base and selfish disposition, excessive ambition, the decay of martial virtues. To this list we might wish to add the problems of seller-manipulation, corporate government and oligopolistic distortion (for a theory of markets need not be a *Loblied* to private enterprise, and in the case of Adam Smith most assuredly was not).

Adam Smith did not adequately explore the question of overdevelopment, partly because the problems with which he was more immediately concerned lay far to the other side of the Golden Mean, partly because he, like the rest of us, did not and could not have all the answers. Perhaps today, however, that which was to Smith *obiter dictum* has become to us *sine qua non.* If so, then in any future discussion of the relationship between men and things, between society and economy, there is no better example to follow than that of the haunted intellectuality of Adam Smith.

Works by Adam Smith

(*MS*)   *The Theory of Moral Sentiments* (1759), Augustus M. Kelley, 1966.

(*LR*)   *Lectures on Rhetoric and Belles Lettres* (lectures given in 1762–63), ed. by John M. Lothian, Thomas Nelson and Sons, 1963.

('ED')   'An Early Draft of Part of *The Wealth of Nations*' (probably written about 1763), in W.R. Scott, *Adam Smith as Student and Professor,* University of Glasgow, 1937.

(*LJ*)   *Lectures on Justice, Police, Revenue and Arms* (lectures given in 1763), ed. by Edwin Cannan, Clarendon Press, 1896.

(*WN*)   *The Wealth of Nations* (1776), ed. by Edwin Cannan, Methuen, 1961.

(*EW*)   *Essays on Philosophical Subjects* (1795), reprinted in J. Ralph Lindgren (ed.), *The Early Writings of Adam Smith*, Augustus M. Kelley, 1967.

Further reading

S. Hollander, *The Economics of Adam Smith* (Heinemann, 1973).
D.A. Reisman, *Adam Smith's Sociological Economics* (Croom Helm, 1976).
A. Skinner and T. Wilson, eds., *Essays on Adam Smith* (Clarendon Press, 1975).